Sexual Contradictions

JANET SAYERS

Sexual Contradictions

Psychology, Psychoanalysis, and Feminism

Tavistock Publications
London and New York

106 806

First published in 1986 by
Tavistock Publications Ltd
11 New Fetter Lane, London EC4P 4EE

Published in the USA by
Tavistock Publications
in association with Methuen, Inc.
29 West 35th Street, New York NY 10001

© 1986 Janet Sayers

Typeset by Folio Photosetting, Bristol
Printed in Great Britain
at the University Press, Cambridge

British Library Cataloguing in Publication Data
Sayers, Janet
    Sexual contradictions: psychology, psychoanalysis, and feminism. — (Social
    science paperback)
    1. Men   2. Women   3. Interpersonal relations
    I. Title   II. Series
    305.3   HQ1090

    ISBN 0-422-78780-9
    ISBN 0-422-78790-6 Pbk

Library of Congress Cataloging in Publication Data
Sayers, Janet
    Sexual contradictions.
    Bibliography: p.
    Includes indexes.
    1. Sex differences (Psychology)   2. Women and psychoanalysis.   3. Women —
Psychology.   4. Men — Psychology.   5. Dominance (Psychology)   6. Feminism.
I. Title.
BF692.2.S29   1985   155.3'3   85-27948
ISBN 0-422-78780-9
ISBN 0-422-78790-6 (pbk.)

Contents

Acknowledgements   vii
Introduction   ix

PART ONE   Non-psychoanalytic psychology   1
  1 Biological determinism   3
  2 Cognitive-developmental theory   12
  3 Social learning   23

PART TWO   Post-Freudian psychoanalysis   33
  4 Psychoanalytic essentialism   35
  5 Melanie Klein   49
  6 Object relations theory   64
  7 Lacanian perspectives   79

PART THREE   Sexual contradictions: theory and therapy   97
  8 Sexual identity and difference   99
  9 Repression and neurosis   120
  10 Introjection and depression   138
  11 Projection and paranoia   150

PART FOUR   Conclusion   165
  12 Feminism and psychoanalysis   167

References   182
Name index   205
Subject index   210

To the memory of
Isabel Schwarz, social worker,
tragically killed last year
while working at Bexley Hospital, Kent.

Acknowledgements

Friends, colleagues, and students have been tremendously kind and supportive to me in working on this book. And the following most helpfully read and commented on its various drafts and revisions: Claire Buck, Diane Cunningham, Gill Davies, Kevin Durkin, Anne Edwards, Mary Evans, Norman Freeman, Bob Hinshelwood, David Morgan, Caroline New, Nanneke Redclift, Leone Ridsdale, Joanna Ryan, Ann Scott, Shirley Toulson, Jeffrey Weeks (who also supplied the title), and Elizabeth Wilson. To all of them my thanks, as to the Women's Studies, Social Work, and Psychology students at the University of Kent from whom I have learnt so much over the years. Barbara Green has valiantly typed and retyped the notes, papers, and references made in the course of my writing about feminism and psychoanalysis. My gratitude to her, to Sean Sayers whose work on dialectics has so much influenced my thinking about these subjects, and to our children – Nicholas and Daniel – whose scepticism about Freud's account of symbolism has kept me mindful of the risks of reductionism associated with it. The above may well not agree with the ideas here expressed, responsibility for which of course rests with me. Their encouragement, however, has been invaluable: for it my heartfelt thanks.

For permission to reproduce copyright material, the author and publisher would like to thank:

p. 21: Mirror Group Newspapers Ltd
p. 45: New Directions Publishing Corp. HD: *Collected Poems 1912–1944*. © 1982 by the Estate of Hilda Doolittle.

p. 59:   Outsider Archive, Art House, London.
p. 87:   New York Academy of Medicine (Illustration taken from
         Icones Anatomicae (1934: New York Academy of
         Medicine and University of Munich).
p. 129: Mitchell Beazley International Ltd
p. 169: Punch Publications Ltd

Introduction

This book is about the psychology of men's social dominance and women's resistance to it. It is about the subjective aspects of this dominance and resistance, the social and historical determinants of which have been documented elsewhere. Above all it is a plea for the relevance of Freud's work to our understanding and handling of this psychology.

I shall begin by outlining the three main theories currently informing non-psychoanalytic work on the psychology of sexual inequality: first, the theory that it is biologically determined; second, the claim that it is shaped by the child's understanding of sex and gender; and last, the theory that it is conditioned by the rewards and punishments associated with gender conformity and deviance.

The trouble with these theories is that they treat the psychological correlates of existing sexual divisions in society as either more intransigent, or as more mutable than they are in fact. Rejecting biological determinist accounts of this intransigence, feminists have increasingly looked to psychoanalysis as a means of explaining it. It is with the theories to which this has given rise, and the post-Freudian accounts of psychology on which they are based, that I shall be concerned in the second part of this book.

These theories address head on the question as to why women acquiesce in their social subordination. They do not, however, explain women's resistance to it. This is because they, and the post-Freudian theories on which they are based, attend to the way women's psychology is conditioned, either by the differences between the sexes, or by the sameness of the sexes in their social relations. These theories overlook the way that women's psychology is conditioned by their being treated at one and the same time as both the same as, and as different from, men. The great merit of Freud's work is that he did address the way this contradiction shapes women's psychology. For this is the psychological source of women's resistance to their social subordination.

Freud's work is also important for feminism because it draws attention to the defences whereby, instead of realistically confronting such contradictions in our social experience, we all too often deal with them in illusory fashion, through repression, introjection, and projection. In explaining these points, in the third part of the book, I shall outline the clinical methods whereby Freud and his followers have sought to undo these defences so as to enable women and men to become more fully conscious of, and hence more able effectively to deal with the contradictions of their social life. For, paradoxically, this practical aspect of psychoanalysis has been relatively ignored in recent feminist uses of it despite the fact that feminism, like psychoanalysis, is primarily concerned with practice.

Consciousness of the contradictions in which women are placed by virtue of their sex is a precondition of feminism. In so far as psychoanalysis brings about such consciousness, it is therefore clearly relevant to the women's movement. On the other hand such consciousness does not of itself alter the social conditions that produce it. It is here, as I shall point out in conclusion, that feminism takes off from psychoanalysis. Whereas psychoanalysis interprets our consciousness of the world, feminism seeks to change it.

PART ONE

Non-psychoanalytic psychology

1
Biological determinism

> For the Earthly Adam's being Form'd before Eve, seems as little to prove her Natural Subjection to him, as the Living creatures, Fishes, Birds and Beasts being Form'd before them both, prove that Mankind must be subject to these Animals. (Mary Astell 1700)

> Men are naturally more suited to be aggressive and assertive and dominant and women more suited to be submissive and give way and be the peacemakers. (Yvonne Stayt 1984)

Feminists today still have to confront the claim, as did Mary Astell three hundred years ago, that women's 'Subjection' is given by 'Nature'. For it is still regularly argued that this subjection is determined by the biological fact of women's childbearing, and by their being physically weaker than men. I have reviewed such arguments elsewhere (Sayers 1982).

Here I shall deal with the psychology of this subjection and of men's social dominance. I shall start, in this chapter, with the view, expressed by Cotswold housewife Yvonne Stayt quoted above, that this psychology is biologically determined. Perhaps the most influential version today of this view is that put forward by the Stanford psychologists, Eleanor Maccoby and Carol Jacklin, in their review of psychological sex differences. It is therefore with their work that I shall begin.

Maccoby and Jacklin claim that psychological sex differences in dominance and aggression must be psychologically determined since these differences are universal. As evidence they quote a study by Omark, Omark, and Edelman (1973) of 4 to 8 year olds in the USA, of 5 to 9 year olds in Switzerland, and of 8 to 10 year olds in Ethiopia showing that in all three countries the boys were higher than the girls in hierarchies of 'toughness', and were more often involved in aggressive interaction in the sense of 'hitting or pushing without smiling'. The universality of sex differences in aggression, say Maccoby and Jacklin like others before them (for example Hutt 1972), is also shown by Whiting and Edwards' (1973) observations on the behaviour of 3 to 11 year old children in Kenya, Okinawa, India, the Philippines, Mexico, and the USA. According to Maccoby and Jacklin, the younger boys in this study were found to be more dominant than the younger girls, the older boys more often to react with aggression to peer attack, and boys of all ages to engage in more rough-and-tumble play and 'mock fighting', and to be more verbally aggressive than the girls. In fact, however, as Todd Tieger (1980) – another Stanford psychologist – points out, these differences are not found when Whiting and Edwards' data are analysed country by country. He goes on to suggest that, in so far as this analysis does reveal significant sex differences in aggression – in rough-and-tumble play for instance – these differences seem to have been due to social rather than biological factors since they were not found in those cultures in which boys are required to look after younger siblings, and in which girls are not expected to fulfil specifically 'feminine' duties. Socialization, says Tieger, would also seem to account for the finding that sex differences in aggressive response to provocation only occurred among the older children. Why else was this sex difference not found among the younger children too?

Even were sex differences in aggression to be universal among children – and the evidence to date has mainly been collected on children living in Europe, the USA, or countries under their influence – this would not prove that the greater aggressivity of boys is biologically determined. The universality of this psychological sex difference could equally be explained as due to the effect on children of the social fact that, in all cultures, men tend to be the dominant sex.

This dominance may well be related to biology. But biology – women's childbearing, say – contributes to the determination of this dominance differently in different social groups. In our society, for instance, childbearing has contributed to the social subordination of women in the upper class by way of the concern of this class that its womenfolk produce legitimate heirs to its property (Engels 1884). Among the unpropertied classes, by contrast, women's childbearing contributes to their social subordination by way of the fact that employers are unwilling to cut their profits by providing the maternity and paternity leave, and the creche facilities, that would enable women of this class to do the same jobs, or contribute equally with men to their household income (Brenner and Ramas 1984; but, as Jane Lewis 1985 and others point out, this does not explain why childcare falls to women). Whatever the cause, and it would seem to relate to women's childbearing, men are the main breadwinners in many households, and women defer to them on this account. As the wife of a railway porter put it at the turn of this century: 'we must give our husbands sufficient food or we should have them home and not able to work; therefore we have to go without to make ends meet' (Davies 1915:20). Nor has this situation changed today. Sociologist Marion Kerr reports finding in a recent study 'that men in all two-parent families not only consumed larger portions but also ate meat more often than women and children' – a privilege she relates directly to men's status at home as family breadwinner (Kerr 1985:25). Ironically some men feel that it is not enough that their women give them better food than they have themselves. Like the husband who battered his wife because he felt she had given him 'rubbish for his dinner' even though this was nothing to what she had had herself. While he had eaten steak and kidney pie, potatoes, and peas – and this bought out of a rare bonus, her prize-winnings at Bingo – she had only had 'a couple of spoonfuls of peas . . . to kid him I'd had some' (Campbell 1984:84).

Although the above evidence shows men's dominance over women to be related to their greater wage-earning capacity which is in turn related to their not bearing children, this evidence does not show biology directly to determine men's social dominance. And it certainly does not show psychological sex differences in childhood in dominance and aggression to be directly determined by biology. Maccoby and Jacklin however suggest that biology – women's childbearing – might indirectly contribute to these differences in so far as girls are prepared for motherhood by being brought up to be less aggressive and more nurturant than boys. Were this the case, they say, the cause of sex differences in aggression

'would be biological in that it stems from childbearing, but the implications would be quite different than if there were a more direct biological influence on aspects of aggression itself (as in the case of hormonal sensitizing to certain eliciting stimuli).' (Maccoby and Jacklin 1980:971)

But Maccoby and Jacklin rule out this possibility on the ground that sex differences in aggression appear

'early in life, at a time when there is no evidence that differential socialization pressures have been brought to bear by adults to "shape" aggression differently in the two sexes.' (Maccoby and Jacklin 1975:242)

There are abundant data to show that sex differences in aggression do indeed appear very early in childhood. Maccoby and Jacklin (1975:1980) cite in illustration of this point the finding that boys as young as two are significantly more likely to show 'aggression toward peers' (Pedersen and Bell 1970), 'physical aggression' (McIntyre 1972), 'rough-and-tumble play' (Smith and Connolly 1972), 'wrestling and hitting during rough-and-tumble play' (Blurton Jones 1972), and 'agonistic initiations' (Smith 1974) than pre-school girls.

Maccoby and Jacklin claim that these sex differences cannot, properly speaking, be attributed to socialization, to 'shaping' as they term it, since, far from being rewarded for aggression, boys of this age are more often punished for it than are girls. Surely, however, this is just the kind of thing to draw children's attention to aggression as an important dimension of behaviour on which the sexes are treated differently? It would thus seem to constitute evidence of the socialization rather than biological determination of gender difference. The same can be said of the following phenomena also noted by Maccoby and Jacklin: parents' belief that 'boys are naturally more aggressive than girls'; their worries 'about a boy who is notably unaggressive, seeing it as a sign of being a "sissy" '; and their implicit injunction to boys in punishing them for aggression ' "You are not supposed to fight, but I'm glad you did" ' (Maccoby and Jacklin 1975:340). Isn't this just the sort of interaction most of us would include under the heading of social 'shaping'?

There is now abundant evidence that such 'shaping' occurs from earliest infancy onwards. As Maccoby and Jacklin acknowledge, boy babies are stimulated more than girl babies to 'gross motor behaviour', girls being treated as though 'they were more fragile than boys' (Maccoby and Jacklin 1975:309; see also Smith and Lloyd 1978). The importance of social factors in the inculcation of aggression in boys is also indicated by the fact that the occurrence of 'aggressive incidents' among pre-school boys is influenced by whether they are paired with another boy or with a girl (Smith and Green 1975). Lastly, it is found that, as early as two years of age, boys are more often aggressed against, in the sense of being physically punished and verbally scolded by nursery school teachers than are girls (Hyde and Schuck 1977) such that, compared to girls, they are early exposed to more first-hand experience of aggression.

Not surprisingly, Maccoby and Jacklin do not rest their case for the biological determination of male aggression and dominance on such findings. Nor do they rest it on the purported universality of male aggression among young children. They also argue their case on the basis of the fact that comparable sex differences are found among nonhuman primates. They quote, for instance, the findings reported in de Vore's *Primate Behavior* (1965) which, they say, show that 'a fairly stable dominance hierarchy exists among the males of certain groups, although these hierarchies are more stable in some species than others' (Maccoby and Jacklin 1975:255). E.O. Wilson (1975), in his book *Sociobiology*, likewise argues that since male dominance occurs in human hunter-gatherer societies, and since it is 'widespread although not universal' among nonhuman primates, male dominance in industrial societies must be part of our evolutionary heritage and therefore genetically determined. What these authors fail to mention, however, is that the variations they acknowledge to exist in the incidence of male dominance among monkeys and apes is largely attributable to environmental factors. As primatologist Thelma Rowell (1974) points out in summarizing these data, male dominance among nonhuman primates seems to be an effect of social stress, being especially evident among animals kept in captivity.

In common with many others, Maccoby and Jacklin often equate dominance and aggression although they are not in fact synonymous. They are however also careful to point out that

'In observational work, a dominant animal is defined as one whose threats result in withdrawal by other animals; who prevails in conflicts over females, food, sleeping places, etc.; toward whom submissive gestures are made; and who is likely to be followed by other members of the group when he moves away from the group.'   (Maccoby and Jacklin 1975:255)

Assessed by these criteria, dominant apes are not necessarily the most aggressive (Pilbeam 1973). And this is also true of humans where aggression is more usually associated with social failure than with success and leadership (see, e.g., Dodge 1983).

The data on sex differences in aggression among nonhuman primates show these differences, like those in dominance behaviour, to be environmentally determined, occurring more often in animals adapted to savannah and terrestrial life, less often in animals adapted to tree-living and semiterrestrial conditions (Rowell 1966; Martin and Voorhies 1975). Among humans, environmental factors are likely to be even more crucial in determining aggression since the neocortex is more evolved in humans, and since aggression in them is therefore even more subject to neocortically processed environmental stimuli than is the case in nonhuman primates (McKenna 1983; Nicholson 1984).

The last set of data adduced by Maccoby and Jacklin to support their thesis as to the biological determination of male aggression and dominance is drawn from endocrinology, from:

(1) evidence on the effects of experimentally-induced and naturally-occurring alterations in prenatal levels of the sex steroid hormones, the androgens and oestrogens;
(2) results of postnatal administration of these hormones;
(3) measurement of sex hormone levels in individuals already identified on other grounds as aggressive.

As regards the first type of evidence, Maccoby and Jacklin instance a study by Young, Goy, and Phoenix (1964), in which one of the main androgens, namely testosterone, was given to monkeys. These experimenters report that the female offspring of these monkeys showed increased levels of rough-and-tumble play compared to the female offspring of untreated controls. Rough-and-tumble play, however, is not synonymous with aggression. On its own, therefore, this study cannot be said to demonstrate the hormonal determination of male aggression. As further evidence, Maccoby and Jacklin cite Ehrhardt and Baker's (1973) study of girls who, because of a genetic defect affecting the prenatal functioning of the adrenal cortex, had received more androgen *in utero* than is usual in females. Compared to their normal sisters, say Maccoby and Jacklin, these girls 'more often preferred to play with boys . . . took little interest in weddings, dolls, or live babies, and preferred outdoor sports' (Maccoby and Jacklin 1975:243). However, although such observations on andrenogenital syndrome girls have regularly been cited as evidence of the biological determination of sex differences in aggression and dominance (see, for example, Hutt 1972; Goldberg 1977), they hardly bear on these differences unless we are to believe that preference for playing with boys or for outdoor sports (let alone interest in weddings, dolls, and babies) are indicative of dominance and aggression! A more plausible measure of aggression is initiation of fighting. But, as Maccoby and Jacklin themselves acknowledge, no significant difference has been observed between andreno-genital syndrome girls and their sisters on this measure. Nor did

Ehrhardt and Baker's (1974) later study, using different subjects, find significantly higher levels of aggression among andreno-genital syndrome girls or boys and their age peers. Furthermore, not only does exposure *in utero* to excess levels of androgen not seem to increase postnatal aggressiveness, but neither does prenatal exposure to excess oestrogen seem to decrease this behaviour (Ehrhardt *et al.* 1977; for further critical discussion of this research see Bleier 1984).

What of the evidence as to the effects on aggression of sex hormones given postnatally? Maccoby and Jacklin include here Joslyn's (1973) investigation of three female rhesus monkeys, given regular injections of testosterone between the ages of 6½ and 14½ months, whose aggression increased following treatment such that they were eventually as aggressive as untreated males. However, as Maccoby and Jacklin acknowledge, injection of the so-called female hormone, oestrogen, can have similar effects, at least in mice. And comparable results have also been observed in monkeys: administration of oestrogen increases dominance and aggressive behaviour in castrated 'female' chimpanzees (Birch and Clark 1950); and aggressiveness in females in many primate species is most marked at those times in their menstrual cycle when their oestrogen levels peak (Michael 1968).

Regarding measures of male sex hormone levels in individuals already known to be aggressive, Maccoby and Jacklin quote Kreuz and Rose's (1972) finding that male prisoners who had committed more violent and aggressive crimes during adolescence had higher plasma testosterone levels. Since, however, no correlation was found between these levels and present fighting behaviour, and since one of the main measures of aggression used was that of escape from incarceration (Chasin 1977), it scarcely proves male aggression to be biologically determined! More convincing in this respect is Rada, Laws, and Kellner's (1976) finding that imprisoned rapists who used 'gratuitous violence in committing their crime' had higher testosterone levels than other rapists. In a subsequent study, however, these researchers failed to find any difference in testosterone levels between 'violent and nonviolent rapists' or between rapists and violent child molesters (Rada *et al.*

1983). Leaving aside the question of whether such studies are motivated by the intention of exonerating male violence as biologically determined (see Dusek 1984; Birke in press), it should be pointed out that none of these studies demonstrates any correlation between male hormone levels and present aggressiveness. And even though Rada and his colleagues found an association in child molesters between their testosterone levels and self-reported attitudes of hostility, they did not find any such correlation among the rapists they studied.

Maccoby and Jacklin claim that animal studies do demonstrate a correlation between present aggressiveness and androgen levels. They cite, for instance, Rose, Gordon, and Bernstein's (1972) study showing an increase in testosterone levels in male rhesus monkeys who were low in the dominance hierarchy of their cage-mates but who were then placed with females they could dominate. On the other hand, testosterone levels decrease when animals are defeated in fights, and when their social rank in their dominance hierarchy changes (Lowe 1983). As far as the endocrinological evidence is concerned, therefore, it seems that biology is as much determined by, as a determinant of, male dominance and aggression.

The above evidence clearly demonstrates some involvement of the sex hormones in this behaviour. And it is also clear that these hormones affect dominance and aggression by way of their influence on neural transmission in the brain, particularly on that part of the subcortex known as the amygdala (Nicholson 1984). But, as I have also sought to show in this chapter, the evidence that sex *differences* in this behaviour are directly determined by the endocrine system or by some other aspect of biology is far less convincing. Most psychologists accordingly tend to explain such differences in social terms – as determined by children's and adults' understanding of sex and gender, and by the rewards associated with gender conformity. I shall briefly outline these explanations next.

2
Cognitive-developmental theory

Hearing that one of the administration was becoming a dove on Vietnam, Johnson said 'Hell, he has to squat to piss'. (Strange 1983:10)

US Marine: One of the most destructive facets of bootcamp is the systematic attack on the recruits' sexuality. While in basic training, one is continually addressed as a faggot or girl. . . . Recruits were brutalized, frustrated, and cajoled to a flash point of high tension. Recruits were often stunned by the depths of violence erupting from within. Only on these occasions of violent outbursts did the drill instructor cease this endless litany of 'You dirty faggot' and 'Can't you hack it, little girls'. (Michalowski 1982:330)

Clearly the militarily-minded do not leave it to biology to make men as aggressive as they want them to be. Instead, as the above quotations indicate, they also seek to instil aggression in men by trading on their insecurities about their sexual identity, by implying that not to be aggressive is to be female, to be a girl.

The Harvard psychologist, Lawrence Kohlberg, has suggested that aggression, as well as the other traits culturally associated with masculinity, are regularly acquired in childhood by way of the insecurities the young child feels about its sexual identity (Kohlberg 1966). Young children, he claims, conform with the traits associated with their sex in order to bolster their sense of themselves as male or female, a sense that is only precariously established in late infancy.

Kohlberg's 'cognitive-developmental analysis' of gender development constitutes one of the main paradigms informing current, non-psychoanalytic research into the psychology of gender. Like Freud before him, Kohlberg draws attention to the fact that babies do not know of sexual difference. They do not initially know either of their sex, or that of those around them. This knowledge is, however, rapidly acquired in the first years of life. By two years of age, as we have seen (p. 6 above), boys and girls already differ psychologically from each other in that boys are more likely to be aggressive (but see Hyde 1984). And children also become aware very early on of gender differences such as those in aggression. It is not, however, clear at exactly what age this awareness first comes about. Some studies show children as young as two to have substantial knowledge of the traits differentially associated with masculinity and femininity in our society (Kuhn *et al.* 1978). Others, by contrast, find that children of this age lack the capacity to classify things, let alone traits, by sex, that they are unable for instance to sort toys into 'boy' and 'girl' piles (Blakeman *et al.* 1979). Similar discrepancies characterize the data as to the age when children first verbalize sexual difference. According to Michael Lewis (1981), by eighteen months most children have acquired this capacity in the sense of using the words 'boy' and 'girl' correctly. Others, however, find that many two year olds are unable to do this, that they cannot correctly answer the question, 'Are you a boy or a girl?'. By three years of age, however, children seem to have no difficulty with such questions and, in this sense, seem to be certain of their sexual identity (Thompson 1975).

It is to this development, to what Kohlberg refers to as the acquisition of 'gender identity', that he attributes the childhood origins of psychological sex differences. Whether or not the child can correctly verbalize knowledge of its sex, says Kohlberg, it is this knowledge that causes it to adopt and egocentrically value the attributes of its sex, and to despise those of the opposite sex. This is evident, for instance, in the finding that, given the choice, three and four year old boys select girls' toys as the ones they most dislike (Eisenberg *et al.* 1982).

Kohlberg goes on to argue that, although children quickly know of their sex, they do not initially appreciate the invariance of sex over time. In Kohlberg's terms, they lack 'gender constancy'. As evidence, he quotes the following conversation between a couple of four year olds – Jimmy, just turned four, and Johnny, his four and a half year old playmate:

> 'Johnny: I'm going to be an airplane builder when I grow up.
> Jimmy: When I grow up, I'll be a Mommy.
> Johnny: No, you can't be a Mommy. You have to be a Daddy.
> Jimmy: No. I'm going to be a Mommy.
> Johnny: No, you're not a girl, you can't be a Mommy.
> Jimmy: Yes, I can.'   (Kohlberg 1966:95)

Jimmy, says Kohlberg, lacks gender constancy: he does not realize that one's sex remains constant with age, that if one is a boy one may grow up to be a father but one cannot grow up to be a mother.

There is, however, a problem with Kohlberg's interpretation of the evidence on this point. Jimmy's remarks are perfectly consistent with his knowing that he will always be male. They may simply reflect his wish to be motherly when he grows up, a wish the belief in the fulfilment of which is perfectly compatible with his also knowing that he will grow up to be a man. Furthermore, subsequent evidence shows that most four years olds have no doubts on this latter score at least as indicated by their responses to questions like, 'Are you going to be a mommy or a daddy?', or 'Could you be a daddy if you wanted to be?' (Thompson and Bentler 1973).

On the other hand, children's sense of sexual identity is precarious in that they do not seem to be entirely certain that one's sex remains the same even though one might adopt a hairstyle, wear clothes, or play games associated with the opposite sex (Marcus and Overton 1978). Paradoxically, six year olds seem to be more uncertain about this than three year olds (Coker 1984) perhaps because of the significance they come to attach to sexual difference as a result of going to school.

This uncertainty may explain the anxieties expressed by six year olds about gender deviance as in the following incident:

> 'Peter, just turning six, made the following comments while his father was carrying his mother's purse along with the groceries: "Why are you carrying the purse, Dad, are you a lady or something? You must be a lady, men don't carry purses." ' (Kohlberg 1966:116)

Further evidence on this point comes from Kohlberg's co-worker, Dorothy Ullian. Asked whether a boy should wear a necklace, one of the six year olds she interviewed replied, 'No, because it would look funny and everyone would say he was a girl' (Kohlberg and Ullian 1974:215). Another six year old responded similarly to the idea of a girl with short hair:

> 'She would kind of look like a boy. [Would that be right or wrong?] Wrong, because it doesn't look nice if a boy has long hair and a girl has short hair. [Why?] Because if there was a girl and a boy together, and say the girl has short hair like the boy, some people would say "I like these two boys", but one is really a girl.' (Ullian 1976:35)

Children, like adults, not only associate particular hairstyles, clothing, and possessions with one sex rather than the other. They also regard certain psychological traits, including that of dominance, as more typical of men than women. American psychologists Jerome Kagan and Judith Lemkin (1960), for example, report that the three to eight year old boys and girls they studied consistently described fathers as stronger and smarter than mothers, as the major agent of punishment, and as family boss – an authority they often attributed to his role as family breadwinner. To the question, 'Who is the boss in your house?', writes Kagan, many of the children hesitated and then said that their father was boss, 'Because he has to work for a living', or 'Because he owns the house' (Kagan 1956:257). Kohlberg likewise found that six year olds claim the father to be 'best in the family' because 'he works and makes the money' (Kohlberg 1966:102n). And, he points out, children attribute dominance to the father even where

there is no 'paternal power' as such in their own families
(Kohlberg 1966:159).

Kohlberg and his followers argue that, with development,
children increasingly come to recognize sex roles to be socially
rather than biologically determined and that these roles can
change – that wage earning, for instance, is not confined to men.
This in turn leads them to appreciate that women too can be
dominant, that the association of traits such as dominance with
men is less a matter of biological destiny than an effect of the roles
socially assigned to men. As one eighteen year old put it:

> 'Women get put into a role; by the nature of them being born
> men and women they're put into social positions and their
> social actions are laid out for them and they are expected to do
> certain things and not to do other things. Men are expected to
> be aggressive and dominant, and the characteristics associated
> with masculinity.'   (Ullian 1976:43)

With this recognition of the social as opposed to biological
determinants of gender comes greater tolerance, argue Kohlberg
and Ullian, for gender deviance. This tolerance, they say, first
comes about when gender constancy is established in earlier
childhood, when the child then recognizes that to act like a
member of the opposite sex is not to put one's biological sex at
risk, that psychological gender is not equivalent to biological sex.
And this is evident in the fact that children, girls at least, seem to
stick less rigidly to same-sex interaction once they acquire gender
constancy (Smetana and Letourneau 1984). By adolescence, argue
cognitive developmentalists, boys as well as girls are less slavish in
conforming with, and less insistent than younger children on
others conforming with the norms of their sex.

Ullian implies that the increasing liberalism of children with
age in their gender attitudes is an instance of the generally greater
liberalism of older as compared to younger children in their moral
attitudes. In this she follows Kohlberg's account of moral
development according to which the child's moral choices are first
governed by whether they accord with, and will be seen by others
to accord with, the dictates of external authority. The child, says

Kohlberg, later comes to recognize these dictates to be a matter of social convention which it believes it should obey for the good of society. Later still, children and adolescents subject these conventions themselves to moral scrutiny and evaluate them in terms of whether they are consistent with the ethics of equity, justice, and so on.

Applying this account of moral development to her data on children's gender attitudes, Ullian says that the child first insists on gender conformity as a matter of obedience to the dictates of nature, then as a matter of obedience to the dictates of social convention, and later still comes to relax this insistence as she or he comes to question whether these conventions are fair and just. An example of this last stage, claims Ullian, is the following response of one of her research sample to the question, 'Who do you think should be the head of the family, the boss, the man or the woman?':

> 'I think it should be shared equally. [Why?] Well, the man does go out and earn money, but that doesn't mean he should be boss because . . . . The woman could be the one that goes out and works, and the man could, they could share it equally. They are equals, so one shouldn't domineer over the other one. They should be equal.'   (Ullian 1977:144, 145)

Ullian points out, however, that even though teenagers and adults may thus be egalitarian in their attitudes to men's and women's psychology, they nevertheless often prefer men and women to be psychologically different from each other. For instance one of her student sample said he preferred a woman to be:

> 'aggressive and ambitious in a less obvious way [than a man]. I feel like a moron admitting it, but it is bred into me, and so if I see a woman who is competing with men and who is being openly aggressive with men, it just sets off a mechanism. . . . I say [stereotypes] should be abolished, but I can't help what has been put into me over the years.'   (Kohlberg and Ullian 1974:221)

And it is clear that in adolescence particularly there is an increasing preoccupation with conforming with the norms of one's sex lest one be regarded as deviant – an anxiety that has been held responsible for the drop-out of teenage girls from maths (see, for example, Beckwith and Durkin 1981; Boswell 1985; but see also Eccles *et al.* 1985), science (see, for example, Keller 1983), and sport (see, for example, Nicholson 1984).

A nice example of the way adults prefer others to conform with the stereotypes of their sex, despite the fact that these selfsame adults question existing inequalities between the sexes, comes from a recent controversy within cognitive-developmental theory itself. An erstwhile student and co-worker of Kohlberg's, Carol Gilligan, takes issue with his account of moral development. She argues that it does not do justice to the 'different voice' that she says characterizes women's moral reasoning. (Indeed she comes close to asserting that far from being morally deficient – as Kohlberg, in conformity with the myth of Eve, implies – women are men's moral superiors.) Girls and women, she claims, decide moral questions in terms of their bearing on relationship issues. Such decisions, she says, should be given at least the same worth that Kohlberg accords decisions framed in terms of individual rights to equality and justice. Gilligan maintains that this latter form of reasoning typifies male, not female decision-making.

As evidence she quotes the following response of an eleven year old, Jake, to a moral dilemma in which he was asked whether a man, Heinz, should steal a drug which he could not afford in order to save his wife's life. Weighing up the right to life against that to property, Jake said that Heinz should steal the drug: 'For one thing, a human life is worth more than money, and if the druggist only makes $1,000, he is still going to live, but if Heinz doesn't steal the drug, his wife is going to die' (Gilligan 1982a:26). On the other hand, says Gilligan, another eleven year old, Amy, responded to this dilemma not in terms of the rights of the individuals involved, but in terms of their relationship to each other. Pondering on the problem, Amy said,

'If he stole the drug, he might save his wife then, but if he did, he might have to go to jail, and then his wife might get sicker again, and he couldn't get more of the drug, and it might not be so good. So, they should really just talk it out and find some other way to make the money.' (Gilligan 1982a:28)

Gilligan claims that, in attending to relationship issues rather than to individual rights, Amy's response is typical of the moral reasoning used by girls and women.

Yet Gilligan's own feminism and her criticism of Kohlberg is testimony to the fact that women also make moral judgements in terms of individual rights. It is because he fails to accord equal rights to women and men as individuals, to their moral reasoning, that Gilligan criticizes Kohlberg. And her criticism in this respect is in accord with the general struggle of feminism to have women's rights as individuals respected equally with those of men. Despite this oversight Gilligan's claim that women are not concerned with individual rights has received widespread approval and publicity among feminists as well as non-feminists, and in the feminist as well as non-feminist press (see, for example, Saxton 1981, Gilligan 1982b). The popularity of her thesis is due, I would suggest, to the fact that it provides apparent confirmation of the wishful belief that women are less individualistic and selfish than men, that they are better attuned than men and more empathic than them to emotional and relational issues.

But this belief flies in the face of the evidence that women are not only motivated by care for others, but are also motivated by individual rights and interests, that in this their moral reasoning is similar to that of men. (For evidence on this point see Walker 1984.) Indeed Gilligan's own data bear this out (Broughton 1983). It was not only the boys in her study who responded to the Heinz dilemma in terms of the individual rights it involved. So too did the girls as in the following example of a teenager who responded to it thus:

'I think survival is one of the first things in life that people fight for, I think it is the most important thing, more important than stealing. Stealing might be wrong, but if you have to steal to survive yourself or even kill, that is what you should do. . . .

Preservation of oneself, I think, is the most important thing. It comes before anything in life.' (Gilligan 1982a:76)

Gilligan, however, clearly prefers women to conform with the stereotype that holds them to be more concerned with relational and caring issues than with individual rights. Whereas Kohlberg might have given the above response a relatively high score as evincing principled moral reasoning in terms of rights and duties, Gilligan ranks it low in her scale of moral values. She says it indicates immaturity of moral judgement, that it focuses on 'caring for the self in order to ensure survival' and is therefore inferior to reasoning in terms of 'caring for others', and to the still more advanced level of reasoning that she says typifies the best in women's moral judgement, namely reasoning that is concerned with both care for self and others recognized as in mutual interdependence with each other (Gilligan 1982a:74).

So firmly entrenched and widespread is the preference, here expressed in Gilligan's scale of moral development, for women to conform with the norms of their sex, that appeal can reliably be made to this preference in furthering the cause of anti-feminism. Anti-feminist propaganda has repeatedly sought to achieve its ends by discrediting feminists as deviating from the norms of their sex, as unfeminine – as 'unsexed' (Linton 1883, quoted by Hollis 1979:234), as evincing 'masculo-femininity (viraginity)' and 'psycho-sexual aberrancy' (Weir 1895:819), as seeking 'unisex rest-rooms' and a generally 'desexed society' as anti-ERA campaigners have recently put it (Ehrenreich 1983:145). Mindful of such opposition, women have often been chary of appearing masculine in their behaviour and dress – of seeming too 'strong-minded' as Elizabeth Garrett Anderson once put it – lest they thereby damage the wider cause of women's emancipation. Indeed, Emily Davies, the founder of Girton College, was thrown into a veritable flap by her students dressing as men to do a play, so fearful was she that this would adversely affect women's chances of gaining formal admission to Cambridge (Strachey 1928). A similar anxiety leads women today likewise to make much of their femininity in entering spheres of activity traditionally assigned to men. As an American athlete recently put it: 'a lot of us try, subconsciously maybe, to look as feminine as possible in a race. There's always plenty of hair ribbons in races!' (quoted by Graydon 1983:10).

Cognitive-developmental theory does not explain the persistence into adulthood of the preference that women act in conformity with the feminine norms of their sex, and men with the masculine norms of their sex – a preference evident in the many jokes now made about 'gender-bender' Boy George, and in the fun made of men who do women's chores as not 'real men' (Simmonds 1985:6), and of women who stand up for themselves as not truly women as in the following Andy Capp cartoon:

For Kohlberg implies that once gender constancy is achieved, at around seven years of age, we have no cause to seek gender conformity either for ourselves or others. The fact that adults as well as children nevertheless do prefer such conformity raises the possibility that this preference persists because of the material interests it serves, because of the interests served, men say, by having women be less assertive than themselves as they are enjoined to be by our culture's stereotype of femininity. Or maybe the persistence of this preference into adulthood is due to adults feeling insecure about their sexual identity just as children do, to their seeking to overcome this insecurity by insisting on gender conformity both in themselves and others. Neither possibility is considered by Kohlberg. I shall pursue the latter possibility further in discussing Freud's work (see, for example, p. 135 below). In the next chapter I shall outline a theory that pursues the former possibility, namely that our preference for gender conformity is an effect of the material benefits it brings.

3
Social learning

> One is not born, but rather becomes, a woman. . . . it is
> civilization as a whole that produces this creature, intermediate
> between male and eunuch, which is described as feminine . . .
> the passivity that is the essential characteristic of the 'feminine'
> woman is . . . a destiny imposed upon her by her teachers and
> by society. . . . she is taught that to please she must try to please,
> she must make herself an object; she should therefore
> renounce her autonomy. . . . If she were encouraged in it, she
> could display the same lively exuberance, the same curiosity,
> the same initiative, the same hardihood, as a boy.   (Simone de
> Beauvoir 1949:295,307,308)

Far more obvious than the theory that children and adults
conform with gender stereotypes to bolster their sense of
themselves as male or female, is the theory that this conformity is
an effect of social conditioning, of boys being taught to be
masculine, of girls being taught to be feminine, that only thus will
they please and be rewarded by others. Simone de Beauvoir is not
alone in putting forward this theory of the genesis of existing
psychological differences between the sexes. It is a view regularly
expressed by feminists and others who reject biological
determinist explanations of these differences. Within academic
psychology this view is now known as 'social learning theory'.
And it remains today probably the most widely used perspective
guiding empirical research into the psychology of gender.
   Walter Mischel (1966) was perhaps the first systematically to

formalize this theory as it is used in this research. He and his followers argue that children first come to know of the behaviour associated with their sex through 'observational learning', through observing the behaviour of their parents and siblings, and of other children and adults around them (see, for example, Perry and Bussey 1979). They claim that children learn of the association of aggression, say, with masculinity from the fact that parents and nursery school teachers treat boys more roughly and boisterously than girls, and from their experience in nursery school, for instance, that the boys tend to be more often involved than the girls in rough-and-tumble and aggressive interaction (see pp. 6–7 above).

As evidence that children can acquire sex-typed behaviours through observing it in others, Mischel cites the experimental studies of his fellow behaviourist, Albert Bandura. He cites, for instance, Bandura's study in which three to five year olds were shown a film of someone attacking a large, inflated Bobo doll by sitting on it, punching it in the nose, hammering it, tossing it in the air, and kicking it, all the while abusing it verbally with such remarks as 'Sock him in the nose . . .', 'Hit him down . . .', 'Throw him in the air . . .', 'Kick him . . .', and 'Pow!'. The children were then 'mildly frustrated'. They were given some attractive toys to play with but were then immediately whisked away to another room where there were some more toys including a three foot Bobo doll. The children who had seen the film thereupon set about attacking the doll in the ways they had seen the actor do on the film, the boys being significantly more aggressive than the girls in this respect especially if the actor on film had been a man (Bandura *et al.* 1963).

However absurd or even unethical one might find this study, it does seem to demonstrate that sex-typed behaviours – in this case aggression – can be acquired through observational learning, albeit that subsequent research, stimulated by concern about the harmful effect of television violence, have not replicated Bandura's finding that these effects vary by sex (Milavsky *et al.* 1982).

It is now commonplace to point to the ways television may contribute to children's learning of gender. Children, it is argued, learn of the association of aggression with masculinity from the fact that anger is more often expressed by men than by women on TV (Birnbaum and Croll 1984). Similarly, it is said, children learn of the association of femininity with submissiveness and subservience from the way these traits are so often expressed by women and so seldom by men on TV (Sternglanz and Serbin 1974; Kalisch and Kalisch 1984). That television thus plays a part in children's learning of the stereotypes of masculinity and femininity that they also learn from countless other sources, is also suggested by the fact that the more television children watch the more traditional are their gender stereotypes (McGhee and Frueh 1980, but see Durkin 1985a), and by the fact that when children are shown films in which these stereotypes are transgressed their subsequent gender attitudes are less conformist (see, for example, Cobb *et al.* 1982; Geis *et al.* 1984). It is not, however, clear how long-lasting such effects are, and some have found television portrayal of counter-stereotypes to have no significant effect in changing children's gender attitudes even in the short term (see, for example, Durkin and Hutchins 1984). Furthermore, it is evident that the influence of television in teaching and modifying gender stereotypes varies with the age, sex, and personality of the viewer (Pingree 1978; Eisenstock 1984) – factors not readily subsumable within social learning theory. It should also be pointed out that television may not so much contribute to the acquisition of gender stereotypes as presuppose the viewer's knowledge of them. (See Durkin 1985b for a much fuller discussion of these issues than is possible here.)

Gender stereotypes are also said to be conveyed to children by the books that are read to them (Weitzman *et al.* 1976), by the books they read themselves (Sharpe 1976; Dixon 1977), and by the newspapers (Foreit *et al.* 1980). Some however have questioned whether, apart from sex differences in aggression, the media do in fact now depict males and females as quite so psychologically different as feminists have sometimes claimed (Davis 1984; Collins *et al.* 1984). That books, nevertheless, do seem to contribute to children's learning of gender comes from the finding that, where children are given stories in which the characters do not conform to stereotype, their subsequent gender attitudes are more liberal, this effect being especially pronounced in girls (Flerx *et al.* 1976). And, of course, children also learn of the norms associated with their sex from the organization and content of the school curriculum (see, for example, Koblinsky and Sugawara 1984; Sayers 1984a), and from the structuring by sex of domestic and occupational roles as is evident from children's stereotypes about these roles (see, for example, Franken 1983; C.J. Archer 1984).

Mischel argues that whether children and adults themselves act in conformity with the gender stereotypes they observe depends on the 'reinforcement contingencies' associated with such conformity. He and his followers maintain that male aggression and dominance, for instance, are not simply an effect of boys and men observing such traits to be associated with their sex. They are also an effect of their experiencing aggression to be rewarded for their sex. Moreover, children are likely to come by this experience early in life given that parents so obviously approve of aggression in boys. As one Nottinghamshire mother said of her four year old son: 'I like the way he's rough. He's a proper lad' (quoted by Archer and Lloyd 1982:203).

Experimental evidence that reward for aggression increases the probability of its subsequent occurrence comes again from the work of Bandura (1965), from another study in which he again showed three to five year olds a film of a man hitting and being generally aggressive to a Bobo doll. This time the children were then told that they would get stickers and a drink every time they imitated the behaviour they had seen on film. Under these changed conditions, where the children were offered rewards for copying filmed aggression, the previously observed sex differences in imitative aggression were practically wiped out. This, says Mischel, demonstrates that, although knowledge of the sex-typing of behaviour such as aggression is acquired through observing how men and women act, actual imitation of this behaviour depends on the rewards associated with it. The reason girls are less often aggressive, he argues, is that they are less often rewarded for being aggressive.

Social learning theorists claim that boys are rewarded more

than girls not only by adults but also by other children for being aggressive and masculine in their behaviour. In a recent experiment, for example, it was found both that parents punished their pre-school daughters by ignoring them when they played with boys' toys – with soldiers and war vehicles, for instance – and that other children also punished them by ridiculing them for such 'masculine' behaviour. By contrast, the boys in the study were rewarded both by their fathers and by their peers for playing with these toys (Langlois and Downs 1980). When they play with girls' toys, however, boys are often criticized, isolated, and left to their own devices by other children (Fagot 1977). And children quickly become aware of such sanctions against boys acting like girls. As one five year old put it in explaining why, although it was all right for a boy to play with a G.I. Joe, it was not all right for him to play with a Barbie Doll:

> 'Because if a boy is playing with something, like if a boy plays with a Barbie Doll, then he's just going to get people teasing him, and if he tries to play more, to get girls to like him, then the girls won't like him either. [Why won't the girls like him?] Because they might think it's funny to have a boy playing with girls' stuff.' (Damon 1977:255)

Nor is it any wonder that children should so quickly learn of the negative consequences of deviating from the norms of their sex, such is their exposure to these consequences both in their own immediate day-to-day experience, and in the media. In the British comic, *The Beano*, for instance, Walter the Softy's femininity is the constant butt of the taunts and attacks of Dennis the Menace and his dog, Gnasher.

And, as has been regularly pointed out by feminists, such conditioning does not stop with childhood. Teenagers and adults are also constantly bombarded by the media about the sanctions associated with gender deviance, and the rewards of gender conformity (see, for example, Peck and Senderowitz 1974; Coote and Campbell 1982; Coward 1984). It is clear, for instance, that many women fear to succeed in those spheres of activity traditionally assigned to men lest they thereby be disliked and regarded as 'unfeminine' (see, for example, Horner 1969; Cano *et al.* 1984; but see also Paludi 1984 and Durkin in press). In Victorian times the sanctions against women being 'masculine' in their behaviour were likewise clearly conveyed to them. Thus, for instance, the sexologist Krafft-Ebing then wrote uncharitably of women who think, feel, or act like men as thereby evincing an 'extreme grade of degenerative homosexuality' (Krafft-Ebing 1886:262–63). And one reads of women at the beginning of this century learning to avoid 'manly games because they are unwomanly and unbecoming', never cultivating their minds 'because men dislike clever women', and instead learning 'to sew and knit and keep house and talk prettily' to attract men – an upbringing that seemed particularly futile to many who did not marry (Knight 1984). Similarly we are told today that men 'do not like pushy, ambitious girls' (Wilby 1985:37). The negative consequences of gender deviance continue to be much canvassed. In his popular advice manual, *Pregnancy*, Gordon Bourne even goes so far as to suggest that such deviance can lead to infertility! He writes: 'From a purely biological aspect the masculine type of female and the effeminate type of male are not good vehicles for reproduction and the procreation of the human race' (Bourne 1972:27).

Despite this, however, many women and men feel free to be both masculine and feminine in their behaviour. Their readiness thus to contravene the norms of their sex has been measured by the American psychologist, Sandra Bem (1974), who found that while some women respond to her Sex-Role Inventory (the BSRI) by only owning to those traits socially associated with femininity – traits such as being gentle, shy, understanding, and yielding – others also own to masculine traits – traits such as being aggressive, assertive, independent, and self-sufficient. She reports that the latter type of woman, whom she refers to as 'androgynous', is more adaptable (Bem 1976). And, although many questions have since been raised about the BSRI – about the validity of its femininity scale (Pedhazur and Tetenbaum 1979), for instance, and about whether it measures anything more than a limited subset of the traits associated with femininity and masculinity (Spence 1984) – it and similar sex-role questionnaires continue to be widely used. It is now reported on the basis of research using these questionnaires that women who have 'masculine' as well as 'feminine' traits are less afraid of success (Cano *et al.* 1984; Wittig 1984), make more effective business managers (Blanchard and Sargent 1984), and tend to be regarded by others as better managers than more 'feminine' women and men (Powell and Butterfield 1984). Furthermore, they are also found to be freer of guilt feelings (Evans 1984), and of neurotic and depressive symptoms than their more feminine counterparts (Heiser and Gannon 1984; Elpern and Karp 1984; Tinsley *et al.* 1984; Carlson and Baxter 1984).

These findings imply that women should be urged to be 'androgynous', to express those traits – assertiveness, say – associated with masculinity, as well as those traits – being yielding, say – associated with femininity. Bem herself, however, now takes issue with this conclusion. The 'feminist moral' of such research, she says, is that women and men should stop dichotomizing behaviour by sex (Bem 1981). They should seek to overcome their preoccupation with gender difference, and 'should stop projecting gender into situations irrelevant to genitalia' (Bem 1983:616). Given the manifold ways in which social relations are now structured by sex, however, this solution seems somewhat utopian (Morgan and Ayim 1984). Clearly our current preoccupation with gender difference is not going to disappear overnight! In the meantime it has seemed more fruitful to many feminists to pursue the implications of the above findings, namely that women be encouraged to be 'androgynous', to be masculine as well as feminine in their behaviour. In particular, it has been argued that women should be encouraged to be more masculine, in the sense of being more assertive.

As a result there has been an explosion of assertiveness training techniques. They are now big business, being used for instance by The Industrial Society's Pepperell Unit to teach women management skills (Bingham 1985). Implicitly or explicitly, these techniques use the principles of social learning adumbrated above. Adopting that theory's belief in the effectiveness of observational learning, they seek to teach women to be assertive by getting them to watch others modelling such behaviour. A typical exercise involves getting pairs of women to take it in turns to act out to each other the part of a dissatisfied customer returning shoddy goods to a store, assertively requesting the shopkeeper to replace them (see, for example, Prutzman 1982). Women are also taught to be assertive by being rewarded for it, and by being encouraged to reward and urge themselves to be more assertive. Anne Dickson, for instance, suggests that women reading her assertiveness training manual should instil assertiveness and confidence in themselves by keeping in mind the following precept: 'I have the right to be treated with respect as an intelligent, capable, and equal human being' (Dickson 1982:30).

Such techniques however easily lend themselves to ridicule and satire, being frequently guyed in such sketches as those of the Monty Python team. And this is evidence of the general scepticism as to the likely effectiveness of assertiveness training, and other techniques lauding 'the power of positive thinking', in fundamentally altering our psychology, especially such deep-seated aspects of it as are associated with gender. Nor is this scepticism misplaced given that, although assertiveness is increasingly being modelled by, and rewarded in women, women nevertheless continue to be generally less assertive than men.

Women's relative lack of assertiveness compared to men's more marked assertiveness and dominance persists not only in our society but also in those societies that have undergone revolutionary transformation. Lenin complained of it, for instance, following the October Revolution of 1917. Russian men 'in the Party and among the masses', he said, all too often continue to adopt 'the old slave-owner's point of view of dominance towards women' (quoted by Vogel 1983:123). Nor does this psychology seem to have withered away in today's USSR.

The persistence in men of a psychology of dominance and assertiveness towards women in the capitalist societies of the West, as well as in the socialist societies of the East, despite the greater sex equality modelled and rewarded today in all these societies, demonstrates that this psychology is more entrenched than social learning theory would have us believe. Rejecting this theory, many feminists have instead looked to psychoanalysis as a means of explaining the continuing psychology of men's social dominance and of women's acquiescence in it. For in its theory of infantile sexuality and of the unconscious, psychoanalysis seems to address that which is most deep-rooted in the psychology of gender. In the next part of this book I shall consider four different ways in which feminists have used post-Freudian theory to explain this psychology. I shall start with 'essentialist' accounts that treat femininity and masculinity as given, in essence, by the character of women's and men's biology.

PART TWO

Post-Freudian psychoanalysis

4
Psychoanalytic essentialism

> Nature has given women so much power that the law has very wisely given them little. (Samuel Johnson 1763:157)

> Commenting on an opponent to women's suffrage, Lord Cecil said: 'He might have been recently spanked, and he feels so deeply and bitterly as never to have got over the indignity of having been born of a woman.' (Quoted by Rowbotham 1973a:83)

In *Of Woman Born*, the American feminist and poet, Adrienne Rich, argues that the failure of social change to effect significant reduction in men's attitudes of chauvinism and dominance toward women is due to these attitudes being deep-rooted in men's attempt thereby to compensate themselves for their envy of women's power in bearing and rearing children – 'their terror of blinding / by the look of her who bore them' (Rich 1975:83). Conjuring up this power, she quotes Rilke:

> 'Mother, you created him small, it was you who started him; . . . where are those years when with your delicate figure you simply stood between him and surging chaos?' (Rich 1976:187)

In her own poem, 'Mother Right', Rich depicts the power of woman as mother to be without limit. She contrasts it with that of man, measuring out the boundaries of what is his (Rich 1977:59).

In arguing that men's continuing attitude of dominance toward women stems from envy of the limitlessness of woman as mother, Rich returns to the work of Karen Horney, the foremost feminist of the early psychoanalytic movement. Rich cites Horney's work thus in criticizing Engels' thesis that socialism will bring to an end men's dominance over women. This thesis, she says:

'is an excellent illustration of what Karen Horney means when she says that "it is in the interest of men to obscure [the fact that there is a struggle between the sexes], and the emphasis they place on their ideologies has caused women, also, to adopt these theories." In her delicately worded essay, "The Distrust Between the Sexes", Horney speaks of the resentment and anxiety harbored by all men toward women – even, she says, by "men who consciously have a very positive relationship with women and hold them in high esteem as human beings." Materialist analysis and masculine bias allow Engels to assume that an economic solution will cleanse false consciousness, create a new concept of gender, purge the future of the pathologies of the past. But he fails to understand that it is the mother–son and mother–daughter relationship, as much as, perhaps more than, that between man the buyer and woman the bought, which creates the sexual politics of male supremacism. Even under the pressures of a growing, worldwide, women's consciousness, the overwhelming bias of socialist and revolutionary movements is male, and reflects a wish to have a social revolution which would leave male leadership and control essentially untouched.' (Rich 1976:99–100)

In the essay to which Rich here refers, Horney argues that men have an unconscious dread of women due to phantasies they entertain in childhood about their mothers. Boys, she says, have an innate desire to have sexual intercourse with their mothers. Rebuffed by the mother on this account, as he experiences it, the boy indulges phantasies of revenging himself on her by 'taking by force and stealing . . . killing, burning, cutting to pieces, and choking' phantasies, the primitive content of which derives from the preoccupations of young children with the immediate sensations arising from their bodily processes (Horney 1931:110). But these phantasies in turn lead the boy to fear lest his mother retaliate and attack him in like manner.

Horney wrote at somewhat greater length of the infantile, unconscious roots of this kind of fear in a later paper, 'The Dread of Woman'. Unlike Freud, who had pointed out as Kohlberg now does, that children do not initially know of sexual difference, Horney claimed in this essay that children know of sex difference from the very start of life. Such are the penetrative sensations in his penis, says Horney, that the boy intuitively knows of the existence of the vagina, of an organ in women to be penetrated. He also knows his penis to be much smaller than the mother's vagina. This gives rise to the following anxiety: 'The boy . . . feels or instinctively judges that his penis is much too small for his mother's genital and reacts with the dread of his own inadequacy, of being rejected and derided' (Horney 1932b:142).

Nor, of course, is it only analysts who write of men's fear and distrust of women and the relation of these anxieties to their ideas about the vagina, to *vagina dentata* anxieties. Shakespeare, for instance, in *Much Ado About Nothing*, has the well-named Benedick express just this anxiety:

'That a woman conceived me, I thank her; that she brought me up, I likewise give her most humble thanks; but that I will have a recheat winded in my forehead, or hang my bugle in an invisible baldrick, all women shall pardon me. Because I will not do them the wrong to distrust any, I will do myself the right to trust none.'   (Act I, Scene i)

Horney, however, points out that men and boys not only mistrust women – they also idealize them. They entertain the phantasy of an ideal, 'nurturing, self-sacrificing mother' who is limitless in her ability to 'fulfil all his expectations and longings'. But this phantasy, she says, breeds its counterpart, 'resentment toward capabilities that one does not possess' (Horney 1931:114; see also Chasseguet-Smirgel 1976).

Indeed Horney (1926) claims that boys and men envy women as much on this score as girls and women envy men their penises. In this, however, she overlooks the fact that, given men's social dominance, women are likely to envy men, and the penis that symbolizes this dominance, more than men envy women and their biology. As Juliet Mitchell (1984) points out, Freud's (1937c) insistence on the asymmetrical attitude of the sexes to each other, on their common 'repudiation of femininity', is more plausible than Horney's claim that both sexes equally envy each other.

Undaunted by such loopholes in her argument, Horney went on to maintain that men's envy of women, that their 'womb envy', is the psychological driving force behind their creation of the 'state, religion, art and science'. But, she says, since these creations fail adequately to compensate men for their envy of women, they try still further to compensate for it by seeking to keep women out of 'their domains', by devaluing women and their maternity, and by overvaluing masculinity and male genitality (Horney 1931:115). Furthermore, they seek to justify this discrimination against women by developing theories, such as that of Freud's theory of women's penis-envy, that characterize women as inferior to men – theories that are readily accepted by women as objective and value free, such is the hegemony enjoyed by men's theories and ideas in male-dominated society (see, for example, Horney 1926). In this last respect, of course, Horney's argument hardly seems innovatory today. It was, however, extremely refreshing in 1967 when her collected papers on *Feminine Psychology* were first published, given the then lack of general awareness of the extent to which this is a 'man's world' (see Rowbotham 1973b).

Clearly men's theories of women's inferiority and necessary subordination to them contradict women's interests. Why then, apart from the hegemony of men's ideas in society, do women acquiesce in them and in the justification of men's social dominance that these ideas express? Horney implies that this acquiescence derives in large measure from women's biology making them innately submissive to men. On the *a priori* assumption that the determinants of women's psychology must be equal to those of men, she rejected Freud's view that women's attitudes to men are based on high regard for their anatomy, for the penis. Such a view, she said, is 'decidedly unsatisfying, not only to feminine narcissism but also to biological science' (Horney 1924:38). Instead she explained women's psychology, including their attitudes to men, as grounded in women's biology.

Among these attitudes, she said, is an innate sexual desire in women for men. Ignoring the clinical evidence that led Freud to conclude that heterosexual desire is acquired not inborn, that girls like boys adopt the person who first looks after them (usually the mother or some other women) as their first love object, that the girl's first desire is therefore homosexual not heterosexual, Horney insisted that the girl's first love object is the father, that her heterosexual desire for him is given from birth by 'the great [animal] law of heterosexual attraction' (Horney 1932a:125). Furthermore, she said, women's heterosexual desire is characterized by passive, masochistic submission to men, that this is an effect of female biology. The girl, she says, innately knows of the disparity in size between her father's genitalia and her own, and has an innate desire to be subject to his desire. This is evident, she maintains, from the fact that from early infancy girls entertain phantasies of being raped, phantasies 'that an excessively large penis is effecting forcible penetration, producing pain and hemorrhage, and threatening to destroy something' (Horney 1926:65).

But if, as Horney claims, women innately desire to be the passive, masochistic object of men, then how are we to account for the fact that they also resist this, their assigned feminine destiny? Paradoxically, and despite her own feminism, Horney treated such resistance, where it occurs, as a sign of neurosis in women, as an effect of a defence first formed in childhood against the sexual desire the girl then consciously feels toward her father. Such is the guilt attaching to this desire, and the anxiety lest her vagina be damaged by the father's penis were this desire to be fulfilled, says Horney, that the girl often defends against it and the female-based feelings that give rise to it by denying these feelings and instead asserting her maleness. In this, says Horney, girls draw on their pre-Oedipal desire to have a penis then stimulated in them by envy of the urethral-erotic, exhibitionistic, and masturbatory gratification seemingly afforded boys by their penises (see Horney 1924). Horney goes on to argue that girls and women rationalize this envy, which she says basically stems from neurotic resistance to their femininity, in terms of the social advantages enjoyed by men in male-dominated society.

But if, as Horney claims, girls are essentially passive and feminine in their psychology from whence comes this, their supposed masculine resistance to, and defence against that femininity? As Freud pointed out: 'if the defence against femininity is so energetic, from what other source can it draw its strength than from the masculine trend which found its first expression in the child's penis-envy and therefore deserves to be named after it?' (Freud 1931b:392). That is, one has to suppose the existence of a 'masculine trend', as Freud here terms it, in women's psychology if one is to account for their resistance to their femininity, let alone to the social subordination of women that received notions of femininity express. Horney however rejected such a possibility. She entirely opposed Freud's theory of infantile bisexuality – that girls like boys have masculine as well as feminine, active as well as passive aims and desires from birth. As a result she failed to explain, even in terms of neurotic defence, the psychology of women's resistance to their subordination.

In 1932 Horney left Berlin for Chicago. According to Dee Garrison (1981), her departure had been largely motivated by the hostility of the Freudians in Berlin to her work. Whatever the cause, Horney was now exposed to a very different culture. And it was this, she later wrote, that alerted her to the priority of social over biological factors in shaping women's and men's psychology (see Horney 1939:12–13). She now revised her previous view that the repressed Oedipus complex (for instance the girl's Oedipal desire for her father) is a biologically-determined cultural universal. Instead she argued that it only occurs where the parents are so wrapped up in their own interests that they fail adequately to attend to the interests of the child. Only then, she said, does the child become incestuously attached to the parent. This attachment, she claimed, then occurs as an attempt by the child to allay the anxiety and insecurity instilled in it by its parents' lack of empathic response to its needs.

This, Horney's later theory of the Oedipus complex, has

become commonplace in current ego psychology (see, for example, Kohut 1977 and Lasch's 1979 adoption of it) – a theory that explicitly blames parents, and particularly mothers, for the neuroses of their children. Horney herself, however, remained a feminist in her sympathies despite this woman-blaming drift of her later theory. She continued to reject the Freudian theory that women's passivity and masochism is an effect of penis-envy. But she now explained these traits in social and cultural rather than in biological terms – as determined by women's economic dependence on men. Men, she wrote, prefer their women to be feminine, to be submissive to them. And since women are economically as well as emotionally dependent on pleasing them they therefore conform with these, men's ideals of their sex (Horney 1935). It is this, she said, that also causes girls to respond to any insecurity bred in them by their upbringing by trying 'to cling to the most powerful person around' rather than by trying 'to rebel and fight' (Horney 1950:19 and O'Connell 1980). Even though she now took more account of the social determinants of women's psychology, she still focused on the passive, submissive, 'feminine' aspects to the neglect of the active, so-called masculine aspects of women's psychology that fuel their resistance to their social subordination.

Her theory still implied that there is not much hope of women themselves actively seeking to overcome the discrimination socially exercized against them. Adrienne Rich however seeks to wrest an optimistic conclusion for feminism from the view she shares with Horney, namely that women are essentially feminine, not also masculine, in their psychology. She concludes *Of Woman Born* by envisaging the following solution to the dilemma of women's subordination:

'I am really asking whether women cannot begin, at last, to think through the body, to connect what has been so cruelly disorganized – our great mental capacities, hardly used; our highly developed tactile sense; our genius for close observation; our complicated, pain-enduring, multipleasured physicality. . . . The repossession by women of our bodies will bring far more essential changes to society than the seizing of the means of production by workers. The female body has been both territory and machine, virgin wilderness to be exploited and assembly-line turning out life. We need to imagine a world in which every woman is the presiding genius of her own body. In such a world women will truly create new life, bringing forth not only children (if and as we choose) but the visions, and the thinking, necessary to sustain, console, and alter human existence – a new relationship to the universe.' (Rich 1976:290,292)

Women's supposed 'complicated, pain-enduring, multipleasured physicality' hardly seems a very hopeful basis on which to build resistance to their social subordination whereby, as Rich (1976, 1980) points out, women have all too often been expropriated from their control over childbirth, and from their intimacy and solidarity with other women. On the other hand, given the way women, their psychology, and their bodies are so frequently denigrated or idealized in the interests of men, it remains important to encourage women, as Rich does, to value themselves for themselves. It is therefore no surprise that Rich's writing and poetry should have attracted such a following.

A similar though not so widespread acclaim has been accorded the work of the French philosopher and psychoanalyst, Luce Irigaray. Like Rich, and like Horney in her early work, Irigaray claims that women's femininity is given in essence by their biology. Women, she says, have a distinctive psychology and desire given by the nature of their sexual organs. She writes, for instance, that

'Women's autoerotism is very different from man's. He needs an instrument in order to touch himself: his hand, women's genitals, language. And this self-stimulation requires a minimum of activity. But a woman touches herself by and within herself directly, without mediation, and before any distinction between activity and passivity is possible. A woman "touches herself" constantly without anyone being able to forbid her to do so, for her sex is composed of two lips which embrace continually.' (Irigaray 1977a:100)

Irigaray implies that women's lack of awareness of their specifically feminine desire, which she says is rooted essentially in the character of their bodies, is due to their being alienated from it by men and their needs. Woman's autoerotism, she writes, 'which she needs in order not to risk the disappearance of her pleasure in the sex act, is interrupted by a violent intrusion: the brutal spreading of these two lips by a violating penis' (Irigaray 1977a:100). Furthermore, she says, men alienate women from themselves by coercing them into being passive objects of their voyeuristic desire:

> 'I, too [a woman] captive when a man holds me in his gaze; I, too, am abducted from myself. Immobilized in the reflection he expects of me. Reduced to the face he fashions for me in which to look at himself. Travelling at the whim of his dreams and mirages. Trapped in a single function – mothering.' (Irigaray 1981:66)

Not only are women alienated from their essential femininity in social and sexual intercourse with men, says Irigaray, but, she adds, they are also alienated from their sexuality by the way it is constituted, in male discourse, as lacking in women (a construction of sexual difference that Irigaray portrays as eternal but which today seems to be the effect of our inheritance of nineteenth-century ideas about sexual difference – see Harris 1985 – ideas well documented by feminist historians like Nancy Cott 1978). So captivated, says Irigaray, are women by this discourse, given its hegemony in male-dominated society, that woman 'Not knowing what she wants, ready for anything, even asking for more, if only he will "take" her as the "object" of his pleasure . . . will not say what she wants. Moreover, she does not know, or no longer knows, what she wants' (Irigaray 1977a: 100).

Irigaray counters the discourse, especially that of the psychoanalyst Jacques Lacan that constitutes woman as 'absence of sex' (Irigaray 1977b:63), by asserting the plenitude of woman's sexuality:

> 'Woman has sex organs just about everywhere. She experiences

pleasure almost everywhere. Even without speaking of the
hysterization of her entire body, one can say that the geography
of her pleasure is much more diversified, more multiple in its
differences, more complex, more subtle, than is imagined – in
an imaginary centered a bit too much on one and the
same.' (Irigaray 1977a:103)

Woman, she says, cannot therefore be adequately characterized in
the unitary terms of men's 'imaginary' – femininity is too
'discursive' for that. (A similar point is expressed by feminists who
argue that women are alienated from the truth of their experience
by 'man made language' – see for example Spender 1980 and
Cline 1984.)

Like Rich, Irigaray urges women to reappropriate their
femininity, the essence of which, she says, resides in their biology.
She urges women, in this case her fictive lover:

'Go back through all the names they [men] gave you. . . . This
currency of alternatives and oppositions, choices and negotia-
tions, has no value for us. . . . Instead, let's reappropriate our
mouth and try to speak. . . . We are not voids, lacks which wait
for sustenance, fulfilment, or plenitude from an other . . . . They
neither taught us nor allowed us to say our multiplicity . . . .
Long before your birth, you touched yourself, innocently.
Your/my body does not acquire a sex by some operation, by the
act of some power, function, or organ. You are already a
woman; you don't need any special modification or intervention. . . . How can we shake off the chains of these terms,
free ourselves from their categories, divest ourselves of their
names? . . . Begin with what you feel, here, right away. The
female "all" will come. . . . This "all" can't be schematized or
mastered. It's the total movement of our body. . . . Our
abundance is inexhaustible: it knows neither want nor plenty
. . . . Touch yourself, touch me, you'll "see".' (Irigaray
1980:69–78)

Irigaray is here rejecting Lacan's thesis that femininity is acquired
via the child's Oedipal recognition of sexual difference – of the

'alternatives and oppositions' of the presence/absence of the penis in men and women, of the meaning of the phallus signified by this antithesis. According to Lacan, this recognition is a precondition of the child's becoming a speaking subject, of its entry into the Symbolic, of its recognizing the Name-of-the-Father symbolized by the phallus (see chapter 7 below for a fuller explanation of this point). Irigaray insists, by contrast, that femininity is given prior to Oedipal recognition of sexual difference, of woman as 'lack' or 'void', of the paternal 'function', of the phallic 'organ', that its essence is given 'long before your [woman's] birth', that it is constituted in woman by her relation to her own body, and by her pre-Oedipal relation to her mother's body – 'Touch yourself, touch me, you'll "see" '.

But, as Lacanians have regularly pointed out in criticism of this thesis, femininity is not constituted in and of itself, or in relation solely to other women. It is only by being contrasted with masculinity that femininity acquires its meaning within patriarchy. And it is only as a result of this contrast that feminism comes into being to challenge the social divisions between the sexes expressed in this contrast. In this sense femininity does depend on recognizing women to be different from men – a recognition that Freud located as first occurring in the Oedipus complex.

Claire Buck's criticism of recent feminist appropriations of the work of H.D., a poet analysed by Freud in the early 1930s, illustrates this criticism of feminist essentialism. The following stanza from H.D.'s poem about Freud, 'The Master', has seemed to some feminists to lend support to their separatist and essentialist account of femininity:

> 'for she needs no man
> herself
> is that dart and pulse of the male,
> hands, feet, thighs,
> herself perfect.'
>
> (quoted by Buck 1983:62)

As Buck however points out, not only is it not clear that H.D. intended the poem from which this stanza is taken to proclaim woman's essential femininity, but, even were H.D. to have had this intention, it makes no sense to say that woman is 'perfect' in the sense of being self-sufficient. For woman is dependent on man if only, paradoxically, because her existence as woman is predicated on being contrasted in opposition and antithesis to man.

Irigaray's appeal to women to return to their supposed pre-Oedipal biological essence would found sisterhood on an illusory basis, on that of the pre-Oedipal child's 'imaginary' experience of itself as one with the mother. It thus hardly constitutes a sound basis on which to mount feminist struggle! (See Sayers 1984b for further discussion of this point.) Furthermore, it seeks to return women to a stage prior to knowledge of sexual difference. But this knowledge is a pre-condition of feminism and its struggle against the different and unequal ways in which women and men are currently treated in society.

The thesis that femininity resides, in essence, in women's biology has more often been used, both now and in the past, to justify rather than to question these social inequalities and differences. Nor is there anything new in Irigaray's incitement to women to speak their sexual 'multiplicity', or in Rich's characterization of women in terms of their supposed 'multi-pleasured physicality'. Again, this has more often been used to control than to liberate women. As French historian of ideas, Michel Foucault, points out in another context, the social production and incitement to discourse of our subjectivity as essentially sexual – a production to which, of course, Freud largely contributed – has constituted in our times a major means of alienating us from our needs, from our 'bodies and pleasures' (Foucault 1976:159). Women have all too long suffered the 'hysterization' of 'the feminine body . . . qualified and disqualified – as being thoroughly saturated with sexuality' (Foucault 1976:104).

Women may only be able to mount the cause for their emancipation in terms of the representations of women currently available to them. These representations of women's femininity constitute, in a certain measure, a rallying point in terms of which women can represent themselves to themselves and hence recognize the similarity between their social situation and that of other women. In affirming a particular cultural representation and image of femininity, as here of woman as a plenitude of sexuality, Irigaray and Rich clearly provide a banner around which women's solidarity as a sex can develop and crystallize, a focus for the formation of feminist consciousness, of 'woman identified woman' as Rich's followers sometimes put it. (An analogous point is outlined by Jeffrey Weeks 1981, Sonja Ruehl 1982, and Elizabeth Wilson 1984 in discussing the mobilization and identification of lesbians at the beginning of this century in terms of the then representation of them, on account of the active sexuality that supposedly marked them out from other women, as essentially male in their biology.)

Such mobilization does not, of itself, challenge the social construction of women's sexuality around which it takes place. In so far as Rich and Irigaray mistake the historical genesis of the construction of woman – in this case of woman as saturated with rather than as absence of sexuality – as depicting an eternal given of women's biology, they not only fail to challenge that construction – they positively wallow in it, and would have others do likewise. Irigaray and Rich well describe femininity as it is currently represented and construed. They well describe the supposed plenitude of women's sexuality, and the way this sexuality is at the same time construed (by Lacan for instance) as absent in women. They eloquently describe the passivity, masochism, boundlessness, interiority, caring, and lack of linearity of thought often supposed to differentiate women from men. Adrienne Rich, for instance, lyrically evokes the contrast of woman's thought – 'the unconscious, the subjective, the emotional' – with that of man – 'the structural, the rational, the intellectual' (Rich 1976:66–7). Time and again, in her poetry, she harps on the differences of the sexes: 'the girl . . . all Rubens flesh and happy moans', the boy 'tongue, hips, knees, nerves, brain . . . language'; woman's word her 'pulse, loving and ordinary', man's 'signals . . . dark scribbled flags'; in 'Trying to Talk with a Man', recognizing danger as interpersonal, man externalizing and listing equipment to deal with it; a mermaid 'Diving into the Wreck' with streaming hair, her counterpart 'the merman in his armored body'; and the refugee couple – 'he with fingers frozen around his Law / she with her down quilt sewn through iron nights' (Rich 1975:38,41,59,67,81).

To achieve the ends they seek, however, feminists have to go beyond such stereotypes of sexual difference. The trouble with Karen Horney's early work, and with the work of Adrienne Rich and Luce Irigaray is that it ultimately fails to provide a basis for doing this, for challenging these stereotypes, because it locates their essence in biology. Indeed, far from challenging these stereotypes, Irigaray for one asserts that the object of feminism should be to realize them: 'it's in order to establish their differences,' she says, 'that women are claiming their rights' (Irigaray 1977b:68). This would indeed seem to be one of the only options available to feminism if, as she and the other writers considered in this chapter claim, the essence of these differences is given by biology. Such essentialism, however, fails to account for the fact that women are also 'claiming their rights' to realize the sameness of their aims with those of men, including those of activity, individuality, boundedness, linearity of thought, and so on. Many feminists have accordingly favoured less essentialist versions of post-Freudian theory some of which I shall outline in the following chapters.

5
Melanie Klein

Man was made for Joy & Woe;
And when this we rightly know
Thro' the World we safely go
                            (Blake 1802:119)

Sucking at the mother's breast is the starting-point of the whole
of sexual life, the unmatched prototype of every later sexual
satisfaction, to which phantasy often enough recurs in times of
need. (Freud 1916–17:356)

The American psychologist Dorothy Dinnerstein has recently
returned to the work of another early analyst, Melanie Klein, and to
her account of the way the infant handles its 'joy' and 'woe', its
knowledge of 'good' and 'evil', its experience of gratification and
frustration in relation to the mother, to explain the psychology of
men's social dominance. Whereas Adrienne Rich and Luce Irigaray
use psychoanalytic accounts of this relation to stress the differences
between the sexes in their psychology, Dinnerstein uses Klein's
work to explain the psychological similarity between the sexes in
their psychological acquiescence in men's dominance in society.
   Kleinianism continues to be one of the major strands in British
psychoanalysis today. Many readers, however, will be unfamiliar
with it, so small is the number of people actually engaged in
psychoanalysis, Kleinian or otherwise. I shall therefore first
outline the relevant aspects of Klein's work before going on to
consider Dinnerstein's use of it.

The starting point of this work is Freud's account of the mother-infant relation, and of its mediation by the oral, anal, and genital components of the sexual instinct. In addition, Klein drew on her clinical work with schizoid and depressive symptoms in adults, and on observations made in the course of her pioneering analytic work with children.

On this basis Klein argued that the baby loves and hates its mother from the very start of life, that this ambivalence results from its instinctual endowment of love and hate, and from its experience of being gratified and frustrated by the mother, or more accurately by her breast since it is with this part of the mother that the infant first relates in being fed by her. (As regards bottle-fed babies, Klein argues that they too first relate to the mother as a part- rather than whole-object, that this is an effect of the way the baby's emotional life is determined at first by parts, or components of the sexual instinct – in this case by the component of orality.)

In loving the mother (or her breast), says Klein, the baby experiences her as a good object and as internalized, in phantasy, as a good object within the self. On the other hand, in so far as the baby hates the mother (or her breast), it feels her to be a bad object which its experiences, again in phantasy, as internalized within the self – this time as a bad, rather than good internal object.

Klein goes on to argue that, so precarious is the infantile ego, that it experiences its hatred and the internal object representations of that hatred as disintegrating of itself. It defends against this anxiety by splitting, by spitting out and evacuating its hostility, in phantasy, into the mother. She is then experienced as hating the baby. And this gives rise to persecutory anxiety in the infant lest the mother act on her supposed hatred and attack it. Klein refers to this anxiety, and to the projection and splitting off of hatred that gives rise to it, as 'the paranoid–schizoid position', a state of mind that can occur in both children and adults (see Chapter 11 below).

As evidence of the persecutory anxiety babies experience in relation to the mother, Klein cites the not uncommon observation that the hungry baby often responds with fear rather than eagerness to the mother's attempt to feed it. Here is Klein's account and interpretation of one such instance:

> 'A mother told me that when her infant B was five months old she had been left crying longer than usual. When at last the mother came to pick up the child, she found her in a "hysterical" state; the baby looked terrified, was evidently frightened of her, and did not seem to recognize her. . . . I would suggest that because the mother did not come when she was longed for, she turned in the child's mind into the bad (persecuting) mother, and that for this reason the child did not seem to recognize her and was frightened of her.' (Klein 1952b:102)

Babies, says Klein, often defend against such persecutory anxiety by splitting off the experience of frustration that gives rise to it. Instead they idealize the mother as not at all frustrating, as inexhaustibly bountiful. But this stirs up the contrary emotion of resentment and envy of the mother (of her breast say) now experienced as wantonly depriving the child of her goodness (see, for example, Klein 1957).

Horney, as we have seen, suggested that such envy constitutes the basis of male chauvinism – of men's denigration of the mother and of women generally (see pp. 37–8 above). Klein, by contrast, argues that this envy elicits negative feelings toward the mother in girls as well as boys, that it results in both sexes seeking to spoil and attack the mother and the phantasied and envied contents of her body. This, in turn, gives rise to yet another anxiety – dread lest the mother retaliate by attacking the child and its body in like fashion. Klein writes, for instance, that the child's 'impulse to devour the mother (and her breast)' gives rise to fear of the mother experienced as herself 'a devouring and dangerous object' (Klein 1952b:108n.1).

In sum: Klein argues that the baby's mental image of the mother is distorted by its oral, and later by its anal and genital impulses toward her, that in general 'the picture of the object, external and internalized, is distorted in the infant's mind by his phantasies, which are bound up with the projection of his impulses on to the object' (Klein 1952a:63).

Klein attributes the source of many of the feeding difficulties, phobias, and night-time fears of toddlers to such distorted perceptions of the mother. (It is interesting, therefore, that the dictionary defines 'nightmare' as a 'female monster supposedly sitting upon and seeming to suffocate the sleeper'.) Klein describes, for example, the case of a two year old, Rita, who sought to ward off her night-time fears by an elaborate bed-time ritual which included her having to be tucked tightly up in bed lest a mouse or 'Butzen' bite her. Klein describes as follows the incident in Rita's analysis that led her to conclude that, for Rita, the Butzen represented the mother she feared might avenge herself for Rita's attacks on her:

> 'On one occasion during her analytic session she put a toy elephant to her doll's bed so as to prevent it from getting up and going into her parents' bed-room and "doing something to them or taking something away from them". . . . The meaning of the ceremonial now became clear: being tucked up in bed was to prevent her from getting up and carrying out her aggressive wishes against her parents. Since, however, she expected to be punished for those wishes by a similar attack on herself by her parents, being tucked up also served as a defence against such attacks. The attacks were to be made, for instance, by the "Butzen".'   (Klein 1932:6–7)

Writing about Rita some years later, Klein added

> 'The fear of her mother attacking the "inside" of her body also contributed to her fear of someone coming through the window. The room also represented her body and the assailant was her mother retaliating for the child's attacks on her. The obsessional need to be tucked in with such elaborate care was a defence against all these fears.'   (Klein 1945:402)

In so far as Rita's fear of her mother involved biting imagery its content was oral. Fear of the mother can also have anal content. In this, says Klein, it derives from the child's anal aggression toward her, frequently expressed in children's lavatorial talk of 'wee' and 'poo'. An illustration of this comes from Klein's account of another patient – a three year old, Trude, who would make believe in her analytic sessions that Klein was asleep whereupon she, Trude

> 'used to come softly over to me [Klein] from the opposite corner of the room (which was supposed to be her own bedroom) and threaten me in various ways, such as that she was going to stab me in the throat, throw me out of the window, burn me up, take me to the police, etc. She would want to tie up my hands and feet, or she would lift up the rug on the sofa and say she was doing "Po-Kaki-Kuki". This, it turned out, meant that she wanted to look inside her mother's bottom for the "Kakis" (faeces), which signified children to her. On another occasion she wanted to hit me in the stomach and declared she was taking out my "A-A's" (stool) and was making me poor. She then seized the cushions, which she repeatedly called children, and hid herself with them behind the sofa. There she crouched in the corner with an intense expression of fear, covered herself up, sucked her fingers and wetted herself. She used to repeat this whole process whenever she had made an attack on me. It corresponded in every detail with the way she had behaved in bed when, at a time when she was not yet two, she started to have very severe night terrors. At that time, too, she had run into her parents' bed-room again and again at night without being able to say what she wanted. By analysing her wetting and dirtying herself which stood for attacks upon her parents copulating with each other, these symptoms were removed. Trude had wanted to rob her pregnant mother of her children, to kill her and to take her place in coitus with her father.' (Klein 1932:4–5)

It was, in Klein's view, these phantasied attacks on her mother and her body that had given rise to her night-time fears – fears that had as their unconscious origin anxiety lest her mother retaliate by attacking her, Trude.

Klein claimed that fear of the mother in such cases stems from the child's idealization of her as containing within herself the means of satisfying its every desire, and from its envious attacks on

her for seemingly witholding this goodness from the child. This
alternating idealization and envious attack on the mother is well
illustrated by the play, in analysis of a four year old, Gerald, who
would at one time imagine 'a "fairy-mamma", who used to come
at night and bring nice things to eat, which she shared with the
little boy', while at other times he would imagine a woman
(represented in the analysis by Klein) acting 'the part of a boy who
crept by night into the cage of a mother-lioness, attacked her,
stole her cubs and killed and ate them' only to have her act later
the part of a 'cruel lioness' (Klein 1929:203,208).

Another example of the way the child alternately experiences
the mother and women generally as 'helpful fairy-mamma' and as
'cruel lioness', to use Gerald's terms, and of the way this latter
perception of the mother stems from the child's projection on to
her of its envious attacks on the idealized contents of her body,
comes from Klein's account of the play behaviour of another child
patient, a six year old, Erna. The following incidents illustrate
particularly well the way Klein attributed the envious attacks of
the child as stemming from its experience of the mother as
callously witholding her goodness from the child to bestow on
others, in this case on the father:

> 'Erna began her play by taking a small carriage which stood on
> the little table among the other toys and letting it run towards
> me. She declared that she had come to fetch me. But she put a
> toy woman in the carriage instead and added a toy man. The
> two loved and kissed one another and drove up and down all
> the time. Next a toy man in another carriage collided with
> them, ran over them and killed them, and then roasted and ate
> them up. . . . This third person was given the most various parts
> to play in Erna's games. For instance, the original man and his
> wife were in a house which they were defending against a
> burglar; the third person was the burglar, and slipped in. The
> house burnt down, the man and woman burst and the third
> person was the only one left.'   (Klein 1932:36)

Erna, says Klein, would then imagine a child who

'was incessantly being maltreated and tormented. It was given semolina pudding to eat that was so nasty as to make it sick, while at the same time its mother and father were enjoying marvellous foods made of whipped cream or a special milk prepared by Dr Whippo or Whippour – a name compounded from "whipping" and "pouring out".' (Klein 1932:40)

Klein suggests that Erna's presenting symptoms – her sleeplessness and 'fear of robbers and burglars' (Klein 1932:35) – resulted from projection into her mother of the envy and hostility (expressed in her play by the attacks of the 'toy man' and 'burglar' on the toy couple) she felt toward her mother for apparently gratifying her father's needs at her, Erna's, expense – Erna having 'semolina pudding', as it were, while her parents enjoyed 'whipped cream'!

It can be, and often has been, argued against Klein that such examples have little bearing on normal psychology. Erna was after all, and by Klein's own account, extremely obsessional and neurotic for her age. But other psychologists, studying 'normal' children, point out that they too expect to be attacked by others as they attack them, that the 'eye for an eye' principle of talion governs moral reasoning until quite late in childhood. Piaget, for example, cites as typical the response of a nine year old who, when asked how he would react to someone who had blotted another's book, replied 'I would dirty his album for him, because that would be the fairest punishment. It would be doing the same to him as he did' (Piaget 1932:208).

The domination of mental life by such notions of retaliation usually decreases as the child grows older. As a result the child no longer imbues the mother to the same extent as it once did with its feelings of hostility toward her. The mother accordingly comes to be perceived more as she is, and less in terms of the child's impulses and phantasies about her.

Klein argues that this same effect can be achieved through therapy. Writing of Erna, for instance, she says that as her analysis progressed Erna ceased copying her mother as she once had in 'exaggerated and invidious fashion'. Instead she came to understand and criticize her as 'a real person' (Klein 1932:43,47). Klein claims that child analysis regularly achieves this effect of enabling the child 'to distinguish between his make-believe mother and his real one' (Klein 1932:11).

She goes on to argue that as the child, with or without the help of analysis, progresses from a 'picture of his parents, which was at first distorted into idealized and terrifying figures', to one which is 'nearer to reality' (Klein 1952a:74), so it begins to develop new anxieties – namely, fear lest, in attacking the hated and envied mother, it might thereby have destroyed and lost the loved and idealized mother. For a realistic attitude towards the mother involves recognizing that the loved and hated (and attacked) mother are one and the same person.

Integration of love and hate also involves bringing together their part-object representations. The mother is now related to as a whole object. And this means acknowledging her to be separate and independent of the child. By the same token, it involves the child acknowledging its separateness from, and independence of, the mother. The child now begins to recognize its mother's comings and goings – a recognition fraught with anxiety in so far as the child interprets the mother's absence as due to its 'destructive impulses' (Klein 1952b:121). Hence the pleasure babies take in 'beep-bo' games, says Klein, which stage not only the mother's going away but also her safe return (Klein 1952b:111).

Klein coined the term 'the depressive position' to refer to the constellation of anxieties about loss of the mother that she says result from recognizing her wholeness and separateness from the child. She went on to point out that the child regularly seeks to ward off these anxieties by manically cultivating an attitude of contempt and denigration toward the mother as someone whose loss would not cause it any pain. This involves denying its dependence on her – a denial that is particularly obvious in the vehement and omnipotent tantrum protests of two year olds.

As the child comes to experience its good and loved object representations of the mother as securely lodged within the self, however, it feels itself to have sufficient inner resources to be able to restore and make 'reparation' to the mother for past attacks made upon her in its envious hatred of her. It is thus able to acknowledge the fact of this hatred and hence to develop a still more realistic attitude toward both itself and the mother – as both hating and loving, hated and loved, dependent and independent. And this developing realism, says Klein, is still further facilitated by the 'reality-testing' used by the child to ensure that it has made effective reparation to the mother, that it has not destroyed and lost her through its hatred.

This brings me back, at last, to the starting point of the above exegesis of Kleinian theory; namely to the use made of it by Dinnerstein in explaining our psychological acquiescence in men's social dominance. Dinnerstein argues that, given our present childcare arrangements, in which infants are primarily looked after by women, children permanently side-step the task of working through the persecutory and depressive anxieties Klein describes as involved in developing a more realistic sense of themselves and of the mother, and involved in recognizing their independence and freedom from her. Children, Dinnerstein says, instead retain into adulthood their infantile sense of the mother as 'engulfing' and 'nebulously overwhelming'. Rather than grasping our freedom, she argues somewhat like Erich Fromm (1941) before her, we avoid the pain this involves by turning from the 'quasi-magical' woman of our infancy to dependence on men who, because they are relatively uninvolved in infant care, are not imbued as women are with the primitive phantasies with which we invested the woman who first mothered us in our infancy.

In this Dinnerstein advances a similar argument to that put forward by Klein's follower, Donald Winnicott, when he wrote:

'the tendency of groups of people to accept or even seek actual domination is derived from a fear of domination by fantasy woman. This fear leads them to seek, and even welcome domination by a known human being, especially one who has taken on himself the burden of personifying and therefore limiting the magical qualities of the all-powerful woman of fantasy, to whom is owed the great debt. The dictator can be overthrown, and must eventually die; but the woman figure of primitive unconscious fantasy has no limits to her existence or power.' (Winnicott 1965:165)

Winnicott subscribed to the unequal division of childcare that Dinnerstein argues gives rise to our psychological acceptance of men's social dominance. Dinnerstein, by contrast, questions this division not least because of this, its supposed consequence: 'So long as the first parent is a woman,' she writes, 'then, woman will inevitably be pressed into the dual role of indispensable quasi-human supporter and deadly quasi-human enemy of the self' (Dinnerstein 1978:111–12). She anticipates that, were men only to participate equally with women in looking after babies, children would then grow up having a more realistic attitude toward both women and themselves, and would thereby come to accept their independence and freedom instead of evading it by seeking domination by men:

> 'If a different, apparently blameless, category of person were not temptingly available as a focus for our most stubborn childhood wish – the wish to be free and at the same time to be taken care of – we would be forced at the beginning, before our spirit was broken, to outgrow that wish and face the ultimate necessity to take care of ourselves.' (Dinnerstein 1978:189)

Dinnerstein's argument is very compelling. All too often our attitudes toward women do seem to be imbued with the 'quasi-magical', idealized, envied, derided, and dreaded properties with which Klein says children in the paranoid–schizoid position regularly invest their mothers. And these attitudes are widely expressed both in our culture and in others. They surface, for instance, in religious symbolism – in the Hindu image of the munificent goddess Lakshmi with her contrary incarnation of Kali the destroyer, and in the Christian images of the wanton Eve and of Mary the Madonna. And the same imagery occurs in folklore: the idealized mother and envious step-mother of *Snow White*; the witch of *Hansel and Gretel*, provider of a whole gingerbread house full of

This bifurcated image of woman is nicely illustrated in the above picture by Albert Louden, exhibited at the Serpentine Gallery, London, April 1985.

goodies, who would devour the children she feeds; the bountiful fairy godmothers of *The Sleeping Beauty* and their vengeful counterpart who would have her die. And play has been made on these selfsame contrary images of women in the attempt to expropriate them from their traditional spheres of influence, as when healing women were represented in terms of this antithesis, as endangering rather than curing the body (see, for example, Oakley 1976), and as when women are equated with a nature viewed not only as 'earth mother . . . nurture and fertility' but as also bringing 'plagues, famine and tempests' (Merchant 1980:127; see also O. Harris 1984). Similar play is made on this polarized attitude to women in current anti-feminist propaganda, in the idealized image of traditional femininity and maternity – of 'Mom and apple pie' – contrasted with the image of the working mother and her supposedly necessarily deprived 'latch-key kids'.

Stereotypes of femininity are likewise often imbued with the contemptuous and denigratory attitudes that Klein describes children as regularly cultivating in manic defence against the depressive anxiety involved in recognizing their dependence on the mother and her separateness from them. The feminist poet, Susan Griffin (1981), suggests that these attitudes – as expressed in pornography – derive from the defences adopted in childhood against the pain involved in recognizing the mother's separateness and independence. By another turn of the misogynist screw, however, these attitudes have also been made use of in anti-feminist propaganda, not least by those Kleinians who criticize mothers who go out to work as thereby succumbing to our culture's denigration of motherhood (see for example Menzies 1975; Temperley 1984), and by those Kleinians who see in Klein's theory a valorization of woman's traditional role as mother (see Rustin 1982).

In their accounts of the maternal sources of these attitudes, however, Griffin and Dinnerstein overlook the fact that men, as well as women are also denigrated, feared, and at the same time idealized. (For evidence on this point see, for example, Parker 1985.) Just as bifurcated images of women people anti-feminist and feminist writing (see Sayers 1984b), so too do bifurcated images of men. Such images are commonplace in our culture and its iconography: Greek mythology, for example, includes Kronos, the god who devoured his sons, and Zeus who raped his mother, wreaked vengeance with his thunderbolts, and was king of the gods withal. Likewise the Christian pantheon also contains idealized and hateful images of men – God the father and his counterpart, the Devil, the fallen angel Lucifer (see, for example, Cohn 1985). And folklore is marked by similarly contrary and fantastical images of men – the loving and exploitative Don Juan, the dreadful and tender hero of *Beauty and the Beast*, the devouring ogre of *Jack and the Beanstalk* who would grind men's bones to make his bread!

Dinnerstein's theory fails to explain the occurrence of such fantastical images of men as of women in our culture. By contrast, Klein's theory does account for this. She demonstrates time and again the way our attitudes of idealization, envy and dread – first experienced in relation to the woman who mothered us in infancy

– also characterize our attitudes not only to other women but also to men. She shows that, just as the child hates the mother and fears her retaliation, so too does it hate and dread the father and the men who come to represent him in the child's day-to-day life, in its imaginative play, and in our culture's representation of men.

Two examples from Klein's work may serve to illustrate the occurrence in children of these phantasy-based attitudes toward men. The first comes from Klein's account of her analysis of a three year old, Peter. She writes:

'In his second session, Peter . . . laid a toy man on a bench, which he called a bed, and then threw him down and said that he was dead and done for. He next did the same thing with two little men, choosing for the purpose two toys that were already damaged. At that time, in conformity with the current material, I interpreted that the first toy man was his father, whom he wanted to throw out of his mother's bed and kill, and that the second man was himself to whom his father would do the same.' (Klein 1932:22)

This interpretation, she says, was confirmed by Peter's asking the next day, 'And if I were a Daddy and someone wanted to throw me down behind the bed and make me dead and done for, what would I think of it?' (Klein 1932n:2). Just as children regularly hate their mothers and fear their retaliation on this account, so too do they hate and fear their fathers, as the above incidents in Peter's analysis illustrate.

Klein's account of her analysis during the war years of a ten year old, Richard, likewise bears on the hostility children feel toward men as well as toward women, and on the fear of men that this evokes in them. It was with expression of just such fears – fears of 'boys he met in the street', preoccupation with Hitler's 'cruel treatment of conquered countries' – that Richard began his first session with Klein, fears that related to his own feelings of hostility toward men as evident from the fact that he went on to tell Klein:

'In the evenings he often feared that a nasty man – a kind of tramp – would come and kidnap Mummy during the night. He then pictured how he, Richard, would go to her help, would scald the tramp with hot water and make him unconscious . . . the tramp . . . might get in through the window: perhaps he would break in.'   (Klein 1961:20)

On the basis of such evidence Klein concluded that children transfer on to the father and on to men generally attitudes they first experience in relation to a woman, the mother. And these include not only attitudes of love and hate but also their derivatives, idealization and envy. Just as the baby idealizes and envies the breast, says Klein, so too does it idealize and envy the penis. It was in these terms that Klein explained penis-envy – that is, as transferred breast-envy (see, for example, Klein 1957:199; 1961:424).

Like Horney (see p. 37 above), Klein assumed that envy of men and of parts of their anatomy is equivalent in strength to envy of women and their biology. Neither analyst took account of the way men's social dominance might cause girls to envy boys and men more than boys envy girls and women. In Klein, this neglect is of a piece with her general focus on internal reality at the cost of losing sight of the extent to which this reality is conditioned by external social reality. It is in terms of this latter reality, and specifically in terms of female-dominated childcare, that Dinnerstein explains the persistence into adulthood of the phantasy-dominated attitudes toward woman first experienced in relation to the mother in infancy. Klein, by contrast, attributes the persistence of such attitudes, where it occurs, more to internal than to external factors, specifically to the Death Instinct predominating over the Life Instinct such that the integration of love and hate necessary to a more realistic perception of the mother does not come about (see for example Klein 1952a:67).

Dinnerstein claims support in Kleinian theory for her argument that women's and men's psychological acquiescence in men's social dominance is due to failure to resolve the phantasies elaborated in infancy about the women who then mothered us.

However, as indicated above, Klein's theory does not in fact provide the support Dinnerstein claims to derive from it for her theory. Furthermore, like Rich's use of Horney's theory, Dinnerstein's use of Klein's theory fails to address or explain women's resistance to male dominance in society. Dinnerstein recommends that this dominance should be overthrown and that men should participate equally with women in looking after children, not least because this might result in us no longer seeking to be dominated by men. But she fails to indicate why either sex would ever feel inclined not to be dominated by men. In so far as she argues that our current sexually unequal childcare arrangements lead us happily to acquiesce in this dominance and to accept the social inequalities between the sexes of which our current childcare arrangements are a part, she implies that women and men lack any interest in seeking to secure the shared parenting she advocates.

Nevertheless, women patently do have an interest in achieving sex equality. Klein's instinct-based account of psychology, however, fails to provide a means of explaining women's psychological resistance to that inequality because it does not take sufficient account of the way social factors like sex inequality shape women's psychology, and their psychological resistance to that inequality. By contrast, the develoment of Kleinian theory by the British object relations school of psychoanalysis does take account of the way psychology is shaped by social factors. It is to an outline of this theory as it has been used to account for the psychology of women's social subordination that I shall now turn.

6
Object relations theory

It is well known that by nature women are inclined to be rather personal. They attach themselves to persons. They become fond of people and they are inclined to follow them to their detriment because they are fond of them.   (Judge Ewart James, October 1977)

Trade Union organizer interviewed by Bea Campbell in 1982–83: 'I gave my all to disputes. But when it was over I'd be down, I'd retreat home and of course there I had my emotional sponge.'   (Campbell 1984:137)

In her book, *The Reproduction of Mothering*, the American sociologist and feminist, Nancy Chodorow, uses object relations theory to explain why women are 'inclined to be rather personal', why they tend to be the 'emotional' caretakers of our society. Chodorow goes on to argue that this aspect of women's psychology fits them well for the sexual division of labour whereby they mother while men work. Before detailing her argument and some of the uses to which it has been put in contemporary feminist theory, I shall briefly describe the object relations versions of psychoanalysis on which it is based.

The Scottish psychoanalyst, W.R.D. Fairbairn, is usually credited as originator of object relations theory. Fairbairn was much influenced by Klein's account of the way the infant at first experiences the mother in split fashion as variously a good or bad object. But he rejected Klein's assumption that the ego, involved in this splitting process, exists from birth. On the basis of his clinical work with schizoid patients, who seemingly experience themselves as merged with the analyst, he hypothesized that schizoid states constitute a regression to the earliest stage of development in which the infant has no ego, and no sense of itself as separate from the mother. Following Freud, Fairbairn termed this state one of 'primary narcissism' – one which Freud described as a 'limitless, unbounded – as it were "oceanic" ' feeling, from which the ego only later 'separates off an external world from itself ' (Freud 1930a:251, 255).

The ego, says Fairbairn, only develops gradually. It is formed out of the baby's internal representation of its relation to the mother recognized bit by bit as separate from itself. Like Klein, Fairbairn argued that this representation at first involves images of the infant's gratifying relation to the mother. Unlike Klein, however, he argued that whether the child also internalizes and splits off images of its relation to its mother as bad and hateful depends not on any instinct of hatred in the child, but on the mother's handling of it. Ideally, he says, the mother meets the child's every need as it arises and does not frustrate the baby until it is ready to cope with such frustration without recourse to splitting (see Fairbairn 1944:109–10). The baby only develops a split between good and bad internalized representations of its relation to its mother if she fails it by not accommodating to its needs. It then seeks to deal with this experience, says Fairbairn, by internalizing it. Only given this adverse experience, he claims, do splits develop within the ego. Faced with maternal failure, the ego, writes Fairbairn, becomes divided off into what he refers to as a 'libidinal ego' and an 'internal saboteur', corresponding respectively to its mother's Eve-like temptation and frustration of its needs. (Fairbairn thus returns, in a sense, to the theory adumbrated by Horney in her later work, namely that splits in consciousness only occur where the child's parents fail it by being too involved in their own needs to be able to respond and empathize with those of their children, see p. 40 above. And, beyond this, he returns psychoanalysis in a sense to Freud's early theory, namely that splitting of consciousness only occurs where the people responsible for the child's early care simultaneously excite and fail it by seducing it, see p. 124 below.)

Fairbairn's work is very heavy-going and it is perhaps for this reason that many readers will probably be less familiar with it than with the version of object relations theory put forward by the British paediatrician and psychoanalyst, Donald Winnicott, and popularized by him both through his radio talks and through his many books that are still widely available in paperback. Like Fairbairn, Winnicott argued that the baby is initially psychically merged with the mother. And he went on to argue that 'the good enough mother', as he termed her, likewise experiences herself, at first, as psychically merged with her baby – a state he refers to as 'primary maternal preoccupation'. As a result of this preoccupation or identification, says Winnicott, the good enough mother is able to anticipate and meet her baby's needs as they arise. She thus protects its 'going-on-being', which forms the base of its ego, from being broken up by reaction to the 'impingements' arising from internally or externally determined needs. The good enough mother's adaptation to her baby's needs, claims Winnicott, also fosters its ego development by the fact that, through adapting to its needs, she brings external reality into correspondence with its internal reality. She thus enables the baby to build up an increasingly realistic mental picture of its external world, and of its mother in the first place. Winnicott hypothesizes that, with good enough mothering,

> 'the infant comes to the breast when excited, and ready to hallucinate something fit to be attacked. At that moment the actual nipple appears and he is able to feel it was that nipple that he hallucinated. So his ideas are enriched by actual details of sight, feel, smell, and next time this material is used in the hallucination. In this way he starts to build up a capacity to conjure up what is actually available. The mother has to go on giving the infant this type of experience. . . . Only on such a foundation can objectivity or a scientific attitude be built.' (Winnicott 1945:52–53)

As a result of 'this type of experience', says Winnicott, the child builds up a picture of the mother that it can hold in its mind when she is absent. The baby thus begins to recognize and tolerate her occasional absences, and thus to appreciate her separateness from itself, and its own separateness from her.

According to Winnicott, splits in the ego occur not as a result of any instincts toward love and hate as Klein proposed, but as a result of the mother not being good enough. This happens, he says, when mothers are 'not able to become preoccupied with their own infants to the exclusion of other interests' (Winnicott 1956:302), and when they therefore fail to anticipate their babies' needs as they arise. As a result the baby's needs then emerge in full force to disrupt and fragment its going-on-being which would otherwise constitute the basis of its ego developing in a whole, integrated, and unified manner. When the mother thus fails to accommodate to the baby's needs, he writes, the baby has to learn to accommodate to her needs. As a result, writes Winnicott (1960), the baby's 'true self' goes into hiding behind a compliant 'false self' facade. It is in these terms that Winnicott explains the genesis of splits in the ego, of 'the divided self' as his follower Ronnie Laing (1960) put it.

In effect, unlike Klein, Winnicott treats the child's internal world as a reflection of an essentially uncontradictory external world, as whole and integrated if its mother is good enough and consistent in her care of the child, and as split, divided, and pathological if its mother's care is pathological and not good enough. He thereby overlooks the contradictions in external reality (involved, for example, in the baby's contrary experiences of gratification and frustration) that Klein and Freud recognized to cause consciousness to be split and divided however good or bad the mothering the child receives.

This account of child development, that pathologizes those women who do not adapt well enough to their babies' needs, and blames them for any splits that occur in their babies' consciousness – splits that are, in fact, inevitable given the ambivalences and contradictions intrinsic to social interaction – hardly seems promising stuff out of which to forge a feminist perspective on psychology! Before explaining how Chodorow nevertheless

seeks to turn it to feminist effect, I shall briefly recount one last
object relations type approach to child development – namely,
that of the American psychoanalyst, Margaret Mahler.

On the basis of observations of 'normal' mother–child pairs,
and on the basis of clinical work with schizoid children, Mahler
claims, as did Fairbairn and Winnicott before her, that the infant
is initially unaware of others as external to itself. The baby, she
says, only begins to emerge from this 'normal autistic phase' at
three or four weeks of age when its dawning awareness of its
mother's separateness is then apparent from the way it smiles at
her. But, says Mahler, the baby continues to experience itself as
in 'mutual symbiosis' with the mother, behaving as though it and
the mother were 'a unitary, omnipotent system' (Greenberg and
Mitchell 1983:275). It only emerges from this state, Mahler
claims, during the 'differentiation subphase' when it begins to
learn to crawl and walk and thus to put physical distance between
itself and its mother – a development that she says is followed, at
about eighteen months, by a 'rapprochement crisis' resulting
from its increasing recognition of the illusory character of its
previous sense of itself as in omnipotent symbiosis with the
mother. Mahler points out that, at this stage, the baby now
recognizes its separateness and independence from the mother.
Paradoxically however the baby's recognition of its independence
is dependent on its mother recognizing its independence 'as a
separate, autonomous individual in his own right', on her thus
fostering its further 'separation–individuation' from her (Mahler
1975:330).

The American ego psychologist Heinz Kohut (1971) likewise
draws attention to this latter phenomenon. He says the child's ego
development, its developing a healthy, 'narcissistic', independent
sense of itself, depends on the mother 'mirroring' and
emphasizing, even exaggerating to the child its capabilities and
independence of her – a relation well described by Anthony
Trollope in his chapter on 'baby worship' in his 1857 book,
Barchester Towers (see also Urwin 1984).

How does Nancy Chodorow use these psychoanalytic theories
of child development to arrive at a feminist account of the

psychology of current social inequalities between the sexes? She suggests that this psychology originates in earliest infancy when, according to object relations theory, the infant and mother experience themselves as psychically fused with each other. Adopting this theory, she goes on to claim that the degree to which the mother merges psychologically with the baby at this stage is affected by its sex.

As far as boys are concerned, she says, mothers experience and relate to them from the first as separate and different from themselves because they are different in sex to themselves. That is, she adopts the implications of Winnicott's theory that psychology reflects an essentially straightforward external reality. From the start of his life, she says, the mother promotes the boy's separation–individuation from her by relating to him as different from herself. This process, she claims, is further promoted by boys repudiating their first female-based object relation of mergence with the mother in the process of forging a masculine gender identity. This identity, says Chodorow, is based on negation – on 'that which is not female, or not-mother'. As a result, masculine gender identity is more precarious than feminine gender identity, which is based on affirmation by the girl of her earliest sense of mergence with the mother. This precariousness, writes Chodorow, is a major source of men's sexism, of their 'psychological investment in difference', and of their assertion of 'maleness as that which is basically human' (Chodorow 1979:65).

Men's self-identity, in being based according to Chodorow on negation of their earliest experience of psychic mergence with the mother, is 'essentially abstract' rather than 'personal' in character. In so far as their masculine identity is based on positive identification with men, she adds, it is based on identification with a sex who, because of the current sexual division of labour, is relatively absent from the home during the child's waking hours. Masculine gender identity is accordingly based on 'abstract' and 'positional' identification with the roles occupied by men in society, rather than on personal interaction with them. As a result, claims Chodorow, boys grow up well equipped psychologically for the impersonal and flexible role requirements of modern occupational life, for the 'instrumental' role that sociologist Talcott Parsons (1964) says this involves. This does not however fit them well for child care, characterized by Parsons as being essentially 'expressive', and by object relations theory as essentially involving psychic mergence on the part of the parent with the child.

On the other hand, writes Chodorow, girls grow up with a very different sense of their personal identity, and with very different relational capacities from those of men. Mothers, she says, tend to experience their daughters, on account of their being the same sex as themselves, as more merged and identified with them than are their sons. As a result they do not promote in them the same degree of 'separation–individuation'. Nor is this process promoted in girls, as it is in boys, by their gender development. For, says Chodorow, this development does not involve negation by the girl of her primary sense of herself as one and unified with the mother. Whereas masculine gender identity is based on negation, maintains Chodorow, 'female core gender identity and the sense of femininity, are defined positively, as that which is female, or like mother' (Chodorow 1979:65). In effect Chodorow collapses gender identity into a specific personality style (an analogous point more fully developed by John Broughton, 1983, in relation to Gilligan's work). Women's gender identity, says Chodorow, is formed on a more 'personal' basis than that of men. It is formed out of personal interaction with the women who looked after them in their infancy. As a result, she claims, girls grow up with a continuing sense of themselves as merged with others in their personal relations with them just as they first experienced themselves as merged with their mothers in infancy. She implies that women are thus well-equipped by their child-rearing psychologically to provide the kind of care Winnicott says is essential to healthy child development.

In sum: Chodorow argues that women's mothering serves to perpetuate in women and men the psychological traits deemed needful by psychoanalysts like Winnicott, and by sociologists like Parsons, to their roles as mothers and workers in our society.

Object relations theorists have often condoned this situation, and have criticized women who seek equality with men in the sense of wanting to work as they do when their children are young. And Winnicott's ideas have regularly been cited in argument against the provision of day nurseries that would enable women to realize this goal (Philipson 1982a; Riley 1983). Unlike the object relations theorists on whom she bases her work, Chodorow challenges the unequal division of labour between the sexes whereby childcare is consigned to women, rather than shared between women and men alike. She argues that men should participate equally with women in bringing up children. And she implies that such 'shared parenting' would result in boys and girls both merging on a personal basis with the same-sex parent and differentiating from the opposite-sex parent such that both sexes would then grow up having the capacity both for identifying with others, and for maintaining their separateness and individuality from others in personal relations with them.

Chodorow's feminist prescription for changing men's and women's psychology, and her psychoanalytically based argument for it, has received widespread acclaim and has been reiterated in many contexts, marriage guidance manuals included (see, for example, Lorber *et al.* 1981; Lerner 1983; Rubin 1983). This is in part because the shared parenting she recommends seems so easy to achieve. It has accordingly been much canvassed today, at a time when hopes of obtaining adequate public childcare provision are fast receding. In fact, however, just as socialized childcare is hard to achieve, so too is shared parenting. Achievement of the latter goal depends on effective struggle by women in the privacy of their own households – a form of action that has so far not notably secured any significant increase in men's contribution to childcare (see, for example, C. Lewis 1985). This is partly because such an increase would depend on a massive reorganization of occupational work, on women being paid the same as men, and on men and women equally being able to take time off work to look after children. Chodorow's shared parenting solution to sex inequality also assumes that women have men upon whom they can call to help them with childcare. But they are less and less able to do so. With the soaring divorce rate and so on women are increasingly finding themselves bringing up children on their own.

Chodorow's neglect of this, the current social context of parenting, is of a piece with the object relations version of psychoanalysis on which her work is based. It replaces the individualism of Klein's account of psychology with an account of the mother–child dyad viewed in isolation from the wider social factors that determine it (Riley 1983; Housman 1982; Sayers 1985b).

Be that as it may, Chodorow's thesis has proved very appealing politically. It has also proved emotionally appealing for it speaks to our sense of women as more attuned to childcare, to intimacy with other women (see, for example, Ryan 1983a), and as more immersed generally than men in personal relations with others – adults and children alike. It has accordingly been adopted by many feminist theorists.

Carol Gilligan (1982), for example, uses Chodorow's theory to explain the differences she says typify women's and men's moral reasoning whereby men supposedly reason in terms of individual rights, women in terms of relational issues (see pp. 18–19 above). Nor is Gilligan alone in using Chodorow's theory to explain what she takes to be women's and men's characteristically different modes of thought. Sara Ruddick (1980) uses this theory to explain the genesis of what she claims to be women's distinctive 'maternal thinking'. Jessica Benjamin (1982) likewise explains, in terms of women's mothering, the 'instrumental rationality' which, like many others, she takes to differentiate men's thought processes from those of women, and which she says involves 'emphasis of difference over sameness, separation over identification'. (For documentation of this time-worn and supposed equation of rationality with masculinity see, for example, Lloyd 1984 and Walkerdine in press.) Men's distinctively different style of reasoning from that of women, Benjamin argues, is 'rooted in male rejection of the mother, her nurturance, and her existence as a subject' (Benjamin 1981:215; see also Hartsock 1983:240–47). Similarly, the feminist physicist Evelyn Fox Keller (1982) uses Chodorow's work to explain, in terms of the psychological effects of women's mothering, men's tendency in science to focus on the independent operation of the constituent parts of the phenomena they investigate whereas women (like the biochemist, Barbara McClintock), she says, seem to be more open to recognizing the dynamic interplay of the constituent particles of their objects of investigation.

Some feminists celebrate such differences between the sexes which, following Chodorow, they regard as an effect of women's mothering. Not only do they argue, as do most feminists, that 'the personal is political', but they use Chodorow's work to celebrate 'the personal' as women's particular province and preserve (see, for example, Flax 1978; Rich 1980). Adrienne Rich, for instance, writes glowingly of women's empathy with each other, of their 'lesbian continuum', and contrasts it with men's psychology which she deplores as unempathic, as leading them to seek to disrupt and destroy women's close personal relations with each other. (In this, of course, she ignores the hostility as well as love that inheres in women's relations to each other – a hostility strikingly evident in a recent *Sunday Times* series in which women interviewed as to their worst enemies all cited other women as fitting this bill, her mother in the case of women's refuge campaigner Erin Pizzey, thinner women in the case of novelist Shirley Conran, and feminist women in the case of anti-contraception publicist Victoria Gillick.)

Unlike Adrienne Rich, Nancy Chodorow and many of her other followers draw attention to the crippling effects on women, as well as on men, of the psychological sex differences they claim to be produced by women's mothering – effects they believe will only disappear given the achievement of shared parenting. Gilligan, for instance, draws attention to 'the limitations for both sexes that result from severing the twin anchors of human psychology, attachment and separation' (Benjamin 1983:298). Keller notes the debilitating effects on scientific research of those psychological sex differences that she says lead scientists to focus either on the interdependence and interaction of things to the neglect of their independent operation, or, as she says more commonly happens in male-dominated science, to their focusing on the independent operation of their objects of enquiry to the neglect of the interaction of these objects.

Jessica Benjamin likewise deplores the damaging effects on both women and men of the psychological sex differences she claims to be produced by women's mothering. In this she draws not only on the work of Chodorow but also on that of the German philosopher Hegel, specifically on his account of the dialectic of self-consciousness. According to Hegel, 'self-consciousness exists in and for itself when, and by the fact that, it so exists for another: that is, it exists only in being acknowledged' (Hegel 1807:111). Fully realized consciousness of one's subjectivity, writes Benjamin following Hegel, depends on recognizing the other as an independent centre of consciousness, as capable by virtue of their autonomy of conferring recognition on one's autonomy and independence. All too often, however, this dialectic is resolved one-sidedly: with individuals either asserting their independence and subjectivity at the cost of denying the subjectivity of others, or with their acknowledging the subjectivity of others at the cost of denying their own subjectivity.

Some years ago Simone de Beauvoir (1949) argued that this 'master–slave' resolution, as Hegel termed it, of the dialectic of self-consciousness constitutes the essence of women's oppression in male-dominated society. Men, she implied, affirm their subjectivity – their 'transcendent being' – at the cost of treating woman as 'immanent other'. Women, by contrast, all too often fail to realize their subjectivity and transcendence and instead experience themselves, as they are treated, that is as 'immanent other'. Rejecting psychoanalytic along with biological, economic, and historical explanations of this sex difference (le Doeff 1980), de Beauvoir rested content with describing this difference rather than with also seeking to develop an alternative explanation of it. Jessica Benjamin, by contrast, does seek to explain this difference. She uses Chodorow's theory to do so. This psychological sex difference, she says, originates in childhood from the divergent ways boys and girls resolve their experience of psychic mergence with the woman who then mothers them. Boys, she says, resolve this experience by denying the subjectivity and independence of their mothers and of women generally while asserting their own subjectivity. By contrast, she claims, girls recognize their fathers' subjectivity and that of men generally at the cost of denying their own subjectivity, autonomy, and separateness:

> 'Since boys are forced to achieve their individuality by repudiating dependency and the identification with the mother, they become fit for the stalemate of one-sided or false differentiation. Since girls are denied identification with the father, who stands for difference and separation, they are unable to achieve the accepted form of autonomy. Each gender is able to represent only one aspect of the self–other relationship; each gender plays a part in a polarized whole. One is independent, the other dependent; one master, the other slave.' (Benjamin 1981:210)

A similar one-sidedness marks psychological theory and its account of 'the self–other relationship'. All too often this theory focuses either on the independent agency of the subject in such relations (as does cognitive–developmental theory), or on the dependent passivity and reactivity of the subject in social interaction (as does social learning theory), to the neglect of the fact that the subject is at one and the same time both active and passive, independent and dependent in social interaction; that it is produced through social interaction both 'as capable of assertive action' and as 'fragile and acutely vulnerable' (Urwin 1984:321). By contrast, as I shall demonstrate below (see Chapter 8), Freud did pay attention to this dialectical aspect of social interaction.

Returning to the main theme of this chapter, however, if – as Gilligan, Keller, Benjamin, and Chodorow claim – women do not experience themselves as independent agents in social interaction, then where does women's assertion, not least these authors' assertion of their independence and autonomy, come from? If, as Chodorow says, women only want to merge their subjectivity and interests in those of their children, why is it that they are even now struggling to achieve the shared parenting she advocates so that they might realize the individual needs they have outside of, and separate from their children? If women were simply content to be the immanent objects of men's transcendence, they would not now be struggling to realize themselves as transcendent, autonomous beings.

These authors' neglect of the striving for autonomy and transcendence that fires both their own feminism and that of the women's movement in general is evidence of the captivating effect on feminists, as on non-feminists, of the ideological equation of femininity with lack of autonomy and transcendence, with mergence of the self with others. Despite this equation, however, women in fact do also experience themselves as separate and individuated from others, as having needs as individual subjects in their own right. It is this experience that fuels feminist struggle to achieve the social conditions that would enable women fully to realize all their needs – immanent and transcendent, dependent and independent, alike.

In so far as Chodorow and her followers take women's psychology to be essentially constituted by maternal mergence with, and empathic care of others, they fail to address women's sense of themselves, not only as enmeshed in domestic and personal relations, but as also separate and individuated from these relations. This oversight is not surprising, however, given that women themselves are often unaware of their aspirations to realize themselves as separate, independent beings, so effectively do they conceal these aspirations from themselves as a result of internalizing society's stereotype of women as essentially concerned with the interests of others, not of themselves.

A clinical example may serve to clarify this point, in this case that of the way women conceal their independent strivings from themselves through repression. The example comes from Freud's *Studies on Hysteria* and concerns the case of a middle-aged widow, one Emmy von N. To all appearances Emmy was a paragon of caring femininity. Freud tells us how impressed he was by her 'benevolent care for the welfare of all her dependents, her humility of mind and the refinement of her manners,' which he said, 'revealed her qualities as a true lady' (Freud 1895d:165). Emmy, however, suffered a distressing symptom: a clacking sound that Freud described as interrupting her otherwise highly articulate account of herself. The symptom, it seemed, had originated some years before when Emmy had been sitting by her daughter's sickbed and sought to be particularly quiet so as not to awaken her sleeping child. The emergence of this noisy symptom on just this occasion when Emmy had sought to be quiet for the sake of her child suggested to Freud that, alongside this caring intention, Emmy had then had a contrary, uncaring intention, namely that of making a noise so as to disturb her child. It was, says Freud, the contradiction between these two intentions that had rendered the occasion traumatic to Emmy, and had caused her to repress its memory from consciousness. Now all that remained of the uncaring impulse so noisily expressed on that occasion was her nervous tic which so effectively concealed the selfish impulse it expressed that Emmy seemed to all intents and purposes to be the epitome of caring and empathic femininity that Chodorow takes to be typical of women's psychology.

Chodorow is not of course alone among object relations theorists in assuming that women are generally well endowed by their psychology to merge and subordinate their interests to those of others, particularly to those of their children. So convinced was Winnicott of this that he believed that it was rare for a woman not to be 'a good enough mother', not to be psychically merged and 'maternally preoccupied' with her baby's interests, that it was only the very occasional mother who substituted her interests for those of her baby.

Nor is the equation of women's psychology with preoccupation and mergence with others peculiar to object relations theory. It is the very pervasiveness of this equation in society generally that renders Chodorow's account of women's psychology, framed as it is in terms of this equation, so compelling. On the other hand, as I have sought to show in this chapter, Chodorow fails to address other aspects of women's psychology that are equally important, namely their interests and aspirations as individuals apart from and independent of those with whom they also experience themselves as merged. She thereby fails to address the psychological sources of women's resistance and struggle against those sexual divisions in society that obstruct their realizing these aspirations.

By contrast Freud did address this aspect of women's psychology as I have briefly indicated in describing his account of the case of Emmy von N. Before outlining this aspect of his work in greater detail, however, I shall consider one last, post-Freudian theory of the psychology of sexual difference, namely that of the French psychoanalyst Jacques Lacan – a theory that has been particularly influential on recent British feminist accounts of the psychology of our sexually divided society.

7
Lacanian perspectives

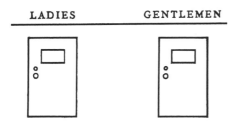

A train arrives at a station. A little boy and a little girl, brother and sister, are seated in a compartment face to face next to the window through which the buildings along the station platform can be seen passing as the train pulls to a stop. 'Look', says the brother, 'we're at Ladies!'; 'Idiot!' replies his sister, 'Can't you see we're at Gentlemen'. Besides the fact that the rails in this story materialize the bar in the Saussurian algorithm . . . for these children, Ladies and Gentlemen will be henceforth two countries towards which each of their souls will strive on divergent wings, and between which a truce will be the more impossible since they are actually the same country and neither can compromise on its own superiority without detracting from the glory of the other.   (Lacan 1957:151,152)

Like Freud before him, Lacan stressed that a pre-condition of the child taking on 'the ideal type of his sex' (Lacan 1958:281) is that it recognize sexual difference, that only thus can it begin to recognize the 'divergent' social destinies of men and women signified by this difference. He therefore rejected the view, put forward by Klein as well as by Horney, that the essence of femininity and masculinity resides in the female and male body without any necessary reference to the difference between them. Lacan's followers also take issue, not only with the essentialism of writers like Horney and Irigaray (see Chapter 4 above), but also with the sociological theory of Nancy Chodorow that gender is constituted by the child's affirmation or denial of its pre-Oedipal experience of itself as one with the mother. Whether the child affirms or denies this experience, they point out, depends on its recognizing the mother to be the same or different from itself – a recognition that Lacan, like Freud, claims not to occur pre-Oedipally but only to occur with the Oedipus complex.

Lacan himself also criticized object relations theory from which, as we have seen, Chodorow derives her account of gender development. Much of his work is devoted to polemical attack not only on this theory but also on the Kleinian theory on which it is based, and on the American version of ego psychology of which Horney's later work was an early example. These post-Freudian accounts of psychoanalysis, says Lacan, wrongly take the ego to be one with its objects. This unity, says Lacan, is 'imaginary'. Freud likewise referred to this unity as 'hallucinatory'.

The baby, says Freud, initially hallucinates itself to be one with its mother, or more accurately with her breast – the first object of its oral desire. Freud arrived at this deduction via consideration of the hallucinatory wish-fulfilment character of dreams. He hypothesized that the hallucinations of dreams recapitulate the processes of thought he believed to be characteristic of waking as of sleeping life in infancy – a process of thought that he accordingly referred to as 'primary'. When it is hungry, he suggested, the baby hallucinates to itself the breast, the presence of which was associated with reduction of its hunger in the past. 'The aim of this first psychical activity', writes Freud, is 'to produce a "perceptual identity" – a repetition of the perception which was linked with the satisfaction of the need' (Freud 1900a:720). But, he argued, since this hallucination does not bring about actual gratification of need, of hunger (see, for example, Freud 1911b), and since it is in contradiction with reality in so far as the breast is actually absent, this hallucinatory wish-fulfilment is repressed into the unconscious. Freud thus argued that unconscious identification with the mother's breast first occurs in its absence. By contrast, Kleinians and object relations theorists argue that this identification first occurs in the presence of the breast. (This explains, in part, the rather uncertain status of the unconscious in Kleinian theory commented on by, for example, Glover 1945.)

Freud claimed that the infantile psyche is dominated by the baby's physical needs, such as those for food and excretion, and that its sexual instinct first comes into being in relation to these needs, that is, in component parts: orality, anality, exhibitionism, sadism, and so on. (I shall discuss this aspect of Freud's theory in greater detail in Chapter 8.) And, just as the baby's physical needs relate to parts of its mother's and its own body – her breast, its faeces, etc. – so it is these parts of her and of its body that are first invested, or 'cathected', by the component sexual instincts. In the course of development, however, these instincts become unified, says Freud, and subordinated to 'genital primacy' (Freud 1905d). Later he was to refer to the stage at which this unification takes place as that of 'phallic primacy' (Freud 1923e). For, he said, boys and girls attach psychological significance initially only to one genital, namely the male genital or phallus. He explained this in anatomical terms as the result of the fact that the penis is 'strikingly visible and of large proportions' (Freud 1925j:355). With the unification of the component sexual instincts brought about with phallic primacy, he argued, the objects cathected by these instincts also come to be unified. The child now cathects its mother as a whole object and also narcissistically cathects itself as a whole object. It is this narcissism, says Freud (1914c), that forms the basis of the ego.

Freud attributed to biology the unification of the component sexual instincts that he regarded as necessary to ego development. Lacan, by contrast, explains this unification as coming about through what he refers to as 'the mirror stage'. He describes the fascination of the six to eighteen month old baby with its mirror image, and the way that, like the mythical Narcissus, the baby seems to mistake this, its reflection, for itself. Lacan suggests that this fascination derives from the fact that the mirror presents the baby with a unified image of itself, whereas the baby, still under the sway of its part-object experience of itself, still experiences itself in bits and pieces, as 'fragmented' (Lacan 1949:4). It is this experience, says Lacan, that lures the baby into identifying with the wholeness of its reflected image. And with this identification, Lacan claims, the ego comes into being. It is formed, he says, on the basis of illusory, not real identity with the other, on identification with an image that seems to be the same as the self but which is not the self. Juliet Mitchell puts Lacan's account of the mirror stage thus: 'Lacan's human subject is a being that can only conceptualize itself when it is mirrored back to itself from the position of another's desire' (Mitchell 1984:254). Lacan goes on to claim that, although the ego is formed in alienation in this process, this stage serves a useful function in being the precondition of the child's being able to represent itself outside itself by the personal pronoun 'I' of language (a capacity that infants and many autistic children lack).

On the basis of his theory of the mirror stage Lacan criticizes those psychoanalysts who seek to strengthen the analysand's ego by fostering his or her identification with the analyst. In Kleinian analysis this involves interpreting the analysand's unconscious anxieties so that she or he might internalize their relation to the analyst as a good object relation around which further ego integration may then occur (see p. 146). Winnicott advocates that the analyst provide a 'facilitating' and 'holding' environment such that integration of the 'true' and 'false' self may take place. Likewise, Heinz Kohut, the late foremost exponent of today's American ego psychology, recommends that, in cases of ego weakness, or 'narcissistic personality disorder' as he terms it, the analyst should promote a 'mirroring' or 'idealizing' transference such that the analysand's ego might thereby be strengthened through mergence with, and through internalization of the idealized aspects of the analyst. (For a useful critique of the way this overlooks the contradictions of love and hate involved in such idealization see, for example, Kernberg 1974 and Russell 1985.)

Overlooking the possibility that such techniques may be necessary to the treatment of schizoid states of mind in which there is a split within the ego (see Freud 1940a and 1940c), rather than between the ego and the id (or between the conscious and unconscious mind), Lacan criticizes them as colluding with our all too persistent tendency to alienate ourselves in identification with others. Some have concluded from this that Lacan altogether dispensed with psychoanalysis as a clinical project. Stuart Schneiderman, for instance, writes in the name of Lacan: 'What is wrong with psychoanalysis is that it has as a goal, and as a reason for being, the medical model of treatment and cure' (Schneiderman 1983:47). Lacan did however regard psychoanalysis as having a therapeutic purpose – namely that of freeing analysands from the illusion of their sense of themselves as unified subjects: 'Who,' he asks, if not the analysts,

> 'will question once more the objective status of this "I", which a historical evolution peculiar to our culture tends to confuse with the subject? This anomaly should be manifested in its particular effects on every level of language, and first and foremost in the grammatical subject of the first person in our languages, in the "I love" that hypostatizes the tendency of a subject who denies it. An impossible mirage in linguistic forms among which the most ancient are to be found, and in which the subject appears fundamentally in the position of being determinant or instrumental of action.' (Lacan 1948:23)

This is part and parcel of Lacan's general critique of Descartes' doctrine – *cogito ergo sum* (I think therefore I am) – and of the philosophy of individualism it expresses. (A much more accessible but similar critique of this philosophy as expressed in ego psychology is provided by Marcuse 1955.) In criticizing this philosophy Lacan's work lends itself to feminism which also seeks to draw attention to the way the philosophy or ideology of individualism falsely presents women, like men, as already 'determinant or instrumental of action' when in fact women are systematically obstructed by society from realizing this, their purported freedom. And Lacan is, of course, right to point to the 'historical evolution' of this ideology which is the product, in our society, of the development of capitalism whereby people have become increasingly liberated from their erstwhile feudal and kinship fetters to dispose of their labour power on an individual basis (see, for example, Macpherson 1962; Scott and Tilly 1975). The obstacles to people realizing this freedom, however, are social and historical. They are not, as Lacan implies, determined by the transhistorical fact that one is not one with one's mirror image. It is because the obstacles to women realizing the individual freedom promised by capitalist society are not eternal but are historical and social that the struggles of feminists over the last three hundred years to overcome these obstacles in order to realize their needs as individuals have not been futile as Lacan's theory of the mirror stage implies them to be. Given that it is precisely the ideals of individualism that have fired this struggle, it is strange to find feminists of all people lauding Lacan's theory on the ground that it demonstrates these ideals to be illusory, on the ground that it undermines 'the subject's coherence as a self-determined actor in its own affairs' (Gallop and Burke 1980:109), and unsettles 'feminism's tendency to accept a traditional, unified, rational, puritanical self ' (Gallop 1982:xii; but see also Abel 1984).

On the other hand, Lacan's theory of the mirror stage is useful in so far as it provides a means of explaining why we are so easily duped into falsely believing that the freedom promised us by our society's ideology of individualism is already ours. For his theory draws attention to the ease with which we are captivated into believing that we are already one with any image, including that of our individual freedom, which presents as a reflection of ourselves. This is well explained by Judith Williamson in her book, *Decoding Advertisements*, in which she shows how advertisements – such as the cigarette advertisement, 'People like you are changing to No. 6' – present us with an image of ourselves as unified, free individuals, free to buy whatever commodities advertizing depicts. Furthermore, advertisements also present us with the illusion that our needs as women are already catered to, as in the slogan, ' "farouche" – the perfume created by Nina Ricci, Paris for all the women you are'. In this, advertisements mystify the fact that our society does not in fact fully cater to women's needs as a sex, that if these needs are adequately to be met we cannot rest content with society as it is but must instead struggle to change and improve it.

How is it that women come to identify as the sex addressed by the above perfume ad? How is it that they come to recognize themselves as the sex addressed by the injunctions of advertisements, and of the media generally: 'Do not act. Do not desire. Wait for men's attention.' (Coward 1984:82)? And how is it that women also resist identifying with such representations of them as mere passive subjects of men's agency, as 'the second sex'? How do women come to resist identifying with our society's representation of them as wife, mother, lesbian, or whatever (a form of resistance that Sartre, 1935, paradoxically might have derided as a species of 'bad faith')? How are we to account for such resistance as testified, for example, by Jill Johnston when she writes: 'I never said I was a dyke, even to a dyke, because there wasn't a dyke in the land who thought she should be a dyke; or even that she was a dyke' (Johnston 1973:48)?

Lacan's theory of the mirror stage provides no means of explaining such resistance. Instead he seeks to explain women's acquiescence in, and identification with our society's representation of them as passive object of men's agency, as mere Echo of men's narcissism. He explains this not in terms of the mirror stage but in terms of what his disciple, Moustafa Safouan (1975) refers to as 'phallo-narcissism', in terms of what Freud referred to as the Oedipus or castration complex.

In his later theory of this complex, Freud argued that it comes about when the oral and anal organization of the infantile libido give way to phallic primacy, and when the child accordingly comes to entertain phallic desires and wishes in relation to its mother (and father). Punished on account of its masturbatory expression of these wishes, says Freud, the child comes to recognize what it has until then only suspected, namely that girls unlike boys do not have a penis. This leads the child to repress its phallic desire for the mother – the girl because she now recognizes herself to lack a penis (the apparent condition of her gratifying this desire, see also Brunswick 1940), and the boy because he fears that were he to gratify this desire he would be castrated as his parents have threatened, and as girls seem to him to have been.

Lacan and his followers recast this theory in social terms. Freud attributed the primacy of the phallus that he said initiates this complex to biology (see p. 81 above). Lacan attributes it to culture, to the centrality given the phallus in patriarchal society. The phallus, he says, symbolizes 'the law of the father' – the exchange of women by men in marriage – an exchange that Lacan, following Lévi-Strauss, takes to be a constant feature of all societies whatever the superstructural variations between them in their elaboration of this exchange. Women and men, says Lacan, constitute the phallus the prime signifier of their desire in so far as they recognize this patriarchal law. And, he maintains, since the mirror stage child identifies with the desire of the other, so it comes to identify with the phallus in so far as this is the signifier of the other's, of say the parent's desire. This imagined identity is only disrupted, argues Lacan, by the castration complex, by the child's discovery that the phallus is 'absent in the mother' (Mitchell 1984:244). Just as absence of the breast led the child to repress into the unconscious its hallucinated identity with it, so absence of the phallus leads the child to repress into the unconscious its hallucinated identity with the phallus. And this initiates it into seeking substitutes for the phallus, just as realization of the absence of the breast initiated it into seeking substitutes for the breast in its lips, thumbs, and so on. The child, writes Lacan, is thus initiated by the castration complex into generating the substitutes, the chains of sliding signifiers of language, in which the phallus is prime signifier. It is thus initiated, he says, into the 'Symbolic', into the proceses of substitution – of condensation and displacement – Freud (for example 1915e) showed to be characteristic of unconscious, primary process thought.

As a result of the castration complex, Lacan claims, the child comes to undertand the meaning of the phallus. Its meaning, like all terms in language, is given, says Lacan following de Saussure, by the antithesis of the presence/absence of that which it signifies. Girls, he implies, come via the castration complex to identify as 'the second sex', as the 'other' of men's agency, desire, and sexual exchange (an age-old definition of woman as mere negative of man articulated by Aristotle in writing of woman as 'female on account of an inability of a sort', and by St Thomas Aquinas in stating that 'the production of woman comes from defect in the active power' – quoted by B. Harris 1984:5 – a definition of woman as man's negative graphically depicted in the extraordinary anatomical diagram of women's sexual organs reproduced below).

The celebrated anatomist Andreas Vesalius's 1543 depiction of the female genitalia, hardly excused, as present editors of his work claim, by the fact of Vesalius's hurried excision of the specimen on which it was based because the woman's lover, a monk, and her family were planning to prosecute Vesalius for snatching her body from its tomb! (See Saunders and O'Malley 1950:170,171.)

Alternatively, if a boy, the child identifies via the castration complex, writes Lacan, as the sex defined as representative of 'the law of the father', of 'the paternal function' signified by the phallus. Like the biblical Adam or Eve beguiled by the serpent into partaking of the tree of knowledge, recognition of sexual difference in the castration complex drives the child, in Lacanian terms, from the pre-Oedipal paradise of 'Imaginary' identification with the mother's desire, into the 'Symbolic Order' of patriarchy within which the phallus is prime signifier.

In terms of Lacan's theory, recognition of genital sex difference in the castration complex at one and the same time individuates the child from the mother and initiates it into patriarchal social relations. At the very moment that the child becomes 'individualized' from the mother (Wilden 1972), from imaginary oneness with her as phallus, it begins to identify with the position either of the father or of the mother in relation to the phallus, with the patriarchal authority it symbolizes or with the mother's subordination to this authority (see also Herik 1980:103). As Anika Lemaire puts it: 'The resolution of the Oedipus liberates the subject by giving him . . . a place in the family constellation, an original signifier of self and subjectivity' (Lemaire 1970:83). In the selfsame process as the child comes into being as an individuated subject, it thereby comes into being as a 'sexed subject'. 'The castration complex', writes Mitchell, 'is the instance of the humanization of the child in its sexual difference' (Mitchell 1984:264).

What has all this to do with feminism? According to Juliet Mitchell, it has the virtue of showing psychoanalysis to be 'an incipient science of the ideology of patriarchy – of how we come to live ourselves as feminine or masculine within patriarchal societies' (Mitchell 1984:221). In her book, *Psychoanalysis and Feminism*, she argues that it is the structuring of the 'imaginary' of the unconscious in patriarchy's kinship terms that accounts for women's deep-rooted acquiescence in patriarchal ideology. It is this, she says, that explains 'why women are everywhere within civilization the second sex, but everywhere differently so' (Mitchell 1974:381). Girls, she says, enter the Oedipus complex wanting 'to take the father's place' and emerge from it recognizing that 'only the boy will one day be allowed to do so' (Mitchell 1974:404).

Mitchell reiterates Lacan's view that, because of the universality of patriarchy, 'the girl's entry into her feminine "destiny"' necessarily involves 'penis-envy, that in its turn must be repressed or transformed' (Mitchell 1974:96). However, she envisages that patriarchy will one day be overthrown. Indeed, she says, this is already under way in that social relations are no longer organized as they once were by kinship, patriarchal or otherwise: 'In economically advanced societies, though the kinship exchange system still operates in a residual way, other forms of economic exchange – i.e. commodity exchange – dominate and class, not kinship structures prevail' (Mitchell 1974:378). Kinship nevertheless still remains crucial to the structuring of social relations even in 'economically advanced societies'. The family, as Michèle Barrett and Mary McIntosh (1983) point out, continues to be a major institution whereby existing social relations and their class and sex divisions are organized and reproduced.

Mitchell, however, points out that this kinship ordering of social relations is nevertheless on the wane, that patriarchal kinship's ideology 'is, in fact, in the slow death throes of its own irrationality' as is 'the capitalist economy itself'. But, she insists, 'only a political struggle will bring their surcease' (Mitchell 1974:413). And, she goes on, 'When the potentialities of the complexities of capitalism – both economic and ideological – are released by its overthrow, new structures will gradually come to be represented in the unconscious. It is the task of feminism to insist on their birth' (Mitchell 1974:415).

In terms of Mitchell's analysis though it is hard to see why women would ever want to insist on such change. If, as she says, women repress in early childhood the desire to accede to the place accorded men in patriarchy, then there is no reason why they should ever consciously seek to accede to that place by struggling for the overthrow of patriarchy and for 'new structures' to replace it. Mitchell's Lacanian-based account of women's unconscious acquiescence in patriarchy neither explains her own feminism nor the resistance of women in general to patriarchy, and to its treatment of women as merely 'the other', 'an object', 'commodity', or 'thing' as Sheila Rowbotham (1972:98) describes women's present subordinate status in society.

Nevertheless, Mitchell's argument has been taken up by many feminists not only in England but also to a lesser extent in the USA where Gayle Rubin's version of it has been particularly influential. Rubin reiterates Lacan's account of the Oedipus complex thus: 'The presence or absence of the phallus carries the difference between two sexual statuses, "man" and "woman" . . . the dominance of men over women . . . [and] the meaning of the difference between "exchanger" and "exchanged" ' (Rubin 1975:191).

The Oedipus complex, she says, not only initiates the child into situating itself as 'exchanger' or 'exchanged', it also initiates the child into society's taboo on homosexuality. It marks the occasion of the girl's first understanding that: 'The mother, and all women by extension, can only be properly beloved by someone "with a penis" (phallus). Since the girl has no "phallus", she has no "right" to love her mother or another woman, since she is herself destined to some man' (Rubin 1975:193). As a result of the Oedipus complex, writes Rubin, the girl recognizes 'the futility of realizing her active desire' (Rubin 1975:195).

If women are to realize this desire, she claims, they must 'call for a revolution in kinship' (Rubin 1975:199), must seek the overthrow of patriarchy such that they are no longer mere subjects of men's desire. Lacan's 'exegesis of Lévi-Strauss and Freud,' she states,

> 'suggests that we should aim . . . for the elimination of the social system which creates sexism and gender. . . . I personally feel that the feminist movement must dream of even more than the elimination of the oppression of women. It must dream of the elimination of obligatory sexualities and sex roles. The dream I find most compelling is one of an androgynous and genderless (though not sexless) society, in which one's sexual anatomy is irrelevant to who one is, what one does, and with whom one makes love.'   (Rubin 1975:204)

Rubin, however, fails to explain how this dream might be realized. For if, as she says, women come to acquiesce via the Oedipus complex in the passive and subordinate lot accorded them within patriarchy, why would they ever actively struggle to achieve its overthrow? Why would they ever struggle against 'the obligatory sexualities' Rubin claims to be a consequence of patriarchy? Nor does Rubin explain her own struggles in this respect; how, having grown up in a culture that she says effectively coerces women into passive heterosexuality, both she and the Samois group with which she has been associated are nevertheless able to realize their active and lesbian desire, albeit in sado-masochistic form. Maybe this is one reason why, in her recent defence of diversity in sexual practice, Rubin (1984) rejects her previous Lacanian argument that she now says wrongly sought to explain in the same terms both sexual practice – that of heterosexuality – and gender identity.

Juliet Mitchell still regards Lacanian theory as a useful basis for explaining heterosexuality. She argues, in Lacanian terms, that 'So long as we reproduce ourselves as social beings through a heterosexual relationship, human society must distinguish between the sexes . . . for human society to exist at all, men and women must be marked as different from each other' (Mitchell 1980:234–35). Like Rubin, however, though for different reasons, Mitchell is now sceptical of the usefulness of Lacan's texts to feminism, of whether they 'ultimately get us beyond the dilemma of the relationship between patriarchy and capitalism' (Mitchell 1983:7). Perhaps it is their doubts on this score that have led feminists, interested in Lacan's work, to attend less to his account of the general psychological consequences of patriarchy, than to his account of the specific ramifications in language of patriarchal social relations. A nice example of this comes from the work of the feminist historian, Sally Alexander, who draws attention to Lacan's stress on the way 'sexual identity' is formed as 'the human infant enters language, that is as s/he is spoken to and about and s/he learns to speak' (Alexander 1984:132). Alexander provides an extremely interesting account of the way sexual difference came to be spoken and written about in the 1840s as a result of the way people at that time experienced the then changeover to factory production as eroding what now seemed to them to have been natural and God-given differences between the sexes in the organization of home and work. But this is not sufficient, on its own, to explain the resistance of the women of the period (say of the Owenite women) to the differential treatment of their sex then so widely written and talked about.

Mitchell is also doubtful whether Lacan's account of language can in fact be developed in non-idealist ways. 'I don't think',

she says, that Lacan's ' "materiality" of language is quite
enough' (Mitchell 1983:7). Others are more sanguine on this
score, arguing the value of Alexander's 'turn to psychoanalytical
theory' since it 'permits the location of subjectivity and sexual
difference in the unconscious and in language rather than in
nature' (J. Lewis 1985:116). Jacqueline Rose believes that Lacan's
work – specifically his use of structural linguistics to insist that the
meaning of any linguistic element, or signifier, is given by its
relation to the other elements of language and is thus not fixed – is
not only relevant to our understanding of subjectivity but also to
the materiality of feminist politics. Its usefulness in this respect,
she says, resides in the fact that it questions

> 'the register of the absolute fixity . . . of the category of woman.
> . . . psychoanalysis challenges other notions of the political
> which require a total identity of the group to which they refer
> and the corresponding stress on "woman" as fantasy goes right
> back to the point . . . that psychoanalysis, and indeed certain
> aspects of feminism (because I wouldn't want to homogenise
> feminism) demanded a theory which challenges the category of
> woman in that way.'   (Rose 1983:7, 15–16)

In this Rose reiterates the claim of another of Lacan's followers,
Julia Kristeva, who writes, 'a feminist practice can only be
negative . . . In "woman", I see something that cannot be
represented, something that is not said, something above and
beyond nomenclatures and ideologies' (Kristeva 1974:137).

It is true that the ideologies and nomenclatures of patriarchy
that categorize woman as object of man's agency, authority, and
exchange, do not thereby represent any eternal or fixed truth
about woman, biological or otherwise. But neither is this category
a mere phantasy. Woman might not be 'all', as Irigaray claims (see
p. 44 above), but neither is she nothing. The category 'woman' is
useful to feminism in that it serves to represent the reality of
women's shared social experience as a sex. Furthermore, it is this
shared experience that constitutes the base of feminist solidarity in
resistance against, and struggle to change the social conditions that
produce it. Simone de Beauvoir (1960:572), for instance, tells how

it was her recognition of the common social experience of women who, 'in differing circumstances . . . had all lived as "dependent persons" ' that galvanized her into becoming a feminist. To imply that such recognition is based on mere illusion and phantasy is to attack the very foundation of women's consciousness of their shared oppression that is the source of feminist resistance to it.

This is not to deny that there are not also differences between women in their experience of their social subordination as a sex, that, in this sense, 'woman' is indeed a sliding signifier, variously signifying 'daughter', 'lover', 'prostitute', 'Black', 'mother', 'worker', and so on. And the meanings of these terms are themselves not fixed but vary in relation to other terms within the signifying practices in which they are embedded. Or, as Zillah Eisenstein puts it, 'None of the processes in which a woman engages can be understood separate from the relations of the society which she embodies and which are reflected in the ideology of society. . . . The term "mother", for instance, may have a significantly different meaning when different relations are involved – as in the "unwed mother". It depends on what relations are embodied in the act. . . . The social relations of society define the particular activity a woman engages in at a given moment. Outside these relations, "woman" becomes an abstraction' (Eisenstein 1979:47; something akin to this notion of 'social relations' or 'signifying practices' is conveyed in non-analytic psychology by the terms 'scripts' and 'schemas', see, for example, Durkin 1984 and Bem 1981 respectively).

These relations and practices constitute the basis of relatively autonomous sites of struggle, and vary in the degree to which women put themselves at risk in 'coming out' in terms of them – whether as 'mother', 'lesbian', 'prostitute', or whatever. Lacanians are also surely right to take issue with those who, in thus coming out, identify the whole 'truth' of their experience with such labels – a fault that detracts from some otherwise laudable manifestoes on behalf of the women they represent (see, for example, Cline 1984). For this is to commit the error, in Lacanian terms, of collapsing the signifier – whether it be that of 'lesbian', 'woman',

or whatever – into its signified, of 'imagining' oneself to be one
with the words that represent one in language, of collapsing
'word-presentations' into their 'thing-presentations' (see Freud
1915c), treating 'words or other representations of things-in-
themselves' as 'the things-themselves' (Meltzer 1978:48). It treats
these signifiers as in themselves adequately denoting woman's
'true self', in the sense in which Winnicott uses this term.

On the other hand the Lacanian feminist project of deconstruct-
ing the category 'woman' can proceed too far. It carries with it the
implication that in the final analysis each woman should engage
with the specificity of the social practices that produce her in her
subjectivity and singularity – a fragmentation and pluralization of
women's struggle to improve their social lot that feminists have
rightly sought to transcend in forging the collective consciousness
and movement of women necessary to their overcoming the social
obstacles to their realizing their common needs as a sex. (Jeffrey
Weeks, 1985, points out that a similar problem of fragmentation
faces gay politics in its current valorization of 'sexual diversity'.)
In feminism such 'deconstructionism' overlooks the fact that, just
as the various signifiers of womanhood are related to each other,
so too are women's struggles around the practices marked by these
signifiers. As Michèle Barrett and Rosalind Coward point out:

> 'Women may come to the women's movement through
> different experiences – of job discrimination, sexual violence,
> difficulties over childcare for example. But the women's
> liberation movement could only operate if it is recognised that
> cutting across these different experiences there is a level of
> structural and general division between women and men. It is
> on the basis of the operation of the general categories of
> women and men in this society that the women's movement
> seeks to develop a sense of collectivity and a strategy for
> change.' (Barrett and Coward 1982:88)

It is not altogether surprising that, when they use Lacanian
theory, feminists often lose sight of the social realities that go to
make up the category 'woman', and that constitute the basis of
feminism's struggle to improve women's social lot, that they

overlook the fact that the ideologies, phantasies, dreams, psychical, and subjective reality that constitute the signifiers of femininity are determined by their signifieds, by the material reality of women's day-to-day lives. (For a fuller discussion of the relation of signifier to signified, of psychical to material reality, see S. Sayers 1985.)

This oversight is no surprise because Lacan was entirely opposed to considerations of material reality. He contemptuously rejected the 'reality principle' of Freudian theory, for instance, as 'the expression of a scientific prejudice most hostile to the dialectic of knowledge' (Lacan 1949:6). His 're-reading' of Freud is accordingly open to the charge levelled by Freud against Jung. He replaces the realism of Freud's theory with an idealist and mystical version of it. Of Jung's work, Freud wrote,

> 'For sexual libido an abstract concept has been substituted, of which one may safely say that it remains mystifying and incomprehensible to wise men and fools alike. The Oedipus complex has a merely "symbolic" meaning: the mother in it means the unattainable, which must be renounced in the interests of civilization; the father who is killed in the Oedipus myth is the "inner" father, from whom one must set oneself free in order to become independent.' (Freud 1914d:62)

Much the same can be said of Lacan's theory!

Juliet Mitchell is right to be wary of the pretensions of Lacanianism to provide a materialist account of the construction of women within language. And she is right to doubt the capacity of Lacanianism to contribute much of use to feminism about the relation of patriarchy and capitalism. Furthermore, as I have also sought to show in this chapter, Lacanianism as it has so far been developed fails to explain or usefully to further our undertanding of women's resistance and struggle against 'capitalist patriarchy', as it has been termed by Zillah Eisenstein (1979) among many others. In this last respect Lacanianism is no different, though often a great deal more obscure, than the other post-Freudian theories considered above and against which it sets itself as the only true heir to Freud.

PART THREE

Sexual contradictions: theory and therapy

8
Sexual identity and difference

> If feminism's underlying demand is for women's full inclusion
> in humanity (whether that inclusion is strategically posed in
> terms of equal rights, socialism or millenarianism) then the
> dilemma for a feminist political strategy may be summed up in
> the tension between the plea for equality and the assertion of
> sexual difference.   (Alexander 1984:126)

Feminism, as Sally Alexander points out, starts from recognition
of the contradiction between women's need to be treated equally
with men and the fact that they are treated unequally and
differently from them. The reason the post-Freudian theories so
far considered fail adequately to explain women's psychological
resistance to their social subordination is that they do not attend
sufficiently to the way this contradiction determines women's
psychology. These theories either attend, as does Dinnerstein's, to
the similarities to the relative neglect of the differences between
the sexes in the social experience that shapes their psychology.
Alternatively, they attend to the differences in the social
experience that shape women's and men's psychology to the
relative neglect of the similarities in social experience that also
shape their psychology. This is the case in varying degrees with
the feminist versions of the post-Freudian work of Horney, object
relations theory, and Lacan.

A similar one-sidedness marks non-psychoanalytic psychological theory. Most of its accounts – those of behaviouristic and
cognitive psychology – focus on the similarities between the sexes

to the neglect of their differences. (This is pointed out, for instance, by John Archer 1984.) A minority commit the opposite error and focus on the differences between the sexes to the neglect of the similarities in the biological and/or social factors that shape their psychology. This is the case, for example with the theories considered in the first three chapters of this book.

The great merit of Freud's work in this respect is that, virtually alone among psychologists, and albeit very inadequately, he took account of the way women's and men's psychology is determined at one and the same time by the similarities and differences of their biological and social lot. Furthermore, he provided a pointer to the reason this contradiction is so generally overlooked by other psychologists. Psychology, feminist and non-feminist alike, tends to focus on the immediate manifestations of consciousness. Indeed, some feminists, in the name of the maxim that 'the personal is political', make a virtue of attending only to what women's immediate consciousness tells them of their personal experience. But, as Freud discovered, immediate consciousness often makes it its business to iron out and thereby conceal the contradictions in social life that determine it. It is therefore little wonder that these contradictions, and the way they shape our psychology, should be overlooked by theories that focus simply on the unified, smooth-functioning appearance of 'conscious self-perception' as Freud put it, of 'lived experience' as ethno-methodologists now put it. Freud accordingly recommended that, if psychology is 'to fathom the profusion and complexity of the processes of the mind', it must model itself on the procedures adopted in the natural sciences:

'In our science as in the others the problem is the same: behind the attributes (qualities) of the object under examination which are presented directly to our perception, we have to discover something else which is more independent of the particular receptive capacity of our sense organs and which approximates more closely to what may be supposed to be the real state of affairs.' (Freud 1940a:195–96)

Pursuing this method in his own work, Freud discovered that 'the real state of affairs' as far as psychology is concerned is that it is determined at one and the same time by the similarities and differences between women and men in their social experience.

This discovery was not forced on Freud by any sympathy with the cause of women's emancipation. His upbringing was hardly conducive to instilling any such sympathy in him. His biographer, Ernest Jones, recounts for instance how his sister's piano-playing was sacrificed by his family to his, Freud's, studies and ambitions. Nor did Freud's work, as a young man, in translating Mill's *Subjection of Women* endear him to the cause of women realizing their ambitions in the ways open to men. Of this book's argument, he wrote to his wife-to-be, Martha Bernays:

> 'It is really a still-born thought to send women into the struggle for existence exactly as men. . . . I believe that all reforming action in law and education would break down in front of the fact that, long before the age at which a man can earn a position in society, Nature has determined women's destiny through beauty, charm and sweetness . . . [to be] in youth an adored darling and in mature years a loved wife.'   (quoted in Jones 1954:193)

Freud was later to encourage women analysts in their professional aspirations – Lou Andreas-Salomé, for instance, and his daughter, Anna (whom, to his discredit, he himself analyzed from 1918 to 1921, and again from 1924 to 1925, see Peters 1985). He nevertheless remained convinced to the end of his life that women should be subordinate to men. In the posthumously published *Outline of Psycho-Analysis*, for instance, he asserted, 'It does little harm to a woman if she remains in her feminine Oedipus attitude . . . . She will in that case choose her husband for his paternal characteristics and will be ready to recognize his authority' (Freud 1940a:99).

As feminists are all too well aware, this view informs not only Freudian theory but also its clinical practice. In *The Interpretation of Dreams* Freud had written of the equal substitutability of one unconscious wish for another. Writing many years later about psychoanalytic practice, however, he implied that in women only certain wishes can properly be substituted for the wish for a penis. 'The unsatisfied wish for a penis', he wrote, 'should be converted into a wish for a child and for a man, who possesses a penis' (Freud 1937c:355).

Women's other wishes, such as the wish to be educated and employed like men, were accordingly dismissed by generations of analysts as neurotic, even though they were, in principle, no more unrealizable and therefore no more neurotic in this sense than the wish to have a child or a man.

Freud's recognition of the way women's and men's psychology is shaped by the contradictions of their social experience came from his clinical work, and from the investigation of neurotic symptoms, slips of the tongue, jokes, and dreams to which this work gave rise. Study of these phenomena that disrupt the apparent unity of consciousness led to the discovery that they are the product of contradictory aims and intentions as I have already briefly indicated (see pp. 76–7 above). This, in turn, led Freud to a beginning appreciation of the contradictions of family and social life that are the source of the mental conflicts that go to make up the so-called 'psychopathology of everyday life', and that cause the splitting of consciousness into a conscious and unconscious mind.

I shall explain these points by beginning, in this chapter, with an outline of Freud's account of the similarity yet difference in the social experience that shapes the psychology of girls and boys in infancy. Freud argued that, whatever its sex, the infant experiences as sexually pleasurable its interactions with those who feed, clean, clothe and generally attend to its physical needs (physical aspects of childcare curiously neglected by many of the psychoanalytically informed feminist theories considered above – a neglect due perhaps to the transformation of human needs brought about by recent social and economic developments, and by the benefits accruing from them to the middle class from which feminism draws its main support, Sayers 1983). That the infant experiences its physical interaction with its mother as sexually pleasurable is evident, says Freud, from the way babies seek to repeat aspects of this interaction. He points out, for example, that the baby tries to recapitulate the pleasure of being breast-fed by going on sucking at its lips or thumb even when sated. And it seeks to repeat the pleasure it derives from being cleaned and attended to at its toilet by holding on to its faeces so as to recapitulate the anal stimulation it then enjoyed.

That this pleasurable experience is not merely sensual but sexual is evident, maintains Freud, from the fact that adult neurotics recall this experience in relation to symptoms they more immediately associate to current events in their lives that are manifestly sexual (a two-stage account of the genesis of neurotic symptoms explained more fully by Laplanche and Pontalis 1968; see also Sayers 1985a). Freud's patient Dora, for example, recalled the pleasure she gained as an infant from sucking her thumb in association to neurotic symptoms she attributed more immediately to her father's friend's attempted sexual seduction of her. Clinical evidence bearing on the characterization of the anal pleasures of infancy as sexual comes from another of Freud's case histories, that of the Rat Man. This man's symptoms included an obsession with the idea of an Eastern torture in which a basin of rats is inverted on the victim's buttocks so that they bore into the anus. And this obsession was clearly related by the Rat Man to sexual matters, to his relation to his girl friend whom he feared might be subjected to this torture. If further evidence is wanted that anality and orality are sexual, argued Freud, one only has to consider the 'perversions', the way oral and anal pleasures figure in activities such as kissing, fellatio, cunnilingus, buggery, and so on.

Freud points out that babies not only seek to repeat the pleasures they derive from interaction with others in auto-erotic form – in the thumb-sucking, say, or in faecal play. They also seek to repeat these pleasures, as they first experience them, namely in social form. Such repetition – both auto-erotic and social – is made all the more possible, says Freud, by the mobility of the sexual instinct evident from the analysis not only of neurotic symptoms but also of dreams that indicates the substitutability of the aims and objects of the sexual instinct as they are represented in the unconscious. In this, he said, the sexual instinct differs from the 'ego' or 'self-preservative' instincts of hunger, thirst, defecation, and so on which are only gratified by particular aims and objects: hunger, for instance, being only satisfied by feeding and food. Although the sexual instinct first comes into being 'anaclitically', on the back of the social processes whereby the baby's physical needs are satisfied, maintained Freud, it quickly comes to be satisfied by a variety of other objects and aims. The oral component of the infant's sexual instinct, for instance, is satisfied not only by food, but also by the child's lips and thumb. It is satisfied not only by the passive aim of being suckled and fed, but also by the active aim of giving suck and feeding others.

Sexual aims can thus take a passive or an active form. Although these aims later come to be equated with femininity and masculinity respectively, says Freud, the similarity of boys' and girls' early experience leads them equally to indulge both aims in the process of seeking to recapitulate the sexual pleasures they derive from this experience. Initially, Freud points out, boys as well as girls seek to recapitulate this pleasure in the passive form in which they first experience it:

> 'The first sexual and sexually coloured experiences which a child has in relation to its mother are naturally of a passive character. It is suckled, fed, cleaned, and dressed by her, and taught to perform all its functions. A part of its libido goes on clinging to those experiences and enjoys the satisfactions bound up with them.'   (Freud 1931b:384)

On the other hand these passive aims are quickly replaced, in girls as well as in boys, by active aims. 'In the first place, he writes, being suckled at the breast gives place to active sucking' (Freud 1931b:384). Writing of the girl's active aims, as they are consciously expressed in infancy, Freud says:

> 'We seldom hear of a little girl's wanting to wash or dress her mother, or tell her to perform her excretory functions. Sometimes, it is true, she says: "Now let's play that I'm the mother and you're the child"; but generally she fulfils these active wishes in an indirect way, in her play with her doll, in

which she represents the mother and the doll the child.'
(Freud 1931b:384)

Likewise children seek to master the painful experience of separation from the mother by staging the active part, as they experience it, of the mother's going away and return. Freud describes just such an instance in *Beyond the Pleasure Principle*, telling how his eighteen-month-old grandson symbolized and hence gained some measure of control over this experience by playing with a reel attached to some string which he threw over the side of his cot saying 'o-o-o-o' (signifying *'fort'* or 'gone') as it disappeared, and then pulled up again with a joyful *'da'* or 'there'. (For examples of the way this account of the development of symbolization, language, and thinking has been taken up in post-Freudian theory see Klein 1930 and Bion 1970, and for a Lacanian critique of this work see Rose 1982).

Irrespective of its sex, the child seeks to repeat not only the active but also the passive aspects of the anal as well as oral pleasures it derives from, or 'produced' in it by, its interactions with those who first look after the physical needs associated with these pleasures. (For a Foucauldian description of this process see Urwin 1984.) Freud records, for example, how Little Hans, aged three, would repeat the passive, exhibitionistic pleasure involved in this interaction by getting others to watch and supervise his toilet as his parents had. He told his father how, on his summer holidays, ' "when I widdled, Berta and Olga watched me." . . . "Berta always looked on at me too" (he spoke with great satisfaction and not at all resentfully); "often she did. I used to widdle in the little garden where the radishes were, and she stood outside the front door and looked on at me" ' (Freud 1909b:184,222). And Hans would also contrive to repeat the active, voyeuristic pleasure, as he experienced it, of the one (Berta in this instance) who watched him at his toilet. His father records, for example, the following conversation with Hans:

'I: "Have you often been into the W.C. with Mummy?"
He: "Very often"
I: "And were you disgusted?"

He: "Yes . . . No"
I: "You like being there when Mummy widdles or does lumf?"
He: "Yes, very much" ' (Freud 1909b:224)

Similarly, and despite the cultural association of scoptophilia with masculinity expressed in stories of Peeping Toms (see, for example, Mulvey 1975; Kaplan 1974; but see also Betterton 1985), girls also seek to repeat the voyeuristic pleasure, as they experience it, of the one who supervizes their toilet. Like boys they too contrive to watch others at their toilet, their mothers say (see, for example, Ophuijsen 1924).

The similarity in the pleasure derived by boys and girls from having their genitals rubbed in the course or being cleaned and dressed by those who look after them in their infancy likewise gives rise to active as well as passive sexual aims in both sexes. In its passive form, says Freud, the child experiences this aspect of its physical care as one of being passively seduced by its mother or nursemaid – a pleasure it seeks to recapitulate and intensify by inciting her into 'repeated touching and rubbing' of its genitals (Freud 1931b:386). One mother, for instance, told him how, when she was trying a pair of knickers on her three year old daughter, she had 'passed her hand upwards along the inner surface of the child's thigh, whereupon the little girl shut her legs together on her mother's hand, saying: "Oh Mummy, do leave your hand there. It feels so lovely" ' (Freud 1909b:182n.1). And Freud tells how boys likewise seek to repeat the so-called 'feminine' pleasure of being passively seduced, as they experience being clothed and cleaned by the mother. He tells how Hans, aged four and a half,

> 'was given his usual daily bath by his mother and afterwards dried and powdered. As his mother was powdering round his penis and taking care not to touch it, Hans said: "Why don't you put your finger there?'
> Mother: "Because that'd be piggish."
> Hans: "What's that? Piggish? Why?"
> Mother: "Because it's not proper."
> Hans (laughing): "But it's great fun." ' (Freud 1909b:182)

Not only is the cultural equation of passivity with femininity no bar to boys consciously expressing such passive genital aims, but neither does the biological fact of sex difference act as any bar initially on boys also consciously voicing the wish to be passively seduced by men as by women, a wish expressed in the form of a day-dream recounted thus by Hans to his father: ' "Daddy, I thought something: I was in the bath, and then the plumber came and unscrewed it. Then he took a big borer and stuck it into my stomach" ' (Freud 1909b:226). Nor is the fact of biological sex difference any bar at first to boys believing that they can have a baby just as their mothers can: ' "I'll have one if I want to," said the four year old Hans, "when I'm married to Mummy" ' (Freud 1909b:252).

Such is the similarity of their experience of being physically looked after as one of genital seduction that girls and boys equally seek to recapitulate this experience not only in passive form, but also in active form by taking the part of the one they experience as seducing them. 'Active wishful impulses directed toward the mother', says Freud, regularly arise in girls 'during the phallic phase' – impulses that seem, from other evidence, to have as their object that of getting the mother with child (Freud 1931b:386–86). Freud likewise tells how his patient the Wolf Man recalled, as a child, repeating in active form the genital pleasure he had derived from being the passive object of his sister's attentions. When he was three she had played with his penis, telling him the while extraordinary stories about his nursemaid (his Nanya) who, she said, did the same thing with the gardener – how 'she used to stand him on his head, and then take hold of his genitals' (Freud 1918b:248). Seeking to recapitulate the active part of his sister as he had then experienced it, writes Freud, and of his Nanya as his sister had described her supposed exploits with the gardener, the Wolf Man attempted actively to seduce his Nanya by masturbating in front of her.

The Wolf Man's Nanya, however, clearly disapproved of his masturbation. She responded by making 'a serious face . . . children who did that, she added: got a "wound" in the place' (Freud 1918b:253). Hans's mother responded similarly to his masturbating, telling him, ' "If you do that, I shall send for Dr A to cut off your widdler" ' (Freud 1909b:171).

At first, says Freud, both boys and girls respond to such reprimands, as they do to their other social interchanges, that is by seeking to recapitulate them in both the passive and active forms in which they experience them. Passively, this can take the form of indulging phantasies of being punished and beaten. And, although masochism of this sort is culturally equated with femininity, boys initially indulge these phantasies just as girls do. Freud (1919e) tells how men as well as women recall the masturbatory pleasure they derived as infants from masochistically imagining themselves being beaten. The three year old Wolf Man, for instance, would identify with boys he imagined being beaten on the penis. And he also sought to gratify the masochistic desire expressed in this day-dream by being naughty so that he would actually be beaten by his father. Freud's colleague Jeanne Lampl de Groot likewise tells of a patient of hers who recalled the 'feeling of shuddering pleasure' she had derived as a child from masochistically identifying with hospital patients whom she would imagine having 'to endure the most frightful pains and tortures' including that of being 'flayed alive' (Lampl de Groot 1928:343).

On the other hand, the child's experience of being punished also gives rise, in girls as well as boys, to the active aim of being the sadistic agent as they experience it rather than the masochistic object of such punishment. For girls, says Freud, punishment of masturbation 'becomes a motive for rebelling against the person who prohibits it' (Freud 1931b:379). Boys respond similarly. The Wolf Man, for instance, reacted to his Nanya's admonitions against his masturbation by tormenting her 'till she burst into tears', by 'being cruel to small animals', and by indulging day-dreams of 'beating large animals (horses)' (Freud 1918b:255). Hans gave vent to similar sadistic phantasies – phantasies that again had their source in his experience of being told off. He told his father:

'Hans: "I should just like to beat her [Mummy]."

I: "When did you ever see any one beating their Mummy?"

Hans: "I've never seen any one do it, never in all my life."

I: "And yet you'd just like to do it. How would you like to set about it?"

Hans: "With a carpet-beater." (His mother often threatens to beat him with the carpet-beater.)'   (Freud 1909b:241)

Not only does the adult's punishment, explicit or implicit, of the child's masturbation give rise in boys and girls to both sadistic and masochistic aims, but it also leads them to recognize what they have until now only suspected, namely that girls do not have a penis. Up until this time, says Freud, both boys and girls believe that the little girl has a penis which is 'still quite small. But when she gets bigger it'll grow all right' (Freud 1908c:194). The girl now recognizes that she indeed does not have a penis. At first, says Freud, she explains this difference 'by assuming that at some earlier date she had possessed an equally large organ and had then lost it by castration' (Freud 1924d:320–21). She interprets it, in the light of her parents' disapproval of her masturbation, as 'a punishment personal to herself' (Freud 1925j:337). Boys, says Freud, likewise interpret the lack of a penis in girls as the effect of the punishment they fear might be theirs given their parents' disapproval of their masturbation and of the incestuous desire it expresses. Like the girl, the boy also first 'believes that is is only unworthy female persons that have lost their genitals – females who, in all probability, were guilty of inadmissible impulses similar to his own' (Freud 1923e:311). The boy then recognizes that his mother, and that all women, lack a penis.

Recognition of this biological fact, occurring as it does in the stage of phallic primacy, when the child narcissistically cathects itself as a whole object (see p. 81 above), means that the boy now cathects himself as a being differentiated from women in having a penis. The boy now equates gratification of his previously consciously expressed desire to take his mother's place in sexual relations with his father as involving being like her, castrated as he construes her lack of a penis. He accordingly represses this desire because its gratification is now in seeming contradiction with his new-found narcissistic cathexis of his penis as signifier of his maleness. But, although this desire now equated with being a woman is thereby repressed, it is not thereby done away with. This desire continues to be expressed. Grown men often consciously entertain the day-dream of being 'a woman submitting to the act of copulation' (Freud 1911c:142). Judge Schreber, whose autobiography Freud analysed, clearly expressed this wish. Furthermore, claims Freud, all men and boys unconsciously hallucinate this wish not merely as though it were fulfilled, as did Schreber in his day-dreams, but as actually fulfilled. This is evident from the study of psychosis when the primary processes of hallucinatory thought escape the opposition to their expression of the secondary processes of realistic and conscious thought. Schreber, for example, gave expression to just such an hallucinatory idea during his psychotic breakdown when he experienced himself actually to be a woman. He then had 'a feeling that enormous numbers of "female nerves" have already passed over into his body, and out of them a new race of men will proceed, through a process of direct impregnation by God' (Freud 1911c:147). During his illness, writes Schreber, he 'possessed female genitals . . . felt a stirring in my body, such as would arise from the quickening of a human embryo . . . male semen had . . . been projected into my body, and impregnation had thus taken place' (Freud 1911c:164n.2).

Nor are such delusions confined to the ravings of lunatics. Freud shows that the hallucination of being a woman in sexual intercourse with a man constitutes a regular feature in the psychology of men who are in no way psychotic. In their case this hallucinated wish-fulfilment is not directly expressed as it can be in psychosis where hallucinatory primary process thought dominates waking as well as sleeping life. Instead this wish is then expressed in disguised form, as in 'normal jealousy', says Freud, when

'a man will not only feel pain about the woman he loves and hatred of the man who is his rival, but also grief about the man, whom he loves unconsciously, and hatred of the woman as his rival . . . [even] consciously imagining himself in the position of the faithless woman.' (Freud 1922b:197–98)

Being a woman carries with it not only the biological connotation of not having a penis. It also carries what Freud referred to as a 'sociological' connotation (Freud 1905d:141n.1). Freud never paid much attention to the details of the sociological, or social elaboration and articulation (material, ideological, symbolic, and discursive – see, for example, Alexander 1984) of sexual difference or to the social subordination of women it expresses. And he paid no attention at all to the way this elaboration, and the production of subjectivity involved in it, varies historically, cross-culturally, and even within the space of each woman's individual biography – as daughter, sister, lover, wife, mother, worker, old woman, and so on. Freud simply referred to this cultural elaboration of sexual difference as entailing an equation of femininity with passivity and of masculinity with activity – an equation that succinctly expresses men's social dominance and women's subordination to it but which also has obvious shortcomings. Freud pointed out, for instance, that contrary to this equation, women are recognized to be active in mothering (Freud 1933a) – regarded by many as the quintessence of femininity. He also pointed out that women, lesbians at least, are recognized to be active in their sexual desire, albeit, as he indicated, this desire is then derided as evidence of their masculinity, of their lack of femininity (Freud 1920a – a derision that is particularly hard for women to bear in so far as their lesbianism is constituted by repudiation of men and masculinity, see Merk 1985).

Not only did Freud say little of the specific content of the social elaboration of sexual difference that he referred to simply as involving the equation of femininity with passivity, masculinity with activity. He also said little of how the child acquires its knowledge of this connotation of sexual difference. He confined his observations on this question to the suggestion that the child acquires this knowledge through watching its parents' sexual and social intercourse with each other:

'Whatever detail it may be that comes under their observation
– whether it is the relative positions of the two people, or the
noises they make, or some accessory circumstance – children
arrive in every case at the same conclusion. They adopt what
may be called a sadistic view of coition. They see it as
something that the stronger participant is forcibly inflicting on
the weaker . . . . The sadistic theory of coitus . . . has in part
divined the nature of the sexual act and the "sex-battle" that
precedes it. Not infrequently, too, the child is in a position to
support this view by accidental observations. . . . In many
marriages the wife does in fact recoil from her husband's
embraces, which bring her no pleasure, but the risk of a fresh
pregnancy. And so the child who is believed to be asleep (or
who is pretending to be asleep) may receive an impression from
his mother which he can ony interpret as meaning that she is
defending herself against an act of violence. At other times the
whole marriage offers an observant child the spectacle of an
unceasing quarrel, expressed in loud words and unfriendly
gestures; so that he need not be surprised if the quarrel is
carried on at night as well, and finally settled by the same
method which he himself is accustomed to use in his relations
with his brothers and sisters or playmates.' (Freud 1908c:
199–200)

On the basis of witnessing this, 'the primal scene', says Freud,
the child begins to acquire the sociological equation of femininity
with passivity, of masculinity with activity: in this case with
sadism and violence. Furthermore, argues Freud, the child
identifies with the part of both partners in this scene as it
understands the pleasures they experience in it. This two-fold
identification by the child, he writes, consists of 'the impulse to
put himself in the place of the active man, and . . . the impulse to
identify himself with the passive woman' (Freud 1914d:54).

Up until then, as we have seen, Freud maintains that boys, like
girls, give full conscious expression to the passive, masochistic aim
now equated with being a woman. What happens to this passive
aim in boys and men when its gratification comes to be equated

with femininity? According to the theories outlined in the first part of this book, passive and non-aggressive aims are held to be relatively lacking in boys given their biological and hormonal make-up (see Chapter 1), to be avoided until the child acquires gender constancy (see Chapter 2), or only to gain expression given their appropriate reinforcement and reward (see Chapter 3). By contrast, Freud held passive aims to continue to be expressed by boys and men even when they come to be equated with femininity. Indeed, he argues, 'in many relations in life it is indispensable' for men to adopt 'a passive attitude towards another man' even though this might be unconsciously equated with being a woman, with being castrated (Freud 1937c:356). Freud also reminds his readers that men regularly express passive aims, most blatantly in the 'perverse' forms taken by male masochism in which men derive orgasmic pleasure from imagining themselves, or from actually being 'gagged, bound, painfully beaten, whipped, in some way maltreated, forced into unconditional obedience, dirtied, and debased' – from situations evocative of femininity, of being 'in a characteristically female position' (Freud 1924c:416).

Dramatized in this way it is no surprise that men and women often repudiate femininity and the social subordination of women that it expresses. Freud however shows that even when boys and men repudiate or repress their 'feminine' or passive aims on account of the contradiction of the gratification of these aims with men's narcissistic investment in their masculinity, these aims continue to be expressed. They are then expressed, however, in a form that at best affords them merely illusory gratification (not the real gratification Freud claimed to be obtained through perversion say), such is the opposition of the ego to their actual gratification given its association with femininity, with being castrated as the boy construes being a woman.

This may be illustrated once again by reference to the case of the Wolf Man. When he was three, as we have seen, this man had apparently sought actual gratification of his desire to be the passive object of his father's beatings, by being naughty so as to be punished by him. Freud claims that this passive, masochistic aim in relation to his father was repressed in the Wolf Man when, following his Nanya's threatening him with castration for masturbation, he recalled having seen his parents making love, his father penetrating his mother from behind so that he could see she had no penis. Construing this as meaning that, were he to take his mother's place as his father's sexual object he would then be castrated as his mother seemed to be, the Wolf Man repressed this his previously consciously expressed desire. But, despite being repressed, says Freud, its passive aim continued to be expressed, albeit it was now expressed in neurotic form, in a form that could at best only afford it hallucinatory not actual gratification. The Wolf Man stopped being naughty and instead became a nervous and anxious child, phobic of animals and particularly of a picture of a wolf that reminded him of the position of his father as he had seen him in sexual intercourse with his mother: 'the man upright, and the woman bent down like an animal' (Freud 1918b:270). Later he became obsessively religious, identifying in his rituals with the sufferings of Christ at the hands of God the Father. Later still he passively submitted to the atheistical views of his tutor even though they were diametrically opposed to his own religious convictions.

If this can be the fate of boys' passive aims once they are equated with femininity, what is the fate of girls' active aims once their gratification is equated with masculinity, with having a penis? Freud argues that when the girl recognizes that, unlike boys, she does not have a penis, she then represses into the unconscious her previously consciously expressed phallic sexual aims toward her mother. For she now recognizes gratification of these aims to be in contradiction with reality, that she lacks the wherewithal to put these aims into effect. The hallucination of her phallic, incestuous desire as fulfilled, however, is no more done away with by thus being repressed into the unconscious, writes Freud, than is the analagous hallucinatory wish-fulfilment in men, namely that of being the female object of phallic penetration by a man. Freud shows that the desire to be a man, to penetrate phallically the mother, continues to be expressed in girls and women following their recognition of genital sex difference either directly as in psychosis, when this difference may be 'disavowed' (Freud 1927e), or indirectly as in neurotic symptoms and dreams.

The following dream of Freud's patient, Dora, is a case in point:

'I was walking about in a town which I did not know. I saw streets and squares which were strange to me. Then I came into a house where I lived, went to my room, and found a letter from Mother lying there. She wrote saying that as I had left home without my parents' knowledge she had not wished to write to me to say that Father was ill. "Now he is dead and if you like you can come." I then went to the station and asked about a hundred times: "Where is the station?" I always got the answer: "Five minutes". I then saw a thick wood before me which I went into and there I asked a man whom I met. He said to me: "Two and a half hours more". [In repeating the dream she said: "Two hours".] He offered to accompany me. But I refused and went alone. I saw the station in front of me and could not reach it. At the same time I had the usual feeling of anxiety that one has in dreams when one cannot move forward. Then I was at home. I must have been travelling in the meantime, but I know nothing about that. I walked into the porter's lodge, and enquired for our flat. The maidservant opened the door to me and replied that Mother and the others were already at the cemetery. I saw myself particularly distinctly going up the stairs, and after she had answered I went to my room, but not the least sadly, and began reading a big book that lay on my writing table.' (Freud 1905e:133–34)

In psychosis, as I have indicated, the unconscious hallucination of being a member of the opposite sex may be fully available to consciousness, such is the dominance then of waking as of sleeping life by the primary processes of hallucinatory thought. Normally, however, hallucinatory dream thoughts can only be expressed in consciousness provided that they are subject to 'secondary revision' whereby the contradictions of which they are constituted are ironed out. Only thus does the dream constitute a sufficiently coherent unity to be consciously recollected and narrated. Its unconscious, or 'latent' primary process thoughts can then only be retrieved, says Freud, by focusing on the elements of the manifest dream that have escaped secondary revision, namely those that disrupt its narrative unity.

Applying this method of analysis to Dora's dream, how come the anomalous appearance in it of a wood given its general urban character of streets, squares, and station? Why, asked Freud, having overlooked the means whereby she got home from this strange town, did Dora then distinctly recall 'going up the stairs' to her flat? And, why given the generally impressionistic character of the dream, the precise amendment as to time – the 'two hours'? It was Dora's associations to these, the dream's incongruous elements, that revealed its unconscious thought. The square of the dream reminded her of a postcard sent her by a male admirer. In the dream she unconsciously identified with this man. The 'station', 'thick wood', and 'cemetery' are all symbols of female genitals, and 'going upstairs' symbolizes their entry. The 'two hours' of the dream reminded Dora of an occasion when she had stood this long 'in front of the Sistine Madonna, rapt in silent admiration' (Freud 1905e:136). All in all, therefore, the dream represented herself as a man entering a woman's genitals, those of her mother. It represented, albeit in disguised form, the hallucinatory fulfilment of the phallic incestuous desire which, according to Freud, is first consciously expressed by girls in early childhood and is then repressed into the unconscious as a result of the castration complex when its fulfilment is then equated with being a man, and therefore recognized to be impossible.

An example of the way this selfsame wish can likewise be expressed in neurotic symptoms as fulfilled comes from another of Freud's cases, namely that of a young woman whom he describes as having felt impelled each night to go through the following elaborate bed-time ritual:

'The big clock in her room was stopped, all the other clocks or watches in the room were removed, and her tiny wrist-watch was not allowed even to be inside her bedside table. Flowerpots and vases were collected on the writing-table so that they might not fall over in the night and break, and disturb her in her sleep. . . . the door between her room and her parents' bedroom should stay half-open – the fulfilment of which she ensured by placing various objects in the open doorway . . . . The pillow at the top end of the bed must not touch the wooden back of the bedstead. The small top-pillow must lie on this large pillow in one specific way only – namely, so as to form a diamond shape. Her head had then to lie exactly along the long diameter of the diamond.' (Freud 1916–17:304,305)

Freud points out that if one is to understand the psychological meaning and cause of such symptoms, as of dreams, it is not so much their more plausible, as their more implausible elements that require investigation. This patient explained her ritual as designed to ensure silence while she slept. Why, then did she insist on the bedroom door being kept open? And why her insistence on the pillows being placed just so on the bed? For surely neither of these requirements had anything to do with ensuring silence? The girl's associations to these, her obsessional symptoms' anomalies indicated that, for her, the large pillow represented her mother, the small top-pillow herself, while its being placed diamond-wise on the larger pillow recalled the way the open female genitals are depicted in graffiti. In lying on these diamond-placed pillows therefore she enacted, albeit unconsciously, the openly expressed phallic desire of the infant toward the mother as fulfilled: 'she herself was playing the man,' writes Freud, 'and replacing the male organ by her head' (Freud 1916–17:308).

If, as Freud claims, girls at first consciously entertain phallic desire for their mothers in infancy and then repress this desire on account of their recognizing its contradiction with the reality of their not having a penis, of their not being male, what then becomes of the psychological attributes of maleness brought into being and produced in them as in boys by the social experiences of their infancy? In repressing the hallucination of themselves as biologically male, as having a penis, what becomes in girls and women of the traits socially equated with being a man – traits equated by Winnicott (1971:95) for instance with 'doing' rather than 'being', traits equated by American students with being 'aggressive', 'independent', 'not at all emotional', 'objective', 'dominant', 'active', 'competitive', 'logical', 'worldly', 'self-confident', 'ambitious', and 'never conceited about appearance' (Broverman *et al.* 1970)? What happens to these traits and aims socially associated with masculinity when girls and women repress into the unconscious the hallucination of themselves as male?

These aims continue to be elicited in girls and women, as in boys and men, by the fact that our society encourages everyone, regardless of sex, to believe themselves to be active, independent agents of their own destiny. At the same time, however, women's social experience also teaches them that there are fewer opportunities open to them than to men to their realizing this, their supposed freedom as individuals.

The aim of realizing this freedom in practice is contradicted by the social restrictions on women's spheres of activity. Gratification of this aim, however, is not in contradiction with biological reality as is gratification by women of the phallic incestuous desires consciously expressed by them in infancy. There is therefore no reason on this score why women's 'active' aims, produced in them as in men by their social interactions and relations, should be repressed into the unconscious. And, to the extent that these aims remain conscious, they constitute the psychological source of women's individual and collective resistance to the social obstacles to their realization.

Jeffrey Weeks makes a somewhat similar point when, commenting on the work of Michel Foucault, he writes: 'the individual subject is not a product of a single discourse, is not trapped in a prison of dominant meanings, but is in a sense "inter-discursive", with the potentiality for challenging and reversing the forms of definition, deploying one system of meaning against another' (Weeks 1982:113). Jean Anyon (1983) and Barbara Hudson (1984) likewise point out that adolescent girls' resistance to their social lot comes about through the contradiction of the fact that their social experience produces them at one and the same time as both identical with boys in their capacity for individual achievement, and as different from them in their femininity.

All too often girls and women succumb to these contradictions. They regularly disown their so-called 'active', individualistic aims on account of the social association of these aims with masculinity, and on account of their consequent contradiction with girls' and women's narcissistic or egoistic investment in their femininity – an investment that Freud said first comes about with the recognition of sexual difference through the castration complex. Oftentimes, says Freud, as a result of this complex a girl will give up 'her phallic activity and with it her sexuality in general as well as a good part of her masculinity in other fields' (Freud 1931b:376).

These 'masculine' aims are not, however, thereby done away with. They persist since the social conditions that first brought them into being persist. As indicated above, women, just like men, are incited by their social experience from infancy onwards into seeking to repeat the pleasure they derive from this experience by becoming not merely the passive objects of others, but also by becoming active in social interaction with them. To the extent, however, that actual gratification by women of this latter aim is opposed by consciousness, it may then be repressed into the unconscious as occurs in neurosis, turned against the self as occurs in depression, or only recognized in others as occurs in paranoia. I shall explain this in greater detail in the following chapters. In the process I shall outline the methods whereby Freud and his followers, particularly Melanie Klein, sought to undo the defences of repression, introjection, and projection involved in neurosis, depression, and paranoia respectively. Psychoanalysis, I shall argue, thereby seeks to enable women (and men) to become more fully conscious of the contradictions giving rise to these defences so as to become more capable of realizing rather than disowning their aims, active as well as passive, masculine as well as feminine.

9

Repression and neurosis

> What is now called the nature of women is an eminently artificial thing – the result of forced repression in some directions, unnatural stimulation in others.   (John Stuart Mill 1869:451)

> When I have promised my patients help or improvement by means of a cathartic treatment I have often been faced by this objection: 'Why, you tell me yourself that my illness is probably connected with my circumstances and the events of my life. You cannot alter these in any way. How do you propose to help me, then?' And I have been able to make this reply: 'No doubt fate would find it easier than I do to relieve you of your illness. But you will be able to convince yourself that much will be gained if we succeed in transforming your hysterical misery into common unhappiness. With a mental life that has been restored to health you will be better armed against that unhappiness.'   (Freud 1895d:393)

The main object of Freud's clinical practice was to undo the defence of repression so that his patients might handle the sexual contradictions giving rise to it realistically rather than neurotically. I shall describe the main features of this, the clinical method of Freudian psychoanalysis, by outlining the way Freud developed this method in response to the obstacles he encountered in treating neurosis – obstacles that led him finally to recognize, albeit only rudimentarily, that one of the ultimate causes of neurosis lies in sexual inequality and difference.

Freud only arrived at this conclusion toward the end of his life. The theme of neurosis as the effect of repressed sexual conflict was, however, a feature of his psychoanalytic theory and practice from its very inception. It was on this point that Freud eventually took issue with Josef Breuer from whom he first learnt the 'cathartic treatment' of hysteria. Breuer attributed the frequent occurrence of hysteria among the women of his class not so much to the conflicts as to the monotony of their social lot which, he said, bred in them a tendency towards day-dreaming. It was, he argued, the ideas occurring to them in their day-dreams, or 'hypnoid states' as he termed them, ideas that were thus dissociated from normal consciousness, that constituted the source of their neurosis.

At first Freud went along with Breuer on this point, at least to the extent of concluding with him that it was no good seeking to treat hysteria by the 'rest cure' method then widely canvassed by the physician Weir Mitchell (Freud 1895d:350), a method that had included, in the case of his patient, the American feminist writer, Charlotte Perkins Gilman, the prescription that she 'never touch pen, brush or pencil as long as you live' (Hedges 1973:47)! Such treatment, argued Freud, could hardly relieve women of their hysterical symptoms for it sought to set in train the very social conditions that had produced these symptoms in the first place.

It seemed that these symptoms could, however, be relieved by having the patient articulate, under hypnosis, the ideas they expressed. Breuer attributed the success of this, his cathartic treatment of hysteria, to its bringing the pathogenic ideas expressed in it into associative connection, through verbalization, with consciousness such that they could then be corrected and revised. His patient, Anna O., later to become a pioneer women's rights campaigner, accordingly referred to this method of treatment as a 'talking cure' (Breuer 1895:83).

So impressed was Freud by the apparent success of Breuer's treatment of Anna O. that he adopted the method himself. The aim of bringing dissociated ideas into connection with those of consciousness became fundamental to the psychoanalytic technique he was now to develop. Freud was, however, sceptical as to the validity of Breuer's explanation of the dissociation of ideas from consciousness that occurs in hysteria, namely as the effect of their having first occurred in a hypnoid state. He argued that this dissociation is the effect of defence, of the ego's opposition to the ideas dissociated from consciousness because of the conflict between these ideas and the ego's other, conscious ideas. The resistance of his patients to being hypnotized, and to recalling these dissociated ideas to consciousness was, he maintained, a manifestation of this selfsame defence.

Faced with this obstacle, namely that of the resistance of his patients to being hypnotized, Freud abandoned hypnotism as a method by which to treat neurosis. In France he had observed Bernheim persuade his hypnotic subjects to recall the ideas he had put to them under hypnosis by simply commanding and pressurizing them to recall these ideas when they were awake. Encourged by this observation, Freud decided to abandon the hypnotic method of suggestion whereby Breuer had got his patients to recall the ideas expressed in their symptoms. Instead he simply insisted, as Bernheim had, that his patients recall these ideas that otherwise only seemed recoverable through hypnosis. Later Freud was somewhat to modify this technique. Instead of pressurizing his patients to recall the ideas expressed in their symptoms he adopted the method of 'free association', requesting the patient to 'put himself into a state of quiet, unreflecting self-observation, and to report to us whatever internal perceptions he is able to make – feelings, thoughts, memories – in the order in which they occur to him' (Freud 1916–17:328).

Applying this method (which puts psychoanalysis as much at risk of contamination by suggestion as the techniques it replaced and claimed to better, see Grünbaum 1984), Freud found again and again that patients related their symptoms not so much to the monotony, but to the sexual conflicts of their lives. Thus, for example, in the case of Elisabeth von R. described in *Studies on Hysteria*, Freud discovered, by use of the method of free association, that her symptoms (pains in her legs and difficulties in walking) were the product of a conflict in her between her desire for her brother-in-law and her loyalty to his wife, her sister. So painful was this conflict to her that she had repressed it from consciousness. Now all that remained of it in consciousness were the pains in her legs that served to represent somatically its mental content. By overcoming Elisabeth's resistance to becoming conscious of this conflict, says Freud, it was possible both to dispel the hysterical symptoms that up until then had represented it, and to determine whether she might not act on her desire by marrying her brother-in-law since her sister was now dead.

Freud also recognized women's social subordination to have contributed to the 'over-determination' of Elisabeth's symptoms. He tells, for instance, how her difficulties in walking served to represent not only her repressed desire but also her dependent status as a woman – her pain at 'standing alone', her feeling of helplessness, of not being able to 'take a single step forward' (Freud 1895d:221). Nor was Elisabeth von R.'s the only case in which he related women's neurotic symptoms to their social subordination. He tells, for instance, of a woman who expressed, through a slip of the tongue, the conflict produced in her by the subordinate status of her sex. 'Her sick husband,' she said, 'had been to the doctor to ask what diet he ought to follow for his health. The doctor, however, had said that a special diet was not important. She added: "He can eat and drink what I want." ' (Freud 1910b:112). Freud similarly tells of a patient of Ferenczi's who expressed the mental conflict produced in her by the social subordination of her sex not by a slip of the tongue (which involves suppression rather than repression of the ideas it expresses, see Timpanaro 1974:127) but by generalized forgetfulness. Ferenczi describes the woman thus:

'At the moment I am treating a patient, a spinster getting on in years, in whose mind the most familiar and best-known names fail to appear, although her memory is otherwise good. In the course of the analysis it has become clear that this symptom is intended by her as a documentation of her ignorance. This demonstrative parade of her ignorance is, however, really a reproach against her parents, who did not let her have any higher education.' (Freud 1910b:79)

Nor have the patients of psychoanalysis been alone among women in suffering neurosis and hysteria on acceding to their socially assigned feminine destiny in ways involving repression of the active aims that otherwise fuel their resistance to that destiny. A leading spokeswoman of the mid-nineteenth century American women's rights movement, Lucy Stone, for instance, suffered hysterical loss of her voice on marriage and the birth of her first child (Rossi 1974). Similarly Cora Caplan (1983) describes how, in the earlier years of the nineteenth century, Elizabeth Barrett Browning suffered hysteria with the onset of the menarche.

In 1896 Freud flirted with the idea that the main sexual conflict underlying hysteria or neurosis is that produced by sexual seduction in childhood. He had already reported one such case in 1895, the case of an eighteen year old, Katharina, who recalled in association to her neurotic symptoms her father's attempted seduction of her when she was fourteen. The next year Freud reported that his patients, men and women alike, regularly recalled such experiences in association to their symptoms, experiences of being seduced in early childhood by a member of the family household of their infancy, often by a nursemaid or governess, or by siblings who had themselves been victims of sexual abuse by one of the family servants. It was, said Freud, the opposition of the ego to remembering this experience, and the resulting repression of this memory from consciousness, that constituted the fundamental aetiological cause of the hysterical symptoms that somatically represented it. Where memory of this experience did not conflict with the ego, he argued, sexual seduction in childhood did not produce hysteria (see Freud 1896c).

On hearing Freud's announcement of this theory, the sexologist Krafft-Ebing dismissed it as 'a scientific fairy-tale' (Jones 1954:289). Freud himself quickly came to view the theory in something of the same light. Only a year after first propounding it, Freud abandoned the seduction theory for the same reason as he had earlier abandoned the use of hypnosis in therapy, namely because treatment in terms of this theory failed to alleviate his patients' symptoms. That is, he abandoned this theory because it proved wrong in practice – a testing of theory against practice that characterizes science in general (see, for example, S. Sayers 1985). 'The first group of factors', he wrote to his friend Edward Fliess in September 1897, that had led him to reject the theory,

> 'were the continual disappointment of my attempts to bring my analyses to a real conclusion, the running away of people who for a time had seemed my most favourably inclined patients, the lack of complete success on which I had counted, and the possibility of explaining my partial successes in other, familiar, ways. (Freud 1950a:215; for Freud's full correspondence with Fliess about the demise of his seduction theory see Masson 1985)

Freud now believed that the stories of childhood seduction with which his patients had regaled him were indeed a species of 'fairy tale'. (See Malcolm 1984 for a very readable and intelligent discussion of the current rumpus about this development in Freud's theory.) Freud maintained that these stories were phantasies elaborated in defence against the conflict between the ego and the incestuous desires of childhood to which it was opposed.

Many (for example, Bartlett 1954) have concluded that, with the replacement of the seduction theory by a focus on phantasy and infantile sexuality, Freud lost sight of the material as opposed to psychical reality that determines consciousness. But this is to overlook the fact that Freud continued to regard consciousness as determined by material reality, by the material reality of inheritance and biological constitution for instance to which he now gave more attention (compare, for example, Freud's 1896c and 1905e accounts of hysteria). More importantly, he regarded the phantasies, the psychical reality, he now viewed as the principal constituents of neurosis as produced by social reality, by the contradictions in it between the anti-social aims – autoerotic, perverse, and incestuous – elicited in the child by the family's physical care of it and society's taboos and injunctions against the open expression of these aims.

Having previously regarded children as sexual innocents, Freud now came to regard them as sexual beings. As we have seen, he explained this sexuality as elicited in the child by the physical care and attention bestowed on it by its parents and nursemaids, care that, whether or not it involves actual sexual seduction, is regularly experienced by the child as a form of seduction (see pp. 106–07 above). Less than a month after writing to Fliess of his rejection of the seduction theory, Freud wrote to him of his dawning suspicion that all children entertain sexual desire toward members of their families:

'I have found in my own case too, falling in love with the mother and jealousy of the father, and I now regard it as a universal event of early childhood. . . . If that is so, we can understand the riveting power of *Oedipus Rex* . . . the Greek legend seizes on a compulsion which everyone recognizes because he feels its existence within himself. Every member of the audience was once, in germ and in phantasy, just such an Oedipus, and each one recoils in horror from the dream-fulfilment here transplanted into reality, with the whole quota of repression which separates his infantile state from his present one.' (Freud 1950a:265)

If neurotics are to be relieved of their symptoms, Freud now argued, it is necessary to enable them to become conscious and hence to resolve the incestuous conflicts that he believed these symptoms to express. As long as these conflicts remain unconscious, he said, they remain 'relatively unchangeable'. On the other hand, once such conflict is rendered conscious it is then 'subject to a process of wearing away'. In this, he suggested, unconscious conflicts are like the relics of Pompeii: 'their burial had been their preservation: the destruction of Pompeii was only beginning now that it had been dug up' (Freud 1909d:57).

The process of rendering conscious the unconscious phantasy elaboration of sexual conflict that Freud now believed to be expressed in neurotic symptoms may be illustrated by reference to his account of the case of Dora. Dora, in actual fact a woman by the name of Ida Bauer, was referred by her father for treatment with Freud. She suffered a variety of neurotic symptoms – hysterical fainting fits, nervous cough, a 'tickling in her throat', and anorexia. Anorexia and other eating disorders in women are now often attributed to women's obsession with the control, or lack of control, they are able to exercise over their lives (see, for example, Lawrence 1984; Maisner and Pulling 1985). Freud likewise explained such disorders in terms of control, specifically in terms of the control involved in repression: sexual repression. Dora's associations to her symptoms led him to conclude that in her case her oral symptoms represented, in hallucinatory form, the fulfilment of her repressed and displaced incestuous desire, that they unconsciously represented herself in fellatio with her father, the recourse Freud assumed her father's lover, Frau K., to have adopted in her sexual relations with him, given the fact of his, Dora's father's, impotence.

Freud (1908d) attributed the widespread occurrence of neurotic symptoms in women of Ida Bauer's class to the fact that, in the interests of securing a husband of good family for their daughters, these women's parents taught them from their earliest childhood to suppress their sexuality until it could result in them making a good match. Ironically, however, this socialization had the effect of subverting the very institution it was intended to promote. Often sexuality was thereby rendered so disgusting to women that they regarded marriage, on account of the sexual relations it entails, as loathsome. Elizabeth Blackwell, for instance, the first woman in the USA to gain a medical degree, confided in her reminiscences that as a young woman she 'hated everything connected with the body and could not bear the sight of a medical book'. She only persisted in studying medicine, she said, so as to place 'a strong barrier between me and all ordinary marriage' (Rossi 1974:327,328). Freud (1894a) also tells of women likewise disgusted by the idea of marriage, of a woman unable to go out because of her anxiety lest her sexual desire thereby be aroused, whose social activity had become so restricted by agoraphobia that she could not possibly meet an eligible suitor.

Freud went on to point out that, even when women do marry they often remain so incestuously attached to the parents by whose authority they repress their sexuality that they are unable to enjoy sexual relations with their husbands. They are accordingly loath to conceive and become mothers as their socialization had intended. Some women, writes Freud (1912d) are only able to enjoy sexual relations once the condition of its prohibition is restored, as in adultery. Others instead find sexual gratification of a kind in neurotic symptoms, and in over-sexualizing their relations to their children. This, however, prematurely awakens their children's sexuality. And, since their children are no more able to express their sexuality than were their mothers, the way is thereby prepared for them to become neurotic in their turn.

This is a far cry from the theories considered in Chapters 4 to 7, that imply that the family acts in essential accord with its interests in reproducing its sexual divisions (Sayers 1985b). It might be argued, however, that this is no objection to these theories in that families no longer repress their daughters' sexuality as they once did, and given that women are now freer to indulge their sexual desire outside marriage (although the accompanying illustration clearly indicates the continuing hold of the equation of sex with marriage).

In fact, however, families still treat their daughters' expression of their sexuality with greater disapproval than that of their sons. The situation decribed by Simone de Beauvoir (1949:299–300) whereby families positively elicit and encourage their sons' sexuality while greeting their daughters' with silence, if not with overt disapproval, persists today. This may explain why women not only had an 'incapacity to tolerate undisguised sexuality' in Freud's day (Freud 1905c:144), but are still less open than men in acknowledging their sexuality. They are still less willing than men to acknowledge as sexual, situations and relationships that are patently erotic (see, for example, Sartre 1943; Wilson 1984; Newton 1984). And, of course, women are still frequently sexually dissatisfied in marriage – a dissatisfaction fed off by the purveyors of Mills and Boon romance, which panders to women's repressed sexuality. This repression continues to contribute to the widespread occurrence of neurosis in women.

Freud points out that neurosis affords the sufferer hallucinatory

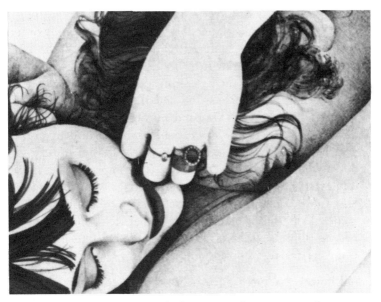

Cover illustration of Alex Comfort's sex manual, More Joy of Sex.

gratification of her (or his) repressed sexual desire. This 'primary gain', as Freud termed it, constitutes a major obstacle to neurotics giving up their symptoms so as to deal more realistically with the conflicts that produce them and thus gain actual, as opposed to merely illusory gratification of the needs and desires these symptoms express.

This obstacle to cure is compounded by the fact that neurotics also derive real, or 'secondary' gain from their symptoms in the sense of being physically looked after by others on account of them. Indeed, said Freud of the women of his class and time as have many before and since (see, for example, Nightingale 1859; Delamont and Duffin 1978; Webster 1981; Uglow 1983), such was the social lot of these women that they often had little option, other than that of illness, whereby to gain physical care and attention to their needs and wants:

'A woman who is roughly treated and ruthlessly exploited by her husband will fairly regularly find a way out in neurosis, if her constitution makes it possible, if she is too cowardly or too moral to console herself secretly with another man, if she is not strong enough to separate from her husband in the face of every external deterrent, if she has no prospect of supporting herself or obtaining a better husband and if in addition she is still attached to this brutal husband by her sexual feelings. Her illness now becomes a weapon in her battle with her dominating husband – a weapon which she can use for her defence and misuse for her revenge. To complain of her illness is allowable, though to lament her marriage was probably not. She finds a helper in her doctor, she forces her usually inconsiderate husband to look after her, to spend money on her, to allow her at times to be away from home and so free from her married oppression.'   (Freud 1916–17:430)

Freud however adjured doctors not to collude in this way with their neurotic patients. In order that neurotics gain actual, as opposed to merely illusory gratification of the sexual wants and desires their symptoms express, he said, it is necessary to enable them to become conscious of the conflicts that produce these symptoms 'within the framework of the patient's life' (Freud 1898a:275). Treatment of these symptoms in some other context, say in a mental hospital, cannot bring about their permanent relief since such treatment does not deal with these symptoms in the social context that produces them.

Freud also came to recognize that it was necessary to tackle these conflicts as they occur in the analytic situation itself. This was dramatically borne in upon him by Dora's summary termination of her analysis barely three months after it had first begun. She had, it seems, made up her mind to this course of action two weeks before actually giving Freud her notice. In this she had behaved like Frau K.'s maid who had given Herr K. a similar period of notice when he reneged on his sexual promises to her. Dora, it seemed, had unconsciously identified Freud with Herr K. Furthermore, since analysis of her dreams showed that she unconsciously equated Herr K. with her father, it seemed that she had unconsciously equated Freud not only with Herr K. but also with her father. Freud believed that, if only he had rendered conscious to Dora her unconscious transference on to him of her attitudes to her father and to Herr K., he might thereby have forestalled her breaking off her treatment with him before her cure was complete. As it was, it seems, she remained a neurotic to the end of her days (see Marcus 1976).

Analysis of the transference now became the *sine qua non* of psychoanalytic therapy (an aspect of analysis most illuminatingly discussed by Janet Malcolm 1982). The transference, said Freud, might constitute an obstacle to treatment as it had in Dora's case. On the other hand it can also be turned to therapeutic effect. It does the analyst 'the inestimable service', wrote Freud, 'of making the patient's hidden and forgotten erotic impulses immediate and manifest. For when all is said and done, it is impossible to destroy anyone *in absentia* or *in effigie*' (Freud 1912b:108).

Only by analysing these impulses as they become manifest in the transference, argued Freud, is it possible to restore the patient to her (or his) desire, described thus by Blake:

'What is it men in women do require?
The lineaments of Gratified Desire.
What is it women do in men require?
The lineaments of Gratified Desire.'

(Blake 1787:100)

At the time he analysed Dora, Freud implied the 'lineaments of gratified desire' to be innately heterosexual. Musing on the Dora case some years after treating her, however, he came to recognize the bisexuality of her desire. He realized that his failure to analyse her transference on to him of her unconscious heterosexual desire toward her father had not been the only reason he had failed to cure her of her neurosis. He came to recognize this failure to have also been due to his neglect of the homosexual component of the unconscious phantasy sustaining her symptoms. Freud came to regard her oral symptoms as constituting the hallucinatory fulfilment of her desire, not only to take Frau K.'s supposed place in heterosexual relations with her father, but also her desire to take her father's place in sexual relations with Frau K., to be Frau K.'s lover.

As we have seen, Freud argued that, in their sexual relations, Dora's father and Frau K. must have resorted to fellatio since he, Dora's father, was impotent. But this is most illogical. As Lacan points out, 'cunnilingus is the artifice most commonly adopted by "men of means" whose powers begin to abandon them' (Lacan 1951:67). It seems more likely that Dora's symptoms represented herself in cunnilingus with Frau K., rather than in fellatio with her father. Freud's overlooking of this possibility bears on yet another obstacle to the analytic cure of neurosis – namely, that of the analyst's transference or 'counter-transference' on to the analytic situation of his (or her) unconscious phantasies. In overlooking the possibility that Dora's oral symptoms expressed the homosexual phantasy of herself in cunnilingus with Frau K., and in focusing instead on trying to persuade Dora that her symptoms represented repressed heterosexual desire for her father and for Herr K., Freud seems unconsciously to have identified with these two men. He seems unconsciously to have sought to meet Dora's father's interest in persuading Dora to accede to Herr K.'s desire so that he, her father, might freely enjoy Herr K.'s wife (see Ramas 1980; for an account of the way Freud's counter-transference likewise obstructed his treatment of a manifest lesbian see Merk 1985). Furthermore, Freud unconsciously identified Dora with the maid with whom Her K. had had sexual relations (Moi 1981), a fact that only came to light later when he analysed the reason why 'one name and only one occurred to me – the name "Dora" ' by which to conceal Ida Bauer's identity (Freud 1901b:302). The reason, he discovered, was that 'Dora' was the name of a maid, his sister's maid.

Unlike some of his followers (see p. 161 below) Freud did not turn the discovery of the obstacle to treatment constituted by the counter-transference to therapeutic effect. Nor did he consider the possibility of bisexuality in the transference and counter-transference, that analyst and analysand unconsciously treat each other as opposite as well as the same as their biological sex.

Freud did however insist, on the basis of the failure to which his neglect of the bisexuality of desire had led in Dora's treatment, that cure of neurosis depends on uncovering the homosexual as well as heterosexual phantasies that sustain it (Freud 1908a). Only then can patients begin to act on the aims expressed in their neurosis so as to obtain real as opposed to merely phantastical or hallucinatory gratification of these aims.

But actual gratification of bisexual desire is obstructed by the fact of sexual difference. This desire cannot be gratified, as it seems to be in early childhood and in neurotic symptoms, by one and the same object. For, in reality, one's sexual object is either the same sex as oneself (i.e. constitutes a homosexual object-choice), or is opposite in sex to oneself (i.e. constitutes a heterosexual object-choice). It cannot be both at the same time. The reality of sexual difference means that homosexual and heterosexual desire cannot be gratified by one and the same object (see Freud 1930a:296).

Freud came to regard the biological fact of sex difference, specifically the defences set up on account of the child's construction of this difference in the castration complex, as the ultimate obstacle to the psychoanalytic cure of neurosis. He arrived at this conclusion on the basis of his enquiry into the finding that neurotics not only derive pleasure of a sort from their symptoms (i.e primary and secondary gain) but also derive pain from them and cling to their symptoms on this account. It seems, says Freud, that neurotic symptoms serve to recapitulate both the gratifying and frustrating aspects of the past experience they unconsciously express. He explained this by suggesting that, alongside the pleasure principle (of the libido, or Life Instinct) that seeks to gratify present need by repeating situations that were associated in the past with gratification of this need, there is also a principle of un-pleasure (of the Death Instinct) that seeks to repeat these situations in order to master and get rid of the feelings of frustration and un-pleasure associated with them as in the *fort-da* game of his grandson (see p. 105 above). In this the Death Instinct seeks to abolish stimulation. It seeks to restore the organism to zero stimulation, to the state of inanition that precedes and succeeds life. By contrast the Life Instinct seeks to create the means whereby the needs of the living might be gratified and met. These two instincts thus express the contrary aspects of pleasure and pain involved in all social interaction. They are antithetical aspects of one and the same process – namely of 'the repetition compulsion' (see Freud 1920g; cf. Engels' remark as to 'the negation of life . . . being essentially contained in life itself', Engels 1875–83:388).

Freud suggests that the Life and Death Instincts become split apart through the Oedipus complex. He says that the libidinal and incestuous object choices of the id are repressed into the unconscious as a result of this complex on account of their gratification then being equated with castration, such is the child's then construction of sexual difference. On the other hand, he says, the self-destructive impulses of the Death Instinct that are associated with the idea of castration, and with the prohibition of incestuous desire that gives rise to this idea, go to form the super ego. The super ego, he says, is formed out of identification with the father's prohibition of incest. It is set up by the ego in defence against the danger seemingly constituted to it by gratification of the incestuous desires of the id that, given the child's construction of sexual difference, seems to entail castration (see Freud 1923b; for a recent discussion of the problems this poses for explaining the female super ego see Millot 1985). The 'negative therapeutic reaction', says Freud, whereby neurotics cling to their symptoms in obstinate self-punishment is the work of the super ego. The super ego thereby attempts to go on punishing the incestuous desires of the id that are expressed in neurotic symptoms.

Freud accordingly concluded that the obstacle to cure constituted by the negative therapeutic reaction can only be removed by analysing the resistance of the ego, specifically of the super ego, to cure. In order to do this, says Freud, it is necessary to get the neurotic to review the defences first established in infancy by the super ego against the incestuous object-choices of the id so as thereby to free the active and passive aims otherwise fixated to these repressed desires. Up until this point in therapy, writes Freud, the analyst can count on forming a 'therapeutic alliance' with the healthy part of the analysand's ego to work at freeing the

libido from its fixation to the incestuous desires of infancy –
desires that the analyst interprets to the analysand on the basis of
the hypotheses and 'constructions' he, the analyst, forms about
these desires on the basis of the information provided by the
analysand in analysis (Freud 1937d).

With the analysis of the defences of the ego formed in
childhood against conscious expression by the analysand of his or
her passive and active aims and desires, says Freud, the ego can no
longer be relied upon to facilitate the process of analysis. Instead it
obstructs this process. In men, says Freud, this comes about
because the analysand equates cure with passive submission to the
analyst, which he unconsciously equates with being castrated,
such is the persistence in the unconscious of the childhood belief
that to submit to a man is to be a woman, to be castrated as the
child first construes being a woman – a persistence that is hardly
surprising (see Lewin 1984) given the continuing construction of
woman as lack or absence of sex (see Chapter 4 above). On the
other hand, says Freud, women often resist cure because they
unconsciously equate it with gaining a penis. And this, he implies,
is a manifestation of the defence of the ego first instituted in
childhood against realization of their active aims (sexual and
otherwise) on account of gratification of these aims then being
equated with having a penis, with being male. The obstacle to cure
constituted by this defence of the ego, writes Freud, is often
insuperable:

> 'At no other point in one's analytic work does one suffer more
> from an oppressive feeling that all one's repeated efforts have
> been in vain, and from a suspicion that one has been "preaching
> to the winds", than when one is trying to persuade a woman to
> abandon her wish for a penis on the ground of its being
> unrealizable or when one is seeking to convince a man that a
> passive attitude to men does not always signify castration . . . .
> The rebellious overcompensation of the male produces one of
> the strongest transference-resistances. He refuses to subject
> himself to a father-substitute, or to feel indebted to him for
> anything, and consequently he refuses to accept his recovery

from the doctor. No analogous transference can arise from the female's wish for a penis, but is the source of outbreaks of severe depression in her, owing to an internal conviction that the analysis will be of no use and that nothing can be done to help her. And we can only agree that she is right, when we learn that her strongest motive in coming for treatment was the hope that, after all, she might still obtain a male organ, the lack of which was so painful to her.' (Freud 1937c:252)

Freud believed that with this resistance of the ego to cure, analysis reaches 'bedrock', that in such cases the biological fact of sexual difference constitutes an insurmountable obstacle to cure of the neuroses.

Were it the fact that men could only realize their passive aims by being women (a fallacy played on by the film *Tootsie*), and that women could only realize their active aims by being men, by having a penis, then this would indeed constitute an impassable biological hurdle to their being cured, in the sense of being enabled through therapy to realize both their passive and active aims. In fact, however, the obstacles to such realization are social not biological. Although these obstacles are real enough they are not insurmountable. Women, for instance, have realized, and continue to realize their active and so-called 'masculine' aims by struggling both individually and collectively against the social obstacles to their realization.

Although these obstacles to effective treatment of neurosis can be overcome, as can the other obstacles that Freud encountered in seeking to treat this condition (namely those involved in hypnosis, the transference, bisexuality, and in the gains afforded neurotics by their symptoms), Freud never made the obstacles to cure constituted by the social subordination of women an object of his analytic work. I shall return to this point in my conclusion. First, however, I shall outline two other ways described by Freud whereby women and men seek to elude consciousness of the contradictions involved in their social experience, namely those of 'introjection' and 'projection'. In the process I shall describe the methods of undoing these defences developed not so much by

Freud but by his followers, notably by Melanie Klein. Kleinians have hoped through the use of these methods to enable people to become more fully conscious of the contradictions that give rise to these defences. In this, they set themselves a similar therapeutic goal to that of Freud, namely that of relieving people of their symptoms so that they might be 'better armed against the unhappiness' caused them by the conflicts and contradictions of the social experience that produces these symptoms in them.

10

Introjection and depression

> Why have women passion, intellect, moral activity – these three – and a place in society where no one of the three can be exercised? . . . This system dooms some minds to incurable infancy, others to silent misery. . . . It seems as if the female spirit of the world were mourning everlastingly over blessings, not lost, but which, in her discouragement she feels that she never will have, they are so far off.   (Florence Nightingale 1859:396,404,413–14)

> Women are in a continual state of mourning – for what they never had – or had too briefly, and for what they can't have in the present, be it Prince Charming or direct worldly power. . . . When female depression swells to clinical proportions, it unfortunately doesn't function as a role-release or respite. (Phylis Chesler 1972:44)

The women's movement of Florence Nightingale's day, as of our own, sought to change society so that women might realize their 'passion, intellect, moral activity', and so on, and thus realize themselves fully in the world. All too often, however, non-feminist and feminist women alike succumb to the social obstacles standing in the way of such realization. As we have seen in the last chapter, women may repress their 'masculine' aims such that they are then not realized but are instead expressed in neurotic form. Alternatively, women often deal with the obstacles to their realizing these aims by turning them against themselves, by 'introjecting' them such that these aims are then expressed, again unrealistically, in 'misery', 'mourning', and 'depression'.

A tragic illustration of this second type of response by women to the social restrictions on their sex comes from Freud's tale of the Wolf Man's sister:

'As a child she was boyish and unmanageable, but she then entered upon a brilliant intellectual development and distinguished herself by her acute and realistic powers of mind; she inclined in her studies to the natural sciences, but also produced imaginative writings of which her father had a high opinion. She was mentally far superior to her numerous early admirers, and used to make jokes at their expense. In her early twenties, however, she began to be depressed, complained that she was not good-looking enough, and withdrew from all society. She was sent to travel in the company of an acquaintance, an elderly lady, and after her return told a number of most improbable stories of how she had been ill-treated by her companion, but remained with her affections obviously fixed upon her alleged tormentor. While she was on a second journey, soon afterwards, she poisoned herself and died far away from her home.' (Freud 1918b:249–50)

The Wolf Man and his sister grew up in Russia at a time when intellectual activity was no more permitted to women there than it was to the women of Florence Nightingale's England. And this was reflected in such activity being regarded as un-feminine, as masculine (an attitude that persists today both in psychoanalysis, see, for example, Guntrip 1969:261, and more generally, as documented by, for example, Sayers 1984a and Walkerdine 1985). In the case of the Wolf Man this attitude included his unconsciously equating his sister, on account of her intellect, with a man, with the poet Lermontov. Freud tells us:

'A few months after his sister's death he [the Wolf Man] himself made a journey in the neighbourhood in which she had died. There he sought out the burial place of a great poet, who was at that time his ideal, and shed bitter tears upon his grave.

This reaction seemed strange to him himself, for he knew that more than two generations had passed by since the death of the poet he admired. He only understood it when he remembered that his father had been in the habit of comparing his dead sister's works with the great poet's. He gave me another indication of the correct way of interpreting the homage which he ostensibly paid to the poet, by a mistake in his story which I was able to detect at this point. He had repeatedly specified before that his sister had shot herself; but he was now obliged to make a correction and say that she had taken poison. The poet, however, had been shot in a duel.' (Freud 1918b:252)

Freud explained depression, such as had taken its toll on the Wolf Man's sister's life, in terms of its similarity to the grief following bereavement. He suggested, however, that whereas grief is triggered by actual loss of one's loved objects, depression is triggered by the experience of disappointment unconsciously as entailing loss of one's loved objects. It is this unconscious loss that causes the unhappiness of depression, just as it is actual loss that causes the unhappiness of bereavement. Unlike grief, though, depression is much more often marked by guilt and self-accusation. It seems, says Freud, as though the depressed person unconsciously responds to disappointment and frustration by experiencing the person supposedly responsible for these adversities as lost to the self. Instead of addressing their anger against the external and actual causes of their unhappiness people respond in depression by turning this anger against themselves, against their loved objects psychically internalized as phantoms within the self. It is this shadow-boxing, suggests Freud, that constitutes the stuff of the self-accusations and suicidal self-destructiveness of depression (cf. Raps *et al.* 1982). 'The depressed woman', he writes,

> 'who loudly pities her husband for being tied to such an incapable wife as herself is really accusing her husband of being incapable, in whatever sense she may mean this. There is no need to be greatly surprised that a few genuine self-reproaches are scattered among those that have been transposed back . . .

they derive from the pros and cons of the conflict of love that has led to the loss of love . . . far from evincing towards those around them the attitude of humility and submissiveness that would alone befit such worthless people . . . they make the greatest nuisance of themselves, and always seem as though they felt slighted and had been treated with great injustice. All this is possible only because the reactions expressed in their behaviour still proceed from a mental constellation of revolt, which has then, by a certain process, passed over into the crushed state of melancholia.' (Freud 1917e:257)

Why, though, do depressed people turn their anger against themselves rather than use it to confront and actually deal with the external sources of their anger and frustration? Why the self-destructiveness of depression that, unlike neurosis, involves failure to realize physical as well as sexual need? Freud suggests that this is because the attachment of the depressed person to the external causes of their discontent, or at least to the people they unconsciously believe to be the cause of their troubles, is formed on a narcissistic basis. They love these people for what they seemingly reflect of themselves. Disappointed in this love, says Freud, the depressed person withdraws it, their libido, back into the self instead of transferring it on to some other external object or cause. And, as the libido is thus re-introjected into the self so too is the lost object cathected by it.

Perhaps one can explain in these terms women's peculiar vulnerability to depression, their peculiar tendency to turn against themselves the anger they feel about the hardships of their lives. Surveys repeatedly find women to be very much more likely than men to become depressed (see for example Hirschfeld and Cross 1982). And the rates of depression among certain groups of women is staggering. Studies of working-class mothers of young children find almost half of them to be clinically depressed (for example Richman 1974; Brown and Harris 1978). And their depression is clearly related to, though it in no ways deals effectively with, the adversities of their lives. George Brown and Tirrill Harris's study of a sample of women living in London, for instance, found that depression in these women was entirely a function of whether they had undergone the following difficulties: having recently suffered a 'severe life event' interpreted by them as involving loss; having sustained 'long-term difficulties' (housing, financial, health problems, and so on); having no intimate and confiding tie with another adult; being unemployed; having three or more children less than fourteen years old living at home; and having lost their mothers through death before they were eleven.

Faced with similar difficulties men seem more often to respond with outward rather than inward anger and frustration, with outward action rather than depression (see, for example, Weissman and Klerman 1981). This is not however to deny that men do not also respond to hardship with depression as is evident from the rise in depression among men faced with unemployment (Oatley 1984). Men, however, are generally less vulnerable to depression. And this may be due to their feeling less helpless than women, and more able socially and economically to deal with the untoward circumstances of their lives. Certainly depression in women seems to be associated with feelings of helplessness (see, for example, Beck and Greenberg 1974). Depression might also be less common in men because society more readily tolerates their openly expressing their anger at their social lot than it tolerates women giving open vent to their anger (see pp. 26–7 above).

This last point brings me to another factor that may also contribute to women's greater susceptibility to depression. Not only are women enjoined to be more passive and reserved than men about expressing their anger, but so too are they enjoined to be more passive about expressing their love – injunctions which they also clearly internalize. As the poet Coleridge put it: 'The man's desire is for the woman; but the woman's desire is rarely other than for the desire of the man' (Coleridge 1827:50). Or, as Florence Nightingale complained, 'Women crave for being loved, not for loving' (Strachey 1928:25). Perhaps is is this, the 'narcissistic' character, as Freud termed it, of women's passive aim in love, 'of being loved' (Freud 1914c:82), that also contributes to their greater susceptibility to responding with anxiety to 'the danger-situation of loss of object' (Freud 1926d:300).

Freud himself focused in his clinical work on treating neurotic, not depressive, symptoms. As indicated (see p. 134 above), he believed that successful analytic treatment depends upon the analyst being able to make a therapeutic alliance with the healthy part of the analysand's ego. He implied that in depression – or at least in severe depression – the ego is not sufficiently intact, split as it is between narcissistic cathexis of itself and identification with its disappointing loved object, for such an alliance to be established. Kleinians, taking their cue from the work of Freud's pupil Karl Abraham (1924), have been less wary of treating this condition.

Like Freud, Klein regarded depression as arising from disappointment in love, that is from a contradiction within internal, subjective reality between the love and hate caused by such disappointment. In this depression differs from neurosis in so far as the latter is caused not so much by contradictions within internal reality *per se*, as by the contradictions of internal and external reality, by the contradiction say between woman's subjective hallucination of herself as a man and the objective reality of herself as a woman (see pp. 116–17 above).

The defence of repression to which this latter contradiction gives rise is, says Freud, a developmentally later acquisition than the defence of introjection involved in the contradiction of love and hate. Repression, he maintains, depends on recognition of external reality (see, for example, Freud 1911b), including that of sexual difference. Introjection, by contrast, first comes into play when the child is still unaware of external reality as such. Freud maintains that this defence first comes into being when the child's waking as well as sleeping life is dominated by the pleasure principle, rather than by the reality principle. 'Under the dominance of the pleasure principle', he states, the infant psychically takes into itself, or 'introjects', objects which it experiences as 'sources of pleasure' and expels or 'projects' sources of 'unpleasure' (Freud 1915c:133). 'Expressed in the language of the oldest – the oral-instinctual impulses', he says, the infant deals with the contradiction of pleasure and pain inevitably involved in its social interaction with others by making the defensive judgement: ' "I should like to eat this", or "I should like to spit it out"; and, put more generally: "I should like to take this into myself and to keep that out." That is to say: "It shall be inside me" or "It shall be outside me" ' (Freud 1925h:439). And, as we have seen, Freud also argued that it is not only pleasurable feelings that are introjected, that in depression unpleasurable feelings and their object cathexes are also introjected, that depression involves dealing with the external causes of the contradiction between one's feelings of pleasure and unpleasure as though these causes were inside the self.

How does Klein apply this account of depression to its treatment? On the basis of Freud's account of it, Klein argued that depression results from fear lest, in actually expressing one's anger at the frustrations of one's social lot, one might thereby lose those who seem to be not only the source of these frustrations but who are also those whom one loves, and on whom one depends (see p. 56 above). This fear is all the more problematic for women since they are so often economically as well as emotionally dependent on those they love – a point brought out not by Klein but by feminist therapists using her work and more particularly the object-relations versions of psychoanalysis to which it gave rise (see, for example, Eichenbaum and Orbach 1985).

Kleinian treatment of depression involves interpreting, 'working through' (see Freud 1914g), and thus hopefully making conscious the anxiety about object loss unconsciously feared to be the consequence of openly expressing the anger and discontent one feels about one's social lot. It involves interpreting this anxiety as it becomes manifest in the transference. It involves interpreting the analysand's fear lest in openly expressing their feelings of frustration and need (rather than turning these feelings against themselves) the analyst's capacity to help them might thereby be used up and destroyed.

The Kleinian analyst Hanna Segal writes, for example, of how following her agreement to waive the fees of one of her patients on account of her being hard up, the patient the next day 'opened the session by complaining that my waiting-room was very cold. She also thought, for the first time, that it looked very drab and dreary, and she deplored the lack of curtains in the room. Following these associations, she reported a dream. She said that the dream was very simple – she had just dreamt of a sea of icebergs. . . . She said that on waking her first thought was that she was afraid she might soon be in the grip of depression again . . . . She then associated with the icebergs a poem about ancient and deserted ships, looking like swans asleep. They also reminded her of the white and wavy hair of an old friend of hers, Mrs. A., who used to be kind to her, from whom she had had help and whom she had neglected, which caused her a great deal of guilt and sorrow.' (Segal 1973:71)

On the basis of these associations, Segal interpreted to the patient her anxieties lest she had used up and thereby lost Segal's capacity to help her by putting her money worries on to Segal:

'I interpreted that the cold waiting-room was the same as the cold icebergs in her dream; that she must feel that her demands to pay reduced fees or no fees at all had completely exhausted and impoverished me – the waiting-room being drab and dreary and without curtains – that she had in fact killed me, so that I had become like a cold iceberg, filling her with guilt and persecution.' (Segal 1973:71)

Those working at the London Women's Therapy Centre describe this aspect of therapy thus: 'At the point of being able to take in the therapist's caring, the woman may become caught up in worrying and fantasizing about the needs of the therapist. . . . She may feel she needs to take care of the therapist in order to keep her there' (Eichenbaum and Orbach 1985:93,94). Adopting an object relations rather than Kleinian approach, they argue that this aspect of the transference stems from women's experience, as daughters, of being called upon by their mothers to attend to their (the mother's) needs rather than to their own, that mothers thereby prepare their daughters for women's lot of subordinating their needs to those of others.

By interpreting and working through (as in mourning) the patient's anxieties lest they lose the analyst as a helping person by openly expressing the frustration they feel about their social situation, Kleinians hope to enable their clients to be able to recognize that it is safe to express such feelings within the context of the analysis, that the analyst's capacity to help them is not thereby destroyed. And this, in turn, says Klein, enables the analysand not only to recognize but also to internalize the helpful aspects of the analysis.

Interpretation of this aspect of the transference may again be illustrated by reference to Segal's work, this time by reference to her account of her analysis of a four year old girl. Shortly before Segal was due to go on holiday the girl asked Segal to make her a watch out of paper and to attach it to a string. The little girl also asked if she could take the watch home with her. This request, and similar requests made in previous sessions, says Segal, reflected the girl's wish to internalize her experience of the analysis as a helpful experience, a wish that Segal communicated to her thus: 'I interpreted her wish to take inside herself a breast represented by all the treatment she felt she had had and interpreted the string as her wish to keep in touch with me through this good internalization' (Segal 1973:78).

Hopefully such interpretations, however bald they might seem to the lay reader, strengthen the analysand's sense of herself as containing within herself the helpful aspects of her relation to the analyst. And this in turn, according to Kleinian theory, enables the analysand to feel she has the capacity within herself to help and make reparation for any damage she may have done others by expressing her anger and frustration toward them. (This aspect of Klein's account of the depressive position is also discussed on pp. 56–7 above.) As a result the analysand is then more able to express these feelings openly instead of keeping them bottled up within herself as occurs in depression. An example of this comes from Klein's account of a woman, at first numbed with grief at the death of her son. As she began to feel that this external loss had not destroyed her good internal object relations, or therefore her capacity for reparation, the mother began to be able to express the frustration and grief this loss had caused her:

'In the second week of her mourning Mrs A found some comfort in looking at nicely situated houses in the country, and in wishing to have such a house of her own. . . . The solace she found in looking at houses came from her rebuilding her inner world in her phantasy by means of this interest and also getting satisfaction from the knowledge that other people's houses and good objects existed. . . . In her mind she made reparation to her parents for having, in phantasy, killed their children, and by this she also averted their wrath. Thus her fear that the death of her son was a punishment inflicted on her by retaliating parents lost in strength. . . . The diminution of hatred and fear in this way allowed the sorrow itself to come out in full strength.' (Klein 1940:358–59)

In testing out, in the analytic situation, their capacity actually to make reparation to the analyst, Kleinians believe that their clients thereby become still more able to express rather than introject the sorrow and anger they feel toward the analyst and toward others outside the analysis – feelings that are inevitable given the frustrations, conflicts, and contradictions of everyday social life. Only by such outward as opposed to inward expression of these feelings can women (and men) hope to change the social circumstances that give rise to them.

However, in so far as the contradictions in women's feelings of love and hate are the result of social processes that systematically frustrate their capacities to realize their aspirations and needs as a sex, these contradictions cannot effectively be dealt with solely through individual action. This depends on going beyond the individual help afforded women by Kleinian analysis. It depends on women mobilizing collectively on the basis of the anger they individually feel about their social lot in order to change and improve it. As one woman recently put it, describing her experience first of individual despair in face of the nuclear threat and then of empowerment in joining the collective demonstrations of Greenham women against it: 'we owe it to each other to bring them ['our individual responses'] out . . . because our responses are responses to things in the world. In paying them heed, we pay heed to a way of finding out what the world is like, and how to change it' (Seller 1985:140).

Such struggle, in its turn, seems in some measure to be protective against depression. As a member of the Women's Cooperative Guild, struggling at the beginning of this century to gain women a place in local government, put it:

> 'It is rather a puzzle to myself when I look back, how I have managed to make all my public duties fit in with my home duties. In the first place I have had a splendid constitution, and the busy life seems to have suited me. Most of my lectures and addresses have been thought out when my hands have been busy in household duties – in the wash-tub, when baking (and by the way I have never bought a week's baking during my married life of over twenty-one years), or doing out my rooms. Somehow the time passes more quickly, and I have not felt the work so hard when my mind has been filled with other things.' (Davies 1931:133–34)

Today some have sought to combine individual Kleinian or object relations therapy with depressed women with precisely this kind of collective, local political action, so as to get these women to try actively to improve the social conditions of their lives. Such projects aim to put to constructive use the anger depressed women feel about their social lot, and that they otherwise use so destructively against themselves. The clinical psychologist, Sue Holland, is engaged in just this kind of work in the White City, London (see Holland 1984).

Involvement in such action can be tremendously invigorating even though it also carries its own frustrations. As one woman involved in a local tenants association recently put it: 'It was great to be involved in something outside the house, I'd become an imbecile who couldn't talk about anything. I knew no one except family, so I welcomed it with open arms' (Campbell 1984:200). Women have likewise felt enormously stimulated by acting on the anger they feel at the threatened destruction of their communities involved in the planned closures of many of Britain's coal mines. Many have testified to how empowered they were by participating in the recent, year-long miners' action against these closures.

In depressed states of mind women (and men) experience the problems and conflicts of their lives as though they were of their own making. In paranoia, by contrast, such conflicts are dealt with as though they were the making of others. It is to psychoanalytic accounts and treatments of this source of mental suffering in women (and men) that I shall now turn.

11
Projection and paranoia

> Single mother interviewed by Bea Campbell in 1982–83: 'For five months I slept with the baby, it was so cold. And I couldn't let him outside because there was a river just by. So half the time I felt like killing him, and I got agoraphobia, because I was so depressed.' (Campbell 1984:67)

> Having good reason to hate, but not the courage to rebel, women require symbols of danger that justify their fear. . . . but the existence of the dangerous outsider always functions for women simultaneously as deception, diversion, pain-killer, and threat. . . . The hope is that these women, upset by internal conflicts that cannot be stilled by manipulation, challenged by the clarifying drama of public confrontation and dialogue, will be forced to articulate the realities of their own experiences as women. (Dworkin 1983:34–35)

Women are not alone in mistaking the causes of their hatred, or in mislocating that hatred in others who then figure as 'symbols of danger'. Men likewise mislocate and attribute to others feelings they disown in themselves because they are in contradiction with other feelings to which their social experience also gives rise and which they feel more able to acknowledge in themselves. Nor is it only hatred that is thus projected.

The American psychoanalyst Jean Baker Miller (1976), for instance, points out that men often project and disown their feelings of dependence, vulnerability, and emotionality – feelings that are in conflict with our culture's stereotype of men as essentially independent, invulnerable, and unemotional. They often only recognize these, their own feelings as they are expressed by women – the assumed bearers of such feelings in our society.

The British psychologist and feminist, Wendy Hollway, likewise points out that men frequently project their needs for intimacy into women. In doing so, she says, men not only utilize but also contribute to the perpetuation of the stereotype of women as more immersed in intimate relations than men. And this, 'The reproduction of women as subjects of a discourse concerning the desire for intimate and secure relationships,' in turn, 'protects men from the risk associated with their own need (and the consequent power it would give women)' (Hollway 1984:245–46). Men, she points out, regularly utilize the stereotype of women as the sex who are more given to feeling by projecting into them their need for 'doing the feelings'. The woman is then seen as 'getting upset', as needing the man's support. And this obliges him 'to position himself as someone who is strong enough not to have feelings' (Hollway 1984:253).

In this process men make use of socially given stereotypes – of the stereotype of men as powerful and unemotional, and of women as the dependent and emotional sex, stereotypes that reflect women's social subordination. The way in which projection of unwanted feelings thus makes use of pathways already provided by external social reality is nicely illustrated by Freud's account of a case of a youngish man wracked by jealousy of his loyal wife. Here, as Freud explains, the feelings projected and disowned by the man concerned those of unfaithfulness, rather than those of dependency. This man's attacks of jealousy, writes Freud,

'drew their material from his observation of minute indications, by which his wife's quite unconscious coquetry, unnoticeable to any one else, had betrayed itself to him. She had unintentionally touched the man sitting next to her with her hand; she had turned too much towards him, or she had smiled more pleasantly than when alone with her husband. He was extraordinarily observant of all these manifestations of her unconscious, and always knew how to interpret them correctly, so that he really was always in the right about it, and could furthermore call in analysis to justify his jealousy. His abnormality really reduced itself to this, that he watched his wife's unconscious mind much more closely and then regarded it as far more important than anyone else would have thought of doing. . . . Our jealous husband perceived his wife's unfaithfulness instead of his own; by becoming conscious of hers and magnifying it enormously he succeeded in keeping his own unconscious.' (Freud 1922b:200,201)

Tolstoy describes a similar case of jealousy and its tragic outcome for the woman concerned in his 1889 story *The Kreutzer Sonata*. Unfortunately such cases are not confined to fiction. The media regularly reports cases today of men who mistreat, batter, or even kill their wives on account of their infidelity – actual or only supposed (see, for example, Peter Bogdanovich's 1985 account of *Playboy* model, Dorothy Ruth Stratton's murder – a story recently serialized in *The Mirror* and *The Sun*). A survey of refuge women found a quarter of them citing jealousy as sparking the battering incident that led them to leave home for the refuge (Pahl 1985:32).

It is a measure of women's social subordination that sexual jealousy more often leads men than women to murder one of the offending parties – whose offence may be actual or merely imagined. (For evidence on this point see Moi 1982.) This is not to deny women's capacity for infidelity, both in thought and deed. Nor is it to deny that women also often disown such feelings, recognizing them only as they are expressed by others. Freud (1916–17) describes, for example, the case of a fifty-three year old woman, referred to him by her son-in-law on account of her crippling obsession that her husband was having an affair with another woman. In common with the other instances of projection cited above, this woman's projections also made use of cues provided by external reality. Her obsession focused on an anonymous letter she had received telling her of her husband's supposed infidelity. However, she also knew full well that this accusation was false. She knew that the letter had been concocted by her servant, that the servant knew this to be the best way of setting her and her husband against the girl named in the letter – a girl of whom the maid had her own reasons to be jealous. The reason for the woman's persisting delusional jealousy of her husband, it turned out, lay in the fact that she herself wished to be unfaithful to him – a wish that she could not own to in herself, such was its contradiction with her image of herself as his faithful wife. Rather than recognize this desire in herself, and rather than seek actual gratification of it, she had instead obtained the merely illusory gratification afforded by ruminating on this unfaithful desire as supposedly fulfilled for her husband.

Given our society's sexual double standard, that accords more to men than women the right to act on their sexual desire (and that even goes to the length of reviling sexual desire in women as evidence of their deviance, of their 'nymphomania' say), it is perhaps little wonder that women often only recognize this, their own desire, in projected form, as existing in men, not in themselves. Women continue to be cajoled and humoured into this double standard, by jokes say, that present sexual desire in them as wrong, as something not to be owned to by them. Freud points out that the following joke to this effect is legion: 'Mr and Mrs X live in fairly grand style. Some people think that the husband has earned a lot and so has been able to lay by a bit [*sich etwas zurückgelegt*]; others again think that the wife has lain back a bit [*sich etwas zurückgelegt*] and so has been able to earn a lot' (Freud 1905c:66).

Women's consequent denial of their sexual desire, and of their active desire generally, and their resulting mislocation and displacement of such desire in factors external to themselves, has been commented on by non-analytically, as well as by analytically minded psychologists. They have drawn attention to the fact that women regularly fail to recognize their own agency and desire, that they fail to recognize themselves to be their own 'locus of control' as the psychologist David Rotter (1966) terms it, that while men experience control as internal, women experience it as external to themselves (see, for example, Rosenow and O'Leary 1975). Instead of recognizing themselves as in some measure in control of their lives, and instead of recognizing their own agency, women all too often locate and attribute it to factors external to themselves (see, for example, Deaux and Emswiller 1974; but see also Frieze *et al.* 1982).

Such mis-attribution and displacement often occurs in agoraphobia – a condition that affects not only girls and women but also boys and men (see, for example, Freud 1909b) when it then seems to involve 'extrapunitiveness' and fear of loss of control (Hafner 1983a). It is, however, much more widespread among women, often beginning in them in the first years of marriage (Isard 1985). The analyst Alexandra Symonds, for example, describes cases of women, who, unable to express their dependency needs prior to marriage, look to marriage as a place where these needs might be met. Though independent and in control of their lives prior to marriage, they then become fearful of expressing their independence and autonomy once married. Furthermore, they fear expressing the anger and frustration to which this gives rise lest the marriage thereby be destroyed. These negative feelings accordingly grow all the more fearful for not being expressed, for not being tested out against reality (cf. Blake 1794:76; Freud 1915d:148). Instead these women, according to Symonds, defend against the anxiety caused them by these feelings by 'externalizing' them, by locating them not in themselves but in their husbands whom they describe as hostile and aggressive. Their agoraphobia, says Symonds, is likewise due to their projecting their feelings of anger and control into the external world. One woman, for instance, described how she could no longer drive because 'she feared that the car would do something that she did not want it to do' (Symonds 1973:301). Others have described how such phobic anxieties on the part of women are often colluded in by their husbands who gain a sense of their own competence and effectiveness through dwelling on the helplessness to which their wives' agoraphobia reduces them (see, for example, Goodstein and Swift 1974; Hafner 1983b).

In agoraphobia women parody the social restrictions on their social and sexual activity, brought about in England at least over the last couple of centuries by the increasing confinement of middle-class housewives to the suburbs away from social production (Davidoff and Hall 1983), and by the accompanying ideology of woman's place as 'in the home'. Agoraphobia often involves denial by women of any desire in themselves for social and sexual activity, in their getting others to act for them rather than acting on their own behalf (see, for example, Andrews 1966, Fisher *et al*. 1984), by their only recognizing their active desire as it is expressed by others. Freud describes, for example, the case of a woman who, from the analysis of her dreams, seemed unconsciusly to have equated gratification of such desire with being a man. Instead of acting on this, her own desire, she only recognized it in men. It was, according to Freud, her dwelling on this desire, her 'fears of seduction', now projected outside of herself, that constituted the source of her agoraphobia (see Freud 1900a:478–82). Interestingly, non-analytic research likewise suggests that agoraphobia is caused by rumination on, rather than by repression of 'anxiety-eliciting or threatening information' (Turner *et al*. 1983:75). As Freud early pointed out, projection is unlike repression in that in projection 'the content and the affect of the intolerable idea are retained; but they are projected into the external world' (Freud 1895:113). Projection is thus like displacement in which feelings associated with intolerable ideas are retained in consciousness but displaced from the object that first elicited them on to another object. Unlike displacement, however, projection involves failure to recognize oneself as agent of these feelings (Davies 1985).

Agoraphobia clearly affords women certain primary and secondary gains. It does not, however, afford them actual gratification of the desires expressed in their agoraphobia. This condition may serve to caricature women's restricted social lot, and thus send up the timidity, fearfulness, and housebound domesticity supposed to typify femininity. But it hardly constitutes a real challenge to women's social subordination. Indeed, agoraphobia simply reinforces it and its denial of women as themselves agents of their own desire. Moreover, the agoraphobic's paranoia cripples her capacity to challenge the obstacles constituted by that subordination so as to realize her desire, actually and in fact.

The relation of paranoia to projection is perhaps more obvious in another case, that of a thirty year old woman referred to Freud by her lawyer on account of her fear lest her erstwhile lover use compromising photographs against her. She believed him to have had photographs taken of them making love. Given the circumstances of the case, however, this seemed most unlikely. It seemed much more probable, suggests Freud, that the basis of her paranoid ideas lay in her having mislocated and projected outside herself the sexual sensations she had felt when she had been about to make love with this man. She had, it seems, interpreted these sensations, actually internal to herself, as though they derived from an external source, from the clicking of a camera shutter. 'The woman's situation' on this occasion, writes Freud, 'justified a sensation of a knock or beat in her clitoris. And it was this that she subsequently projected as a perception of an external object' (Freud 1915f:155–56). Her paranoia, it appears, stemmed from recognizing sexual agency not in herself but only in projected form, in the supposed agency of her lover conspiring to have photographs taken of her in the sexual act – a projection made all the more plausible by the fact that society more readily assigns such agency to men than to women.

Freud no more made it his business to treat this kind of severe paranoid symptom than he made it his business to treat severe depression. Again it was left to his followers to extend his analytic ideas to the treatment of such symptoms that so much debilitate both women's and men's capacity to obtain actual gratification of the desires they express. The aims expressed in these desires could be used to combat the social obstacles to their realization. In being projected, however, women (and men) experience themselves in the thrall of these desires, as victims of them rather than as agents of their realization. As Melanie Klein points out, projection of one's desires and feelings into others weakens the ego. It can result in the fear that one's 'mind is controlled by other people in a hostile way' (Klein 1946:11), and 'to the feeling that one is not in full possession of one's self' (Klein 1963:302). Projection thus results in a similar experience to that of the alienation felt by workers who feel themselves to be controlled by, rather than in control of the objects they produce (Hinshelwood 1983).

In the context of women's struggle against their social subordination this can involve them over-exaggerating the extent to which they are victims of others, say of men. This results from their projecting into others, into men, for example, the anger they quite rightly feel about their social subordination, and about men's contribution to it. This has the effect of dissipating the anger that otherwise empowers women's struggle against this situation, and against men's aggression toward them, so as to improve their social lot. As Gayle Rubin puts it such projections 'rarely alleviate any real problems, because they are aimed at chimeras and signifiers' (Rubin 1984:297), the expression of psychical rather than material reality.

The Kleinian analyst, Jane Temperley (1984), describes an example of this as it can occur between women and men in their domestic relations. The example is taken from the case of a woman who described her relations with her husband on the one hand as 'idyllic' and on the other as involving him in becoming 'uncontrollably drunk and violent'. She seemed to feel, says Temperley, 'as constricted and irritable' as he did about their relationship. On the other hand, she only seemed to be able to recognize these, her own negative feelings about their relationship as he expressed them by being violent towards her. Projection of this kind, writes Temperley, buys women their friends' sympathy and an 'illusion of innocence'. These benefits of projection are, however, achieved at a cost. As the feminist philosopher Alison Jaggar points out in writing of radical feminists (though the point equally applies to all women on occasion): 'By portraying women as helpless victims . . . some radical feminists have overemphasized men's control over women's minds and in this way may have unwittingly reinforced the power of those whom they wish to subvert' (Jaggar 1983:115). Projection can all too easily involve women divesting themselves of feelings on which they might otherwise act effectively to counter rather than reinforce the abuses they suffer at the hands of men.

How does Kleinian analysis seek to enable women (and men) to repossess, and thereby act constructively on their feelings, rather than become victims of them as they are projected into others – by being recognized and/or elicited in others? Klein argued that the fundamental anxiety underlying projection of unwanted feelings into others is unconscious fear lest these feelings destroy the self – an anxiety related to the sense of lack of integration of the ego that she says is typical of 'paranoid–schizoid' states of mind (see p. 50 above). The defence of projection thus differs in her view from that of the introjection of depression which she believed involves unconscious anxiety more about loss of the other than about loss of the self. Just as she believed that the introjection of depression can only be undone by interpreting the anxiety that gives rise to it – namely, the anxiety lest were the introjected feelings to be expressed they would destroy the other – so treatment of projected and split off feelings involves interpreting the anxiety lest were these feelings to be experienced they would destroy the self.

Non-Kleinian psychologist Dora Ullian argues that this anxiety is particularly strong in women, at least in regard to their aggressive feelings. For, she says, women tend to view themselves 'primarily in relation to other people'. They have a 'fear of being bad' lest this destroy them, so 'fragile and defenceless' do they experience themselves to be. It is this, she writes, that causes women to be 'fearful of aggression' in themselves and in others (Ullian 1984:254). Corroborative evidence comes from Symonds' study of agoraphobia in which one of her patients expressed in a dream the fear lest her aggression destroy herself. She dreamt that 'she strangled several baby birds' which she identified 'as a symbol of herself' (Symonds 1973:297).

Kleinians seek to make conscious, through interpretation, the anxieties expressed in such dreams, the anxieties lest in acting on one's aggression one might thereby destroy oneself. Such anxieties are interpreted in Kleinian analysis as they manifest themselves in the transference. This can be illustrated by reference to Klein's account of her analysis of the following dream of a woman patient in which the patient experienced herself as having

> 'to deal with a wicked girl child who was determined to murder somebody. The patient tried to influence or control the child and to extort a confession from her which would have been to the child's benefit; but she was unsuccessful. I [Klein] also entered into the dream and the patient felt that I might help her in dealing with the child. Then the patient strung up the child on a tree in order to frighten her and also prevent her from doing harm. When the patient was about to pull the rope and kill the child, she woke.' (Klein 1946:20)

Klein interpreted the dream to the patient as expressing her unconscious anxiety lest by acting on her feelings of anger and frustration she destroy or annihilate part of her personality, represented in the dream by the child. The dream, said Klein, also expressed the patient's hope that Klein might protect her from destroying herself with these feelings.

Kleinians hope in this way to enable people to own to their otherwise disowned feelings rather than projecting and splitting them off from themselves. This can include interpreting such splitting and projection as it occurs in the transference, in the analysand's projection of her or his unwanted feelings into the analyst. Such interpretation, however, carries certain risks. For the analysand can all too easily experience such interpretation as confirming her or his sense of their projected feelings as unbearable. The analysand may well experience the analyst as seeking to extrude these feelings, by interpreting their projection, back into the analysand. In this, interpretation of projection may confirm the persecutory anxiety associated with it (see p. 50 above). Hanna Segal describes just such an instance in her account of a middle aged woman patient of whom she writes that if she, Segal, 'appeared in any way affected by the patient's projections, for instance looking paler or having a slight cold, the patient felt that all "the breakdown" was projected into me, which at first made me an object of some concern; but very soon I turned into a persecutor, pouring disintegration and germs back into her' (Segal 1973:61).

Bearing in mind the risks associated with interpreting to the analysand the projection of their unwanted feelings into the analyst, Segal describes another case that usefully illustrates such interpretation. It concerns the analysis of a woman patient's silence in her analytic sessions. 'To begin with,' writes Segal,

'her silence was linked with projective identification, but as it proceeded, the meaning of it kept changing. At first I interpreted it primarily as a communication: I interpreted to her that she wanted to make me experience what it felt like to be cut off and unable to communicate. . . . Later on, as the patient's distress and her need to project in order to communicate, had lessened a great deal, when she was silent the silence was much more aggressive. Now I could interpret the projection into me of feelings of failure and inadequacy, the motives being two-fold: she partly wanted to get rid of such feelings from within herself and partly wanted to project them into me out of revenge, spite and envy. In any of these situations, when she was silent a vicious circle was established, in which her projection into me of painful feelings led to an anxiety that I would push it back into her and therefore the silence would acquire also a defensive aspect – not speaking in order not to let me penetrate her by interpretations; and this in turn had to be interpreted.'   (Segal 1973:121–22)

The concept of 'projective identification', whereby one disowns one's feelings by eliciting them in others, to which Segal refers in the beginning of this passage, has become extremely important in Kleinian treatment of projection. Klein (for example, 1959) used the term to refer to the process whereby one identifies with others on account of projecting one's feelings into them. It is based, says Klein, 'on splitting of the ego and the projection of parts of the self into other people' (Klein 1963:303). The other person, including the analyst, may in turn unconsciously identify with these projections. The Kleinian analyst, Wilfred Bion, describes for instance how the analyst can unconsciously experience himself

'being manipulated so as to be playing a part, no matter how difficult to recognize, in somebody else's phantasy – or he would do if it were not for what in recollection I can only call a temporary loss of insight, a sense of experiencing strong feelings, and at the same time a belief that their existence is quite adequately justified by the objective situation.' (Bion 1955:446)

The analyst's own feelings, he writes, therefore constitute a source of information about the group's feelings. And this also applies in individual therapy. That is, the unconscious counter-transference of the analyst to the analysand, which can constitute an obstacle to treatment (see p. 132 above), is turned by Kleinians like Bion to therapeutic effect as a source of information about the client's feelings. Furthermore, Bion argues, by identifying with and 'containing' the client's projected feelings rather than immediately interpreting them back, thus seemingly confirming the client's experience of these feelings as unbearable, the analyst enables the client to recognize that these feelings can be borne. As a result the analysand might then be more able to own to these feelings in herself (or himself), because they then no longer feel them to be so overwhelming or dangerous to the self as to have to be evacuated, expelled, or projected out of the self. Hopefully the analysand is thereby enabled to recognize and act on these feelings rather than deal with them in the illusory fashion afforded by recognizing these feelings only in projected form, as they are manifest in others.

Kleinians have suggested that by thus 'containing' the analysand's projected feelings the analyst does what women regularly do as mothers (indeed Bion refers to this function by means of the female symbol, ♀). In so far as mothers are capable of 'reverie', of receiving and containing 'the infant's projective identifications whether they are felt by the infant to be good or bad' (Bion 1962:36), they thereby enable their babies to re-introject the feelings involved in these projections in more bearable form (see, for example, Meltzer 1978; Bott Spillius 1983). The sociologist Mike Rustin has accordingly referred to the increasing use of 'reverie' and 'containment' in Kleinian analysis as 'an index of a wider process of feminisation of psychoanalytic theory' (Rustin 1983:69).

In this he tendentiously equates femininity with maternity – not a helpful equation to women. On the other hand the technique of containment he describes may be helpful to women in enabling them to own to, and thereby act upon feelings they otherwise project, so as to change and improve their social situation. I find persuasive in this respect the following case illustration provided by the Kleinian analyst Betty Joseph. She tells how it became possible in the case of one of her women patients to enable her to own to her unwanted feelings of antagonism and control by having her examine these feelings as they seemed to her to be embodied and contained by Joseph, by having her examine the extent to which these feelings were already present in Joseph and were also her own feelings, and the extent to which she had elicited these feelings in Joseph through projective identification:

> 'As we looked at her feelings about my motivation it became clear that in her mind I felt threatened by her, and deeply envious of her as a young intelligent person with her life ahead of her. I would then wish to explore more carefully her picture of me, this old, supposedly lonely, rather embittered person, and her quiet conviction of what I was like, and only very slowly and over a long period, hope to explore how much of these ideas might be linked with actual observations of myself or the way I function, how much projected parts of herself, and so on. This is, after all, in a large part what we mean when we talk about "containing".' (Joseph 1983:296–97)

If this enables women to repossess feelings they otherwise only recognize in projected form so that they can then use these feelings constructively to act on and improve their social lot then Kleinianism is surely consonant with feminism?

Yet although Kleinians seek to make conscious the feelings evoked in women (and men) by the conflicts, frustrations, and contradictions of their social experience, they no more make these contradictions themselves an object of their clinical intervention than do Freudians. In this, the practice of psychoanalysis is in marked contrast with that of feminism which is precisely concerned with addressing, in order to change and remove, the social contradictions of women's lives so that women might thereby fully realize their aims and desires, actually and in fact. It is with this, specifically with a brief sketch of the preconditions of feminist struggle, and of its relation to psychoanalysis, that I shall now conclude.

PART FOUR

Conclusion

12
Feminism and psychoanalysis

> Emancipation should make it possible for woman to be human in the truest sense. Everything within her that craves assertion and activity should reach its fullest expression, all artificial barriers should be broken, and the road towards greater freedom cleared of every trace of centuries of submission and slavery.   (Emma Goldman 1910:214)

> The key issue for women is an expansion of the economy and the creation of secure, full time jobs for women. To ensure this, the two pillars of a free employment programme for women must be on the one hand anti-discrimination and positive action programmes, and on the other the expansion of socialized services, particularly collective child care and the caring services for the sick and the elderly.   (Angie Weir and Elizabeth Wilson 1984:102–03)

Feminists may disagree about the best way to achieve 'greater freedom' for women, whether this is to be secured through fuller participation by women in employment or through some other means. They are, however, agreed in recognizing the current injustice of women's lot whereby our society both promises freedom to all its members – men and women alike – yet systematically discriminates against women realizing this, their supposed freedom.

I have been arguing that a central object of psychoanalytic therapy is to bring about full recognition of such conflicts and contradictions, and of the frustrations to which they give rise in the personal lives of its clients. Psychoanalysis thereby hopes to enable people realistically to act on this consciousness and these feelings so as to deal effectively with the conflicts that give rise to them and thus to gain actual gratification of their needs and desires.

Consciousness of the conflicts of their social lot, particularly those posed women by the discrimination exercised against them, is a necessary pre-condition of effective feminist struggle to change the social conditions causing these conflicts. On the other hand, such consciousness is not sufficient of itself to bring about women's participation in feminist struggle. Indeed, many women, aware of the differential social treatment accorded their sex, positively wallow in it. Like Nancy Cotter, active member of the Moral Majority styled Australian Women's Action Alliance, who proclaims: 'If there's one thing I cherish, it is the fact that I am different from men, that I have a feminine outlook, a feminine approach to life. *Vive la différence!*' (Quoted by Rowland 1984:97). In this she echoes a common sentiment traded on by the accompanying cartoon. Anti-ERA campaigner, Phyllis Schlafly, likewise values sexual difference and recommends women to be different and socially subservient to men. In her 1977 book, *The Power of the Positive Woman*, she urges women to submit to their husband's interests, to give them 'the appreciation and admiration his manhood craves' (quoted by Ehrenreich 1983:163). In this Schlafly reiterates Marabel Morgan's celebration of sexual difference in her popular book, *The Total Woman*, in which she portrays as ideal the woman who 'surrenders her life to her husband, reveres and worships him' (Morgan 1975:96).

Recognizing that women might also have other desires, the desire to be active agents of their own destiny rather than to be simply passive subjects of men's agency, many women, both now and in the past, have urged their sisters to quash this former, so-called 'masculine' desire in themselves and to cherish instead the 'feminine' traits that supposedly distinguish them from men. Hannah More, for example, leading exponent of the moral reforming ideals of the evangelical movement of the end of the

THE SEX QUESTION.
(A STUDY IN BOND STREET.)

From *Punch*, 5 April, 1911

eighteenth century, recommended in her 1777 *Essays Principally Designed for Young Ladies*, that women be cautious, retiring, and reserved, since, she said, they were naturally more delicate, fragile, and morally weaker than men (Hall 1979). In the nineteenth century a whole host of books, written mostly by women, reiterated this same theme – books like *The English Maiden*, *The Feminine Soul*, *Womankind*, *The Afternoon of Unmarried Life*, and *Woman – Her Social and Domestic Character* (Strachey 1928:46). One Sara Ellis, for instance, told readers of her 1842 book, *The Daughters of England*, that there was 'no excuse' for women to act like men. Their proper sphere, she said, was that 'of feeling rather than of action', their 'highest duty' was 'to suffer and be still', and 'to live only in the existence of another' (Hollis 1979:15–16; also see Parker 1984). Similarly, a writer by the name of Eliza Linton told women in her 1883 tract on 'Womanliness' that they should not have the 'passionate ambition, virile energy, the love of strong excitement, self-assertion, fierceness, and undisciplined temper' of men. Instead, she said, they should cultivate in themselves 'all the meek and tender affections, all the unselfishness and thought for others which have hitherto been the distinctive property' of their sex (Hollis 1979:20).

Other women, far from seeking to suppress in themselves or others the 'masculine' aspirations they share with men, have instead sought to realize these aspirations, even donning male garb to do so. Like the women soldiers of the seventeenth century (see Fraser 1984), Sweet Polly Oliver of ballad fame, and the woman pirate, Mary Reed (see Rowbotham 1972). Others, undaunted by the social equation of entry into public life with masculinity, have sought to enter this sphere by taking on men's names, or at least sex-neutral pseudonyms, as did the writers Hilda Doolittle (H.D.) and Molly Keane (M.J. Farrell) in this century, and Charlotte Bronte (Currer Bell) and Marian Evans (George Eliot) last century. (Others, by contrast, charged with being men on account of the excellence of their writing, have retorted by protesting their femininity, like Jane Austen who answered this charge thus: 'What would I do . . . with your manly, vigorous sketches, so full of life and spirit? How could I possibly join them on to a little bit of ivory, two inches wide, on which I work with a brush so fine', quoted in Austen 1837:ix–x.)

While some have taken on men's clothing or men's names to realize themselves in those spheres of activity traditionally assigned to men, others have sought to achieve this end by emphasizing in themselves their so-called masculine psychological aims and impulses. Harriet Martineau, for instance, writes how, when in 1837 she was offered the editorship of an economics journal, she sought to steel herself to the task by telling herself: 'If I do this, I must brace myself up to do and suffer like a man. No more waywardness, precipitation, and reliance on allowance from others! Undertaking a man's duty, I must brave a man's fate. I must be prudent, independent, serene, good-humoured; earnest with cheerfulness' (Martineau 1877:109,110). Others have likewise sought to realize the aims and aspirations socially equated with masculinity by positively embracing this characterization of these, their aims. Radclyffe Hall, for instance, vehemently endorsed the then 'mythic mannish' image of active sexual desire in women, in lesbians at least, in her 1928 novel *The Well of Loneliness* in which she pleaded greater tolerance for those women who seek to put their lesbian desire into practice (Newton 1984). Others have likewise courted rather than rejected the characterization, not so much of their sexual and emotional as of their mental aims and ambitions as masculine. Simone de Beauvoir (see Evans 1985), for instance, writes how, as an intellectual, she identified with the masculinity 'embodied by my father' (de Beauvoir 1958:41). Nor was this surprising given her father's pronouncement: 'Simone has a man's brain; she thinks like a man; she is a man' (de Beauvoir 1958:121)!

In thus seeking to realize their so-called 'masculine' aspirations many women not only fail to challenge the equation of such aspirations with masculinity. They also seek to overlook the social subordination of women that this equation expresses. As one senior woman in management recently put it: 'I only permit myself to see prejudice once a year' (Bingham 1985:35). Similarly the French semiologist, psychoanalyst, and sometime feminist, Julia Kristeva, has sought to minimize her awareness of sex discrimination as it has affected her own life. She claims never personally to have suffered any sense of being 'enslaved, excluded or repressed' (quoted by Jones 1984:66). Many women in the nineteenth century, similarly sought to keep out of mind the restrictions socially imposed on their sex when looking back on their own efforts as individuals to transcend these restrictions. Florence Nightingale, for instance, claimed never to have 'felt the want of the vote' in prosecuting the cause of professional training for nurses. The social reformer, Beatrice Webb, likewise denied having experienced in her own life 'the disabilities assumed to arise from my sex' (Hollis 1979:96,329).

Such wilful oversight of women's social 'disabilities' often carries with it the implication that women have only themselves to blame if they fail to realize the 'masculine' aspirations they share with men. As the feminist literary critic, Margaret Walters, puts it in commenting on Martineau's claim 'that women, like men, can obtain whatever they show themselves fit for', this attitude involves the complacent assumption, 'if I did it anyone can' (Walters 1976:335). De Beauvoir quite clearly acknowledges the way this individualistic attitude informed her early thinking about the woman question. As a young woman, she writes,

> 'I was certainly not a militant feminist . . . my chief conviction was that each individual was responsible for securing his own [salvation]. . . . To accept a secondary status in life . . . would have been to degrade my own humanity . . . . Obviously, the only reason for the problem presenting itself to me in these terms was because I happened to be a woman. But it was *qua* individual that I attempted to resolve it. (de Beauvoir 1960:62)

And, paradoxically, this same individualism runs through *The Second Sex* in which, although she documents the manifold obstacles to women realizing their humanity and transcendence, she implies that any woman can achieve this transcendence if only she tries hard enough as an individual to do so (le Doeuff 1980).

Feminism involves keeping in clear focus at one and the same time the fact that as individuals women share the same aspirations as men, and the fact that as women they are systematically obstructed by our society from realizing these aspirations. The radical feminist, Andrea Dworkin, points this out when she says:

> 'The liberation of women requires facing the real condition of women in order to change it. "We're all just people" is a stance that prohibits recognition of the systematic cruelties visited on women because of sex oppression. Feminism as a liberation movement, then, demands a revolutionary single standard of what humans have a right to, and also demands that the current sexual bifurcation of rights never be let out of sight.' (Dworkin 1983:217)

Not surprisingly awareness of this, the 'sexual bifurcation of rights', leads many women to associate femininity with illness or physical damage to their narcissistic sense of self (a point discussed by Cora Caplan 1985). It often leads them to envy men. As Freud said of the childhood of a young woman brought to him for treatment on account of her rebellion against her father:

> 'A spirited girl, always ready for romping and fighting, she was not at all prepared to be second to her slightly older brother; after inspecting his genital organs she had developed a pronounced envy for the penis, and the thoughts derived from this envy still continued to fill her mind. She was in fact a feminist; she felt it to be unjust that girls should not enjoy the same freedom as boys, and rebelled against the lot of woman in general.' (Freud 1920a:397)

Many women have wanted to be men because of the greater social freedom they enjoy. A contemporary of Freud's patient, for instance, the German trade unionist, Adelheid Popp, tells how, as a young woman she 'would have liked to be a man, to have a right to busy myself with politics' (Rowbotham 1972:80). Similarly the South African feminist and socialist, Olive Schreiner, expressed this selfsame desire in her novel, *From Man to Man* (dedicated to her dead daughter who 'never lived to know she was a woman'), in which she had her heroine dream: 'How nice it would be to be a man'. She fancied she was one, till she felt her very body grow strong and hard and shaped like a man's. She felt the great freedom opened to her; no place shut off from her, the long chain broken, all work possible for her, no law to say this and this is for woman – you are woman' (Schreiner 1927:202). Today the Black American activist, Maya Angelou, likewise tells how, as a child, she 'wished my soul that I had been born a boy'.

But as she recognized, even then, 'becoming a boy was sure to be difficult, if not impossible' (Angelou 1969:74). Realistically women have recognized, both now and in the past, that to gain the freedom socially accorded men, they must needs struggle collectively against the social obstacles impeding women exercising this freedom, that this object cannot be achieved through individual effort alone. Furthermore, they have recognized that, although the success of this struggle depends on men's support, it also crucially depends on women advocating their cause on their own behalf since men cannot be relied upon to do so. For men regularly regard feminism as seeking gains that would entail their, men's loss. This was nicely pointed out by John Stuart Mill in putting the case for women's suffrage to Parliament in 1867, a case women could not themselves put given that they lacked the vote. Replying to those who claimed that women did not need the vote because men could be counted on to look after their interests, Mill said,

'Sir, this is exactly what is said of all unrepresented classes. . . . Workmen need other protection than that of their employers, and women other protection than that of their men. I should like to have a Return laid before this House of the number of women who are annually beaten to death, kicked to death, or trampled to death by their male protectors; and, in an opposite column, the amount of the sentences passed in those cases in which the dastardly criminals did not get off altogether. I should also like to have, in a third column, the amount of property, the unlawful taking of which was, at the same sessions or assizes by the same judge, thought worthy of the same amount of punishment. . . . No sooner do women (like Miss Garrett) show themselves capable of competing with men in any career, than that career, if it be lucrative or honourable, is closed to them. A short time ago women might be associates of the Royal Academy; but they were so distinguishing themselves, they were assuming so honourable a place in their art, that this privilege also has been withdrawn. This is the sort of care taken of women's interests by the men who so faithfully represent them.' (Hollis 1979:302,303)

Not only do women recognize that the success of their cause depends on their prosecuting it to some degree independently of men. They also recognize that, since different groups of women also have conflicting interests, these groups can only advance them by organizing to some degree autonomously from each other. Pointing this out in the 1890s, for instance, the Leeds feminist and trade union activist, Isabella Ford, argued against the rescue work then being conducted by middle-class women on behalf of their supposed working-class sisters: 'The industrial woman', she wrote, 'must be roused to desire and work out for herself her own salvation' (Rowbotham 1973a:54). Today the feminist historian, Judith Walkowitz (1982), likewise criticizes middle-class feminists in so far as they insufficiently recognize the difference of their interests from those of the women involved in pornography and prostitution whom they claim to represent.

Women have often lacked the will to struggle on their own behalf. They have frequently only been galvanized into such action by wider political movements and upheavals. It was just such an upheaval, namely the Civil Wars of the 1640s, that brought about the first stirrings of feminism in England. At this time, apparently, thousands of women among the Levellers put their names to petitions claiming 'equal participation with men in the political process' (Stone 1979:226). Another two hundred years was to go by, however, before middle-class women were to organize collectively to fight for their rights. Not that in the intervening period individual women of this class, and of the aristocracy, did not repeatedly protest against the social lot of their sex. In the decades of political reconstruction that followed the Civil Wars and the restoration of the monarchy, for instance, one Lady Mary Chudleigh proclaimed against the fact that, although men of her class 'disowned' the 'Passive Obedience' required of them under the old-style monarchy, they still required this obedience from women (Stone 1979:164). But there was then no general constituency among women of her class to fight against this, the passive destiny of their sex. Nor did Chudleigh's contemporary, Mary Astell, fare any better in her 1694 project (see Harris 1984:9) of establishing a college for women. Women could not then be mobilized in any numbers to combat the injustice that, as Astell put it, 'If all men are born free, how is it that all women are born slaves?' (Stone 1979:165). Mary Astell was only too well aware of the lack of any collective spirit of resistance among women to the quasi-slavery of their social lot. Women, she wrote, 'Love their chains. . . . They think as humbly of themselves as their Masters can wish' (Mitchell 1976:390).

The political ferment caused in England by the French Revolution of 1789 also proved insufficient to rouse middle-class women to protest against their social subordination. Mary Wollstonecraft then complained of the inconsistency of the fact that while 'men contend for their freedom' they still 'subjugate women' (Wollstonecraft 1792:87). But her fellow countrywomen were not then ready collectively to protest against this situation. Middle-class women who spoke out against it still found themselves to be lone voices among their sex and class even twenty years later when a governess, Miss Weeton, then confided to her diary how she 'burned to learn Latin, French, the Arts, the Sciences, anything rather than the dog trot way of sewing, teaching, writing copies, and washing dishes every day' (Woolf 1938:138). Nor did the collective struggles of women involved in the labour movements of the 1830s (see, for example, Taylor 1983) encourage significant numbers of middle-class women likewise to seek to improve their working conditions, say as governesses. Charlotte Bronte (see Showalter 1977) then protested in vain against the lot of these women when, in her novel *Jane Eyre*, she wrote

'women feel just as men feel; they need exercise for their faculties, and a field for their efforts as much as their brothers do; they suffer from too rigid a restraint, too absolute a stagnation, precisely as men would suffer; and it is narrow-minded in their more privileged fellow-creatures to say that they ought to confine themselves to making puddings and knitting stockings, to playing on the piano and embroidering bags.' (Bronte 1847:141)

Middle-class women only began to organize collectively against this, the 'confinement' of their sex, as they came to recognize that, despite the economic inactivity held out as an ideal for their sex, they needs must work when, like the fictional Jane Eyre, they had no one else to support them. It was recognition of this, and of the fact that women needed better education and more job opportunities if they were to better their situation as governesses, that at last galvanized middle-class women into fighting for this provision. As Miss Buss, pioneer of the campaign for women's secondary school education in England, put it: 'The terrible sufferings of the women of my own class for want of a good elementary training have more than ever intensified my earnest desire to lighten, ever so little, the misery of women brought up "to be married and taken care of" and left alone in the world destitute' (Strachey 1928:127).

This struggle, of course, continues today. Frequently women have lost heart. Like the clients of the nineteenth-century London Women's Employment Bureau who regularly 'shrank back in horror from the notion of seeking new work' (Strachey 1928:98). And women have often given up the struggle to improve their domestic lot despite being supported in this by other women. As one Helen Crawfurd put it in 1922, 'time and again . . . when asked why they continued to live with a tyrant women reply "It was very difficult to leave. I was either going to have a child or was nursing one"' (Rowbotham 1973a:166). How often have not people heard the same tale from battered women today?

Despite these setbacks women continue to fight for better social conditions for their sex. The Black Civil Rights and anti-Vietnam war campaigns of the 1960s inspired women, after a lull of nearly half a century, once more to take up arms on their behalf. The women's movement thereby brought into being goes on today – in the continuing establishment of refuges for battered women (see, for example, Wilson 1983; Pahl 1985), in the persisting attempt to secure greater equality between the sexes as regards domestic chores (see, for example, Ehrensaft 1980; Philipson 1982b; Finch and Groves 1983), in the campaigns to achieve the childcare (see, for example, New and David 1985), education (see, for example, Anyon 1983), work conditions (see, for example, Coote and Campbell 1982), and welfare provisions (see, for example, Brook and Davis 1985) that will meet women's needs alike with those of men. And women are also campaigning for changes and improvements in health care (see, for example, Doyal 1983) and in science and technology generally (see, for example, Fee 1983; Sayers in press) so that they serve rather than put women's and men's lives at risk. This includes the attempt to bring about a feminist science of psychology and psychotherapy (see, for example, Ernst and Goodison 1981; Ryan 1983b; Eichenbaum and Orbach 1985). And women are continuing to lobby for greater equality between the sexes as regards age of retirement and pensions (Drummond 1985) and for changes in taxation and social security so that they might be assessed as individuals in their own right, not as economic appendages to men (see, for example, London Women's Liberation Campaign 1979).

All this is part of the general movement to secure equal civil rights for women – a campaign that includes, in the long term, the struggle to achieve a society in which women might realize these rights in practice. This means fighting to bring about a society free not only of class division, in which, as the adage has it, Adam would delve and Eve spin, but free also of such sexual divisions of labour as well. It entails struggling for a society which will meet the needs of everyone, women and men alike, while at the same time also meeting the different needs of women and men arising from the differences of their biological and social being (see, for example, Vogel 1983).

Freud maintained that the goal of achieving a society free of division – of class division say – is founded on illusion. People, he said, can never 'live together almost without friction'. To think they could, he argued, is to overlook 'the difficulties which the untameable character of human nature presents to every kind of social community' (Freud 1933a: 217,219). It is not therefore surprising that he never regarded achievement of social harmony as the ultimate objective of psychoanalytic therapy.

Nevertheless, Freud did recognize the effectiveness of improvement in social conditions in alleviating individual mental suffering. He acknowledged that changes in his patients' social circumstances could often bring about relief of their symptoms while therapy often proved unable to do so. The patient's social situation, he pointed out, only has 'to take away a motive for being ill, and the patient is temporarily or perhaps even permanently freed from his illness' (Freud 1905e:78). Behaviourist therapists today likewise observe that neurotics regularly get better from 'spontaneous events' and changes in their lives (Rachman and Wilson 1980:49). But, although Freud recognized his patients' symptoms to be related to 'the purely human and social circumstances' of their lives (Freud 1905e:47), he regularly sought to treat these symptoms as though they were entirely the work of processes 'endogenous' to the patient (Ingleby 1985:5). And this in turn has informed the so-called helping professions' general and continuing tendency to mislocate the source of stress in women's lives not in the contradictions and conflicts of their social lot but in their individual psychology (Cloward and Piven 1979). In his focus on the 'psychical reality' of unconscious phantasy Freud all too often overlooked the contradictions in 'material reality' that give rise to such phantasy in the first place. And both he and his followers adjured, and continue to adjure, their patients not to make any major changes in the material reality of their everyday social lives whilst in therapy. It is therefore no wonder that, in so far as this reality and its contradictions, are the source of mental suffering, people seldom obtain permanent relief from this suffering by way of psychoanalytic and psychoanalytically informed therapy and counselling.

In this book I have sought to show how psychoanalysis seeks, through its methods of free association and interpretation of the transference, to enable its clients to become more fully conscious of the contradictions of their social lot so that they might thereby deal with these contradictions more effectively and thus have some hope of realizing their needs and desires. As I have explained, psychoanalysis seeks to undo the ways this realization is obstructed by the dead hold of the past. Ideally, and *pace* Marx (1852), psychoanalysis thereby seeks to liberate women, like men, to become makers of their own history, drawing in the process on the imaginative and creative possibilities, rather than on the nightmarish stranglehold of the phantoms of the past (see Robinson 1984). Psychoanalysis seeks to do this by freeing desire from its fixation to past experience as it comes to be elaborated in unconscious phantasy. It seeks to divest people of the illusion that their needs are already met by such phantasy as it is expressed in the symptoms of neurosis, depression, and paranoia. Instead it works to strengthen the ego's recognition of the constraints of reality, of the fact that if our needs are to be actualized we cannot rest content with the pleasure principle's hallucination of these needs as already fulfilled, but must instead seek to deal with these constraints, to change reality so that it actually begins to meet the needs and desires to which our past experience has given rise. Only by recognizing our needs as currently unfulfilled, writes Freud, can we begin to work to achieve the conditions of their fulfilment, to 'develop the power to change the order of society' (Freud 1905c:155).

The starting point of psychoanalysis, however, is not society but individual suffering (see, for example, Sayers 1973). It regards its object as achieved once it has enabled its patients to become fully conscious of the gap that exists between illusory and actual fulfilment of their needs. Once it has enabled its clients to recognize this gap, and the contradiction between psychical and material reality involved in it, psychoanalysis regards its therapeutic project as complete. It believes that its clients are then in the position to begin effectively to change reality so that their needs might actually be met. By contrast feminism involves recognition that, although individual consciousness of the disjunction between women's needs and the capacity of society to fulfil them is important and that social and economic theory, unlike psychoanalysis, often pays insufficient attention to women's individual and subjective experience of their oppression, there is a need to go beyond such consciousness and individual action based on it, that this is not sufficient on its own to bring about the changes in society necessary to the needs of women being fully met. It recognizes that this depends on social as well as individual change, and on collective as well as individual struggle to achieve it. Psychoanalysis stops short of this recognition. For feminism it is only the beginning.

References

Note: References in the text are to the date when the work in question was first published or produced. The dates for the Freud references conform with those of the *Standard Edition of the Complete Psychological Works of Sigmund Freud* (*S.E.* London: Hogarth) and adopted by the *Penguin Freud Library* (*P.F.L.* Harmondsworth: Penguin). Page references are to the *P.F.L.* edition where this is available, otherwise to the *S.E.*

Abel, E. (1984) Review of *The Daughter's Seduction* and *Freud on Femininity and Faith*. *Signs* **10** (1): 152–56.

Abraham, K. (1924) A Short Study of the Development of the Libido, Viewed in the Light of Mental Disorders. *Selected Papers of Karl Abraham*. London: Hogarth. 1927.

Alexander, S. (1984) Women, Class and Sexual Differences in the 1980s and 1840s: Some Reflections on the Writing of a Feminist History. *History Workshop* **17**: 125–49.

Andrews, J.G.W. (1966) Psychotherapy of Phobias. *Psychological Bulletin* **66**: 455–80.

Angelou, M. (1969) *I Know Why the Caged Bird Sings*. London: Virago. 1984.

Anyon, J. (1983) Intersections of Gender and Class: Accommodation and Resistance by Working-Class and Affluent Females to Contradictory Sex-Role Ideologies. In S. Walker and L. Barton (eds) *Gender, Class and Education*. Lewes: The Falmer Press.

Archer, C.J. (1984) Children's Attitudes Toward Sex-Role Division in Adult Occupational Roles. *Sex Roles* **10** (1/2): 1–10.

Archer, J. (1984) Gender Roles as Developmental Pathways? *British Journal of Social Psychology* **23** (3): 245–56.

Archer, J. and Lloyd, B. (1982) *Sex and Gender*. Harmondsworth: Penguin.

Astell, M. (1700) *Some Reflections Upon Marriage, Occasion'd by the Duke and Dutchess of Mazarine's Case; Which is also Considered*.

Austen, J. (1837) Memoirs of Miss Austen. In *Sense and Sensibility*. London: Richard Bentley.

Bandura, A. (1965) Influence of Model's Reinforcement Contingencies on the

Acquisition of Imitative Responses. *Journal of Personality and Social Psychology* **1**: 589–95.

Bandura, A., Ross, D., and Ross, S.A. (1963) Imitation of Film-Mediated Aggressive Models. *Journal of Abnormal and Social Psychology*. **66**: 3–11.

Barrett, M. and Coward, R. (1982) Letter. *m/f* **7**: 87–9.

Barrett, M. and McIntosh, M. (1983) *The Anti-Social Family*. London: Verso.

Bartlett, F.H. (1954) The Concept of 'Repression'. *Science and Society* **18**: 326–39.

Beck, A.T. and Greenberg, R.L. (1974) Cognitive Therapy with Depressed Women. In V. Franks and V. Burtle (eds) *Women in Therapy*. New York: Brunner/Mazel.

Beckwith, J. and Durkin, J. (1981) Girls, Boys and Math. *Science for the People* **13** (5): 6–9, 32–5.

Bem, S. (1974) The Measurement of Psychological Androgyny. *Journal of Consulting and Clinical Psychology* **42**: 155–62.

Bem, S. (1976) Probing the Promise of Androgyny. In A.G. Kaplan and J.P. Bean (eds) *Beyond Sex-Role Stereotypes: Readings Toward a Psychology of Androgyny*. Boston: Little, Brown & Co.

Bem, S. (1981) Gender Schema Theory: A Cognitive Account of Sex Typing. *Psychological Review* **88** (4): 354–64.

Bem, S. (1983) Gender Schema Theory and its Implications for Child Development: Raising Gender-Aschematic Children in a Gender-Schematic Society. *Signs* **8** (4): 598–616.

Benjamin, J. (1981) The Oedipal Riddle: Authority, Autonomy, and the New Narcissism. In J.P. Diggins and M.E. Kahn (eds) *The Problem of Authority in America*. Philadelphia: Temple University Press.

Benjamin, J. (1982) Chodorow's *Reproduction of Mothering*: An Appraisal. *Psychoanalytic Review* **69** (1): 158–62.

Benjamin, J. (1983) Review of *In a Different Voice* by Carol Gilligan. *Signs* **9** (2): 297–99.

Betterton, R. (1985) How do Women Look? The Female Nude in the Work of Suzanne Valadon. *Feminist Review* **19**: 3–24.

Bingham, S. (1985) Harnessing Womanpower. *The Sunday Times* (13 January): 35.

Bion, W.R. (1955) Group Dynamics: A Re-View. In M. Klein, P. Haimann, and R.E. Money-Kyrle (eds) *New Directions in Psycho-Analysis*. London: Tavistock.

Bion, W.R. (1962) *Learning from Experience*. London: Heinemann.

Bion, W.R. (1970) *Attention and Interpretation*. London: Tavistock.

Birch, H.G. and Clark, G. (1950) Hormonal Modification of Social Behavior. IV. The Mechanism of Estrogen-Induced Dominance in Chimpanzees. *Journal of Comparative and Physiological Psychology* **43**: 181–93.

Birke, L. (in press) *Women, Feminism and Biology*. Brighton: Harvester.

Birnbaum, D.W. and Croll, W.L. (1984) The Etiology of Children's Stereotypes about Sex Differences in Emotionality. *Sex Roles* **10** (9/10): 677–91.

Blake, W. (1787) The Question Answer'd. *Poetry and Prose of William Blake*. London: Nonesuch Library. 1967.

Blake, W. (1794) A Poison Tree. *Poetry and Prose of William Blake*. London: Nonesuch Library. 1967.

Blake, W. (1802) Auguries of Innocence. *Poetry and Prose of William Blake*. London. Nonesuch Library. 1967.

Blakeman, J., LaRue, A., and Olejnik, A. (1979) Sex-Appropriate Toy Preference and the Ability to Conceptualize Toys as Sex-Role Related. *Developmental Psychology* **15** (3): 339–40.

Blanchard, K.H. and Sargent, A.G. (1984) The One Minute Manager is an Androgynous Manager. *Training & Development Journal* **38** (5): 83–5.

Bleier, R. (1984) *Science and Gender: A Critique of Biology and its Theories on Women*. Oxford: Pergamon Press.

Blurton Jones, N. (1972) Categories of Child–Child Interaction. In N. Blurton Jones (ed.) *Ethological Studies of Child Behaviour*. London: Cambridge University Press.

Bogdanovich, P. (1985) *The Killing of the Unicorn*. London: Futura.

Boswell, S.L. (1985) The Influence of Sex-Role Stereotyping on Women's Attitudes and Achievement in Mathematics. In S.F. Chipman, L.R. Brush, and D.M. Wilson (eds) *Women and Mathematics: Balancing the Equation*. Hillsdale, NJ: Erlbaum.

Bott Spillius, E. (1983) Some Developments from the Work of Melanie Klein. *International Journal of Psycho-Analysis* **64** (3): 321–32.

Bourne, G. (1972) *Pregnancy*. London: Cassell.

Brenner, J. and Ramas, M. (1984) Rethinking Women's Oppression. *New Left Review* **144**: 37–71.

Breuer, J. (1985) With Freud, S. *Studies on Hysteria*. *S.E.* **2**; *P.F.L.* **3**.

Bronte, C. (1847) *Jane Eyre*. Harmondsworth: Penguin. 1966.

Brook, E. and Davis, A. (1985) *Women, the Family, and Social Work*. London: Tavistock.

Broughton, J.M. (1983) Women's Rationality and Men's Virtues: A Critique of Gender Dualism in Gilligan's Theory of Moral Development. *Social Research* **50** (3): 597–642.

Broverman, I.K., Broverman, D.M., Clarkson, F.E., Rosenkrantz, P.S., and Vogel, S.R. (1970) Sex-Role Stereotypes and Clinical Judgments of Mental Health. *Journal of Consulting and Clinical Psychology* **34** (1): 1-7.

Brown, G. and Harris, T. (1978) *The Social Origins of Depression*. London: Tavistock.

Brunswick, R.M. (1940) The Pre-Oedipal Phase of the Libido Development. *Psychoanalytic Quarterly* **9**: 293–319.

Buck, C. (1983) Freud and H.D. Bisexuality and a Feminine Discourse. *m/f* **8**: 53–66.

Campbell, B. (1984) *Wigan Pier Revisited.* London: Virago.

Cano, L., Solomon, S., and Holmes, D.S. (1984) Fear of Success: The Influence of Sex, Sex-Role Identity, and Components of Masculinity. *Sex Roles* **10** (5/6): 341–46.

Caplan, C. (1983) Wicked Fathers: A Family Romance. In U. Owen (ed.) *Fathers: Reflections by Daughters.* London: Virago.

Caplan, C. (1985) Psychoanalysis and Nineteenth and Twentieth Century Autobiographies. Talk given to a planning meeting of a series of London History Workshop seminars.

Carlson, H.M. and Baxter, L.A. (1984) Androgyny, Depression, and Self-Esteem in Irish Homosexual and Heterosexual Males and Females. *Sex Roles* **10** (5/6): 457–67.

Chasin, B. (1977) Sociobiology: A Sexist Synthesis. *Science for the People* **9** (3): 27–31.

Chasseguet-Smirgel, J. (1976) Freud and Female Sexuality. *International Journal of Psycho-Analysis* **57**: 275–86.

Chesler, P. (1972) *Women and Madness.* New York: Avon Books.

Chodorow, N. (1978) *The Reproduction of Mothering.* Berkeley: University of California Press.

Chodorow, N. (1979) Difference, Relation and Gender in Psychoanalytic Perspective. *Socialist Review* **9** (4): 51–70.

Cline, S. (1984) The Case of Beatrice: An Analysis of the Word 'Lesbian' and the Power of Language to Control Women. In O. Butler (ed.) *Feminist Experience in Feminist Research.* Manchester: Department of Sociology, University of Manchester.

Cloward, R.A. and Piven, F.F. (1979) Hidden Protest: The Channeling of Female Innovation and Resistance. *Signs* **4** (4): 651–69.

Cobb, N.J., Stevens-Long, J., and Goldstein, S. (1982) The Influence of Televised Models on Toy Preference in Children. *Sex Roles* **8** (10): 1075–080.

Cohn, N. (1985) Review of *Lucifer: The Devil in the Middle Ages* by Jeffrey Burton Russell. *New York Review of Books* (25 April): 13–14.

Coker, D.R. (1984) The Relationships Among Gender Concepts and Cognitive Maturity in Preschool Children. *Sex Roles* **10** (1/2): 19–31.

Coleridge, S.T. (1827) Entry for 23 July. *Table Talk.* London: John Murray. 1851.

Collins, L.J., Ingoldsby, B.B., and Dellman, M.M. (1984) Sex-Role Stereotyping in Children's Literature: A Change from the Past. *Childhood Education* **60** (4): 278–85.

Comfort, A. (1977) *More Joy of Sex.* London: Quartet Books.

Coote, A. and Campbell, B. (1982) *Sweet Freedom: The Struggle for Women's Liberation.* London: Pan.

Cott, N. (1978) Passionlessness: An Interpretation of Victorian Sexual Ideology, 1790–1850. *Signs* **4** (2): 219–36.

Coward, R. (1984) *Female Desire: Women's Sexuality Today*. London: Paladin.

Damon, W. (1977) *The Social World of the Child*. San Francisco: Jossey-Bass.

Davidoff, L. and Hall, C. (1983) The Architecture of Public and Private Life: English Middle-Class Society in a Provincial Town 1780–1850. In D. Fraser and A. Sutcliffe (eds) *The Pursuit of Urban History*. London: Edward Arnold.

Davies, H.A. (1985) The Use of Psycho-Analytic Concepts in Social Work with Children. Unpublished M.A. thesis. Canterbury: University of Kent.

Davies, M.L. (1915) *Maternity: Letters from Working Women*. London: Virago. 1978.

Davies, M.L. (1931) *Life as We Have Known It*. London: Virago. 1977.

Davis, A.J. (1984) Sex-Differentiated Behavior in Nonsexist Picture Books. *Sex Roles* **11** (1/2): 1–16.

Deaux, K. and Emswiller, T. (1974) Explanations of Successful Performance on Sex-Linked Tasks: What is Skill for the Male is Luck for the Female. *Journal of Personality and Social Psychology* **29**: 80–5.

de Beauvoir, S. (1949) *The Second Sex*. Translated by H.M. Parshley. Harmondsworth: Penguin. 1972.

de Beauvoir, S. (1958) *Memoirs of a Dutiful Daughter*. Translated by J. Kirkup. Harmondsworth: Penguin. 1963.

de Beauvoir, S. (1960) *The Prime of Life*. Translated by P. Green. Harmondsworth: Penguin. 1965.

Delamont, S. and Duffin, L. (1978) *The Nineteenth Century Woman: Her Cultural and Physical World*. London: Croom Helm.

de Vore, I. (ed.) (1965) *Primate Behavior: Field Studies of Monkeys and Apes*. New York: Holt, Rinehart & Winston.

Dickson, A. (1982) *A Woman in Your Own Right: Assertiveness and You*. London: Quartet Books.

Dinnerstein, D. (1978) *The Rocking of the Cradle*. London: Souvenir Press.

Dixon, B. (1977) *Catching Them Young: 1. Sex, Race and Class in Children's Fiction*. London: Pluto Press.

Dodge, K.A. (1983) Behavioral Antecedents of Peer Social Status. *Child Development* **54** (6): 1386–99.

Doyal, L. (1983) Women, Health and the Social Division of Labour: A Case Study of the Women's Health Movement in Britain. *Critical Social Policy* **7**: 21–33.

Drummond, M. (1985) A Case of Unequal Treatment. *The Sunday Times* (2 June): 35.

Durkin, K. (1984) Children's Accounts of Sex-Role Stereotypes in Television. *Communication Research* **11** (3): 341–62.

Durkin, K. (1985a) Television and Sex-Role Acquisition. 2. Effects. *British Journal of Social Psychology* **24** (3): 191–210.

Durkin, K. (1985b) *Television, Sex Roles and Children: A Developmental Social Psychological Account*. Milton Keynes: Open University Press.

Durkin, K. (in press) Personality, Social Cognition and Social Context in the Construction of Sex Differences in Human Performance. In M.A. Baker (ed.) *Sex Differences in Human Performance*. Chichester: Wiley.

Durkin, K. and Hutchins, G. (1984) Challenging Traditional Sex Role Stereotypes in Careers Education Broadcasts: The Reactions of Young Secondary School Pupils. *Journal of Educational Television* **10** (1): 25–33.

Dusek, V. (1984) Sociobiology and Rape. *Science for the People* **16**: 10–16.

Dworkin, A. (1983) *Right-Wing Women*. London: The Women's Press.

Eccles (Parsons), J., Adler, T.F., Futterman, R., Goff, S.B., Koczala, C.M., Meece, J.L., and Midgley, C. (1985) Self-Perceptions, Task Perceptions, Socializing Influences, and the Decision to Enroll in Mathematics. In S.F. Chipman, L.R. Brush, and D.M. Wilson (eds) *Women and Mathematics: Balancing the Equation*. Hillsdale, NJ: Erlbaum.

Ehrenreich, B. (1983) *The Hearts of Men*. London: Pluto Press.

Ehrensaft, D. (1980) When Women and Men Mother. *Socialist Review* **10** (1): 37–73.

Ehrhardt, A.A. and Baker, S.W. (1973) Hormonal Aberrations and their Implications for the Understanding of Normal Sex Differentiation. Paper presented at the meeting of the Society for Research in Child Development, Philadelphia.

Ehrhardt, A.A. and Baker, S.W. (1974) Fetal Androgens, Human Control, Nervous System Differentiation, and Behavior Sex Differences. In R.C. Freidman, R.M. Richart, and R. Van De Weile (eds) *Sex Differences in Behavior*. New York: Wiley.

Ehrhardt, A.A., Grisanti, G.C., and Meyer-Bahlburg, H.F.L. (1977) Prenatal Exposure to Medroxyprogesterone Acetate (MPA) in Girls. *Psychoneuro-endocrinology* **2**: 391–98.

Eichenbaum, L. and Orbach, S. (1985) *Understanding Women*. Harmondsworth: Penguin.

Eisenberg, N., Murray, E., and Hite, T. (1982) Children's Reasoning Regarding Sex-Typed Toy Choices. *Child Development* **53**: 81–6.

Eisenstein, Z. (1979) Some Notes on the Relations of Capitalist Patriarchy. In Z. Eisenstein (ed.) *Capitalist Patriarchy and the Case for Socialist Feminism*. New York: Monthly Review Press.

Eisenstock, B. (1984) Sex-Role Differences in Children's Identification with Counterstereotypical Televised Portrayals. *Sex Roles* **10** (5/6): 417–30.

Elpern, S. and Karp, S.A. (1984) Sex-Role Orientation and Depressive Symptomatology. *Sex Roles* **10** (11/12): 987–92.

Engels, F. (1875–83) *Dialectics of Nature*. London: Lawrence & Wishart. 1954.

Engels, F. (1884) *The Origin of the Family, Private Property and the State*. In *Karl Marx and Frederick Engels: Selected Works*. London: Lawrence & Wishart. 1970.

Ernst, S. and Goodison, L. (1981) *In Our Own Hands: A Book of Self-Help Therapy*. London: The Women's Press.

Evans, M. (1985) *Simone de Beauvoir: A Feminist Mandarin*. London: Tavistock.

Evans, R.G. (1984) Hostility and Sex Guilt: Perceptions of Self and Others as a Function of Gender and Sex-Role Orientation. *Sex Roles* **10** (3/4): 207–15.

Fagot, B.I. (1977) Consequences of Moderate Cross-Gender Behavior in Pre-School Children. *Child Development* **48**: 902–07.

Fairbairn, W.R.D. (1944) Endopsychic Structure Considered in Terms of Object-Relationships. *Psychoanalytic Studies of the Personality*. London: Tavistock. 1952.

Fee, E. (1983) Woman's Nature and Scientific Objectivity. In M. Lowe and R. Hubbard (eds) *Woman's Nature*. New York: Pergamon.

Finch, J. and Groves, D. (1983) *A Labour of Love – Women, Work and Caring*. London: Routledge & Kegan Paul.

Fisher, M., Newton, C., and Sainsbury, E. (1984) *Mental Health Social Work Observed*. London: Allen & Unwin.

Flax, J. (1978) The Conflict Between Nurturance and Autonomy in Mother–Daughter Relationships and Within Feminism. *Feminist Studies* **4** (2): 171–91.

Flerx, V.C., Fidler, D.S., and Rogers, R.W. (1976) Sex Role Stereotypes: Developmental Aspects and Early Intervention. *Child Development* **47**: 998–1007.

Foreit, K.G., Agor, T., Byers, J., Larue, J., Lokey, H., Palazzini, M., Patterson, M., and Smith, L. (1980) Sex Bias in the Newspaper Treatment of Male-Centered and Female-Centered News Stories. *Sex Roles* **6** (3): 475–80.

Foucault, M. (1976) *The History of Sexuality. I. An Introduction*. London: Penguin. 1981.

Franken, M.W. (1983) Sex Role Expectations in Children's Vocational Aspirations and Perceptions of Occupations. *Psychology of Women Quarterly* **8** (1): 59–68.

Fraser, A. (1984) *The Weaker Vessel*. London: Weidenfeld & Nicolson.

Freud, S. (1894a) The Neuro-Psychoses of Defence. *S.E.* **3**.

Freud, S. (1895) Draft H – Paranoia. In S. Freud (1950a) Extracts from the Fliess Papers. *S.E.* **1**.

Freud, S. (1895d) With Breuer, J. *Studies on Hysteria. S.E.* **2**; *P.F.L.* **3**.

Freud, S. (1896c) The Aetiology of Hysteria. *S.E.* **3**.

Freud, S. (1898a) Sexuality in the Aetiology of the Neuroses. *S.E.* **3**.

Freud, S. (1900a) *The Interpretation of Dreams. S.E.* **4–5**; *P.F.L.* **4**.

Freud, S. (1901b) *The Psychopathology of Everyday Life. S.E.* **6**; *P.F.L.* **5**.

Freud, S. (1905c) *Jokes and Their Relation to the Unconscious. S.E.* **8**; *P.F.L.* **6**.

Freud, S. (1905d) *Three Essays on the Theory of Sexuality. S.E.* **7**; *P.F.L.* **7**.

Freud, S. (1905e) Fragment of an Analysis of a Case of Hysteria. *S.E.* **7**; *P.F.L.* **8**.

Freud, S. (1908a) Hysterical Phantasies and their Relation to Bisexuality. *S.E.* **9**; *P.F.L.* **10**.

Freud, S. (1908c) On the Sexual Theories of Children. *S.E.* **9**; *P.F.L.* **7**.

Freud, S. (1908d) 'Civilized' Sexual Morality and Modern Nervous Illness. *S.E.* **9**; *P.F.L.* **12**.

Freud, S. (1909b) Analysis of a Phobia in a Five-Year-Old Boy. *S.E.* **10**; *P.F.L.* **8**.

Freud, S. (1909d) Notes Upon a Case of Obsessional Neurosis. *S.E.* **10**; *P.F.L.* **9**.

Freud, S. (1911b) Formulations on the Two Principles of Mental Functioning. *S.E.* **12**; *P.F.L.* **11**.

Freud, S. (1911c) Psycho-Analytic Notes on an Autobiographical Account of a Case of Paranoia (*Dementia Paranoides*). *S.E.* **12**; *P.F.L.* **9**.

Freud, S. (1912b) The Dynamics of Transference. *S.E.* **12**.

Freud, S. (1912d) On the Universal Tendency to Debasement in the Sphere of Love. *S.E.* **11**; *P.F.L.* **7**.

Freud, S. (1914c) On Narcissism: An Introduction. *S.E.* **14**; *P.F.L,* **11**.

Freud, S. (1914d) On the History of the Psycho-Analytic Movement. *S.E.* **14**; *P.F.L.* **15**.

Freud, S. (1914g) Remembering, Repeating and Working-Through. *S.E.* **12**.

Freud, S. (1915c) Instincts and Their Vicissitudes. *S.E.* **14**; *P.F.L.* **11**.

Freud, S. (1915d) Repression. *S.E.* **14**; *P.F.L.* **11**.

Freud, S. (1915e) The Unconscious. *S.E.* **14**; *P.F.L.* **11**.

Freud, S. (1915f) A Case of Paranoia Running Counter to the Psycho-Analytic Theory of the Disease. *S.E.* **14**; *P.F.L.* **10**.

Freud, S. (1916–17) *Introductory Lectures on Psycho-Analysis*. *S.E.* **15–16**; *P.F.L.* **1**.

Freud, S. (1917e) Mourning and Melancholia. *S.E.* **14**; *P.F.L.* **11**.

Freud, S. (1918b) From the History of an Infantile Neurosis. *S.E.* **17**; *P.F.L.* **9**.

Freud, S. (1919e) A Child is Being Beaten. *S.E.* **17**; *P.F.L.* **10**.

Freud, S. (1920a) The Psychogenesis of a Case of Female Homosexuality. *S.E.* **18**; *P.F.L.* **9**.

Freud, S. (1920g) *Beyond the Pleasure Principle*. *S.E.* **18**; *P.F.L.* **11**.

Freud, S. (1922b) Some Neurotic Mechanisms in Jealousy, Paranoia and Homosexuality. *S.E.* **18**; *P.F.L.* **10**.

Freud, S. (1923b) *The Ego and the Id*. *S.E.* **19**; *P.F.L.* **11**.

Freud, S. (1923e) The Infantile Genital Organization. *S.E.* **19**; *P.F.L.* **7**.

Freud, S. (1924c) The Economic Problem of Masochism. *S.E.* **19**; *P.F.L.* **11**.

Freud, S. (1924d) The Dissolution of the Oedipus Complex. *S.E.* **19**; *P.F.L.* **7**.

Freud, S. (1925h) Negation. *S.E.* **19**; *P.F.L.* **11**.

Freud, S. (1925j) Some Psychical Consequences of the Anatomical Distinction Between the Sexes. *S.E.* **19**; *P.F.L.* **7**.

Freud, S. (1926d) *Inhibitions, Symptoms and Anxiety. S.E.* **20**; *P.F.L.* **10**.

Freud, S. (1927e) Fetishism. *S.E.* **21**; *P.F.L.* **7**.

Freud, S. (1930a) *Civilization and its Discontents. S.E.* **21**; *P.F.L.* **12**.

Freud, S. (1931b) Female Sexuality. *S.E.* **21**; *P.F.L.* **7**.

Freud, S. (1933a) *New Introductory Lectures on Psycho-Analysis. S.E.* **22**; *P.F.L.* **2**.

Freud, S. (1937c) Analysis Terminable and Interminable. *S.E.* **23**.

Freud, S. (1937d) Constructions in Analysis. *S.E.* **23**.

Freud, S. (1940a) *An Outline of Psycho-Analysis. S.E.* **23**.

Freud, S. (1940e) Splitting of the Ego in the Process of Defence. *S.E.* **23**; *P.F.L.* **11**.

Freud, S. (1950a) Letters. *S.E.* **11**.

Frieze, I.H., Whiteley, B.E., Hanusa, B.H., and McHugh, M.C. (1982) Assessing the Theoretical Models for Sex Differences in Causal Attributions for Success and Failure. *Sex Roles* **8**: 333–43.

Fromm, E. (1941) *Escape from Freedom*. New York: Avon Books. 1965.

Gallop, J. (1982) *The Daughter's Seduction: Feminism and Psychoanalysis*. London: Macmillan.

Gallop, J. and Burke, C. (1980) Psychoanalysis and Feminism in France. In H. Eisenstein and A. Jardine (eds) *The Future of Difference*. Boston: G.K. Hall.

Garrison, D. (1981) Karen Horney and Feminism. *Signs* **6** (4): 672–91.

Geis, F.L., Brown, V., Jennings (Walstedt), J., and Porter, N. (1984) TV Commercials as Achievement Scripts for Women. *Sex Roles* **10** (7/8): 513–25.

Gilligan, C. (1982a) *In a Different Voice*. London: Harvard University Press.

Gilligan, C. (1982b) Why Should a Woman Be More Like a Man? *Psychology Today* (June): 68–77.

Glover, E. (1945) Examination of the Klein System of Child Psychology. *Psychoanalytic Study of the Child* **1**: 75–118.

Goldberg, S. (1977) *The Inevitability of Patriarchy*. London: Temple Smith.

Goldman, E. (1910) *Anarchism and Other Essays*. New York: Mother Earth Publishing Association.

Goodstein, R.K. and Swift, K. (1977) Psychotherapy with Phobic Patients: The Marriage Relationship as the Source of Symptoms and Focus of Treatment. *American Journal of Psychotherapy* **31** (2): 285–92.

Graydon, J. (1983) 'But it's More than a Game. It's an Institution.' Feminist Perspectives on Sport. *Feminist Review* **13**: 5–16.

Greenberg, J.R. and Mitchell, S.A. (1983) *Object Relations in Psychoanalytic Theory*. Cambridge: Harvard University Press.

Griffin, S. (1981) *Pornography and Silence*. London: The Women's Press.

Grünbaum, A. (1984) *The Foundations of Psychoanalysis: A Philosophical Critique*. Berkeley: University of California Press.

Guntrip, H. (1969) *Schizoid Phenomena, Object-Relations, and the Self*. New York: International Universities Press.

Hafner, R.J. (1983a) Behavior Therapy for Agoraphobic Men. *Behaviour Research and Therapy* **21** (1): 51–6.

Hafner, R.J. (1983b) Marital Systems of Agoraphobic Women: Contributions of Husbands' Denial and Projection. *Journal of Family Therapy* **5** (4): 379–96.

Hall, C. (1979) The Early Formation of Victorian Domestic Ideology. In S. Burman (ed.) *Fit Work for Women*. London: Croom Helm.

Harris, B.J. (1984) The Power of the Past: History and the Psychology of Women. In M. Lewin (ed.) *In the Shadow of the Past: Psychology Portrays the Sexes*. New York: Columbia University Press.

Harris, O. (1984) The Mythological Figure of the Earth Mother: The Politics of Perception in the Central Andes. Paper prepared for the workshop Perception in History and Anthropology: The Problem of 'Otherness'.

Hartsock, N. (1983) *Money, Sex, and Power*. London: Longman.

Hedges, E.R. (1973) Afterword to *The Yellow Wallpaper* by Charlotte Perkins Gilman. Boston: The Feminist Press.

Hegel, G.W.F. (1807) *Phenomenology of Spirit*. Translated by A.V. Miller. Oxford: Clarendon Press. 1977.

Heiser, P. and Gannon, L. (1984) The Relationship of Sex-Role Stereotypy to Anger Expression and the Report of Psychosomatic Symptoms. *Sex Roles* **10** (7/8): 601–11.

Herik, J. van (1982) *Freud on Femininity and Faith*. Berkeley and Los Angeles: University of California Press.

Hinshelwood, R.D. (1983) Projective Identification and Marx's Concept of Man. *International Review of Psychoanalysis* **10**: 221–26.

Hirschfeld, M.A. and Cross, C.K. (1982) Epidemiology of Affective Disorders. *Archives of General Psychiatry* **39** (January): 35–46.

Holland, S. (1984) 'Loss, Rage and Oppression': Neighbourhood Psychotherapy with Working Class, Black and National Minority Women. The Pam Smith Memorial Lecture. London: Department of Applied Social Studies, The Polytechnic of North London.

Hollis, P. (1979) *Women in Public: The Women's Movement, 1850–1900*. London: Allen and Unwin.

Hollway, W. (1984) Gender Difference and the Production of Subjectivity. In J. Henriques, W. Hollway, C. Urwin, C. Venn, and V. Walkerdine. *Changing the Subject: Psychology, Social Regulation and Subjectivity*. London: Methuen.

Horner, M.S. (1969) Fail: Bright Women. *Psychology Today* **3**: 36–8, 62.

Horney, K. (1924) On the Genesis of the Castration Complex in Women. *Feminine Psychology*. New York: Norton. 1967.

Horney, K. (1926) The Flight from Womanhood: The Masculinity-Complex in Women as Viewed by Men and by Women. *Feminine Psychology*. New York: Norton. 1967.

Horney, K. (1931) The Distrust Between the Sexes. *Feminine Psychology*. New York. Norton. 1967.

Horney, K. (1932a) Problems of Marriage. *Feminine Psychology*. New York: Norton. 1967.

Horney, K. (1932b) The Dread of Woman. *Feminine Psychology*. New York: Norton. 1967.

Horney, K. (1935) The Problem of Feminine Masochism. *Feminine Psychology*. New York: Norton. 1967.

Horney, K. (1939)*New Ways in Psychoanalysis*. New York: Norton.

Horney, K. (1950) *Neurosis and Human Growth*. New York: Norton.

Housman, J. (1982) Mothering, the Unconscious, and Feminism. *Radical America* **16** (6): 47–61.

Hudson, B (1984) Femininity and Adolescence. In A. McRobbie and M. Nara (eds) *Gender and Generation*. London: Macmillan.

Hutt, C. (1972) *Males and Females*. Harmondsworth: Penguin.

Hyde, J.S. (1984) How Large are Gender Differences in Aggression? A Developmental Meta-Analysis. *Developmental Psychology* **20** (4): 722–36.

Hyde, J.S. and Schuck, J.R. (1977) The Development of Sex Differences in Aggression: A Revised Model. Presented at the Annual Meeting of the American Psychological Association, San Francisco.

Ingleby, D. (1985) Unpublished review of *The Production of Desire* by Richard Lichtman.

Irigaray, L. (1977a) This Sex Which is Not One. In E. Marks and I. de Courtivron (eds) *New French Feminisms*. Brighton: Harvester. 1981.

Irigaray, L. (1977b) Women's Exile: Interview with Luce Irigaray. *Ideology and Consciousness* **1**: 62–76.

Irigaray, L. (1980) When our Lips Speak Together. *Signs* **6** (1): 66–79.

Irigaray, L. (1981) And the One Doesn't Stir Without the Other. *Signs* **7** (1): 60–7.

Isard, J. (1985) Agoraphobia: Nature, Treatment and Implications for Social Work. Unpublished M.A. thesis. Canterbury: University of Kent.

Jaggar, A. (1983) *Feminist Politics and Human Nature*. Brighton: Harvester.

Johnson, S. (1763) Letter to Dr. Taylor. In R.W. Chapman (ed.) *The Letters of Samuel Johnson, Vol. I 1719–1774*. Oxford: The Clarendon Press. 1952.

Johnston, J. (1973) *Lesbian Nation*. New York: Simon & Schuster.

Jones, A.R. (1984) Julia Kristeva on Femininity: The Limits of a Semiotic Politics. *Feminist Review* **18**: 56–73.

Jones, E. (1954) *Sigmund Freud: Life and Work, Vol. I*. London: Hogarth.

Joseph, B. (1983) On Understanding and Not Understanding: Some Technical Issues. *International Journal of Psycho-Analysis* **64** (3): 291–98.

Joslyn, W.D. (1973) Androgen-Induced Social Dominance in Infant Female Rhesus Monkeys. *Journal of Child Psychology and Psychiatry* **14**: 137–45.

Kagan, J. (1956) The Child's Perception of the Parent. *Journal of Abnormal and Social Psychology* **53**: 257–58.

Kagan, J. and Lemkin, J. (1960) The Child's Differential Perception of Parental Attributes. *Journal of Abnormal and Social Psychology* **61** (3): 440–47.

Kalisch, P.A. and Kalisch, B.J. (1984) Sex–Role Stereotyping of Nurses and

Physicians on Prime-Time Television: A Dichotomy of Occupational Portrayals. *Sex Roles* **10** (7/8): 533–53.

Kaplan, E.A. (1984) Is the Gaze Male? In A. Snitow, C. Stansell, and S. Thompson (eds) *Desire: The Politics of Sexuality*. London: Virago.

Keller, E.F. (1982) Feminism and Science. *Signs* **7** (3): 589–602.

Keller, E.F. (1983) Women, Science, and Popular Mythology. In J. Rothschild (ed.) *Machina Ex Dea: Feminist Perspectives on Technology*. New York: Pergamon.

Kernberg, O. (1974) Contrasting Viewpoints Regarding the Nature and Psychoanalytic Treatment of Narcissistic Personalities: A Preliminary Communication. *Journal of the American Psychoanalytic Association* **22**: 255–67.

Kerr, M. (1985) Sharing in a Common Plight? *Poverty* **60** (Special Issue on Poverty and Food): 22–6.

Klein, M. (1929) Personification in the Play of Children. *The Writings of Melanie Klein (W.M.K.)* **2**. London: Hogarth.

Klein, M. (1930) The Importance of Symbol-Formation in the Development of the Ego. *W.M.K.* **3**. London: Hogarth.

Klein, M. (1932) The Psycho-Analysis of Children. *W.M.K.* **1**. London: Hogarth.

Klein, M. (1940) Mourning and its Relation to Manic-Depressive States. *W.M.K.* **2**. London: Hogarth.

Klein, M. (1945) The Oedipus Complex in the Light of Early Anxieties. *W.M.K.* **2**. London: Hogarth.

Klein, M. (1946) Notes on Some Schizoid Mechanisms. *W.M.K.* **3**. London: Hogarth.

Klein, M. (1952a) Some Theoretical Conclusions Regarding the Emotional Life of the Infant. *W.M.K.* **3**. London: Hogarth.

Klein, M. (1952b) On Observing the Behaviour of Young Infants. *W.M.K.* **3**. London: Hogarth.

Klein, M. (1957) Envy and Gratitude. *W.M.K.* **3**. London: Hogarth.

Klein, M. (1959) Our Adult World and its Roots in Infancy. *W.M.K.* **3**. London: Hogarth.

Klein, M. (1961) Narrative of a Child Analysis. *W.M.K.* **4**. London: Hogarth.

Klein, M. (1963) On the Sense of Loneliness. *W.M.K.* **3**. London: Hogarth.

Knight, J. (1984) Fit for the Spinning House: Margaret Howard Describes the Ordeals of the Unmarried. *The Sunday Times* (23 December): 37.

Koblinsky, S.A. and Sugawara, A.I. (1984) Nonsexist Curricula, Sex of Teacher, and Children's Sex-Role Learning. *Sex Roles* **10** (5/6): 357–67.

Kohlberg, L. (1966) A Cognitive-Developmental Analysis of Children's Sex-Role Concepts and Attitudes. In E.E. Maccoby (ed.) *The Development of Sex Differences*. Stanford: Stanford University Press.

Kohlberg, L. and Ullian, D.Z. (1974) Stages in the Development of Psychosexual Concepts and Attitudes. In R.C. Freidman, R.M. Richart, and R.L. Van De Weile (eds) *Sex Differences in Behavior*. New York: Wiley.

Kohut, H. (1971) *The Analysis of the Self*. New York: International Universities Press.

Kohut, H. (1977) *The Restoration of the Self*. New York: International Universities Press.

Krafft-Ebing, R. von (1886) *Psychopathia Sexualis*. Translated by Franklin S. Klaf. New York: Bell Publishing Company. 1965.

Kreuz, L.E. and Rose, R.M. (1972) Assessment of Aggressive Behavior and Plasma Testosterone in a Young Criminal Population, *Psychosomatic Medicine* **34**: 321–32.

Kristeva, J. (1974) Women Can Never Be Defined. In E. Marks and I. de Courtivron (eds) *New French Feminisms*. Brighton: Harvester. 1981.

Kuhn, D., Nash, S.C., and Brucken, L. (1978) Sex Role Concepts of Two- and Three-Year-Olds. *Child Development* **49**: 445–51.

Lacan, J. (1948) Aggressivity in Psychoanalysis. *Ecrits*. Translated by Alan Sheridan. London: Tavistock. 1977.

Lacan, J. (1949) The Mirror Stage as Formative of the Function of the I as Revealed in Psychoanalytic Experience. *Ecrits*. Translated by Alan Sheridan. London: Tavistock. 1977.

Lacan, J. (1951) Intervention on Transference. In J. Mitchell and J. Rose (eds) *Feminine Sexuality*. London: Macmillan. 1982.

Lacan, J. (1957) The Agency of the Letter in the Unconscious of Reason since Freud. *Ecrits*. Translated by Alan Sheridan. London: Tavistock. 1977.

Lacan, J. (1958) The Signification of the Phallus. *Ecrits*. Translated by Alan Sheridan. London: Tavistock. 1977.

Laing, R.D. (1960) *The Divided Self*. London: Tavistock.

Lampl de Groot, J. (1928) The Evolution of the Oedipus Complex in Women. *International Journal of Psychoanalysis* **9**: 332–45.

Langlois, J.H. and Downs, A.D. (1980) Mothers, Fathers, and Peers as Socialization Agents of Sex-Typed Play Behaviors in Young Children. *Child Development* **51**: 1237–247.

Laplanche, J. and Pontalis, J.-B. (1968) Fantasy and the Origins of Sexuality. *International Journal of Psycho-Analysis* **49** (1): 1–18.

Lasch, C. (1979) *The Culture of Narcissism*. New York: Norton.

Lawrence, M. (1984) *The Anorexic Experience*. London: The Women's Press.

le Doeuff, M. (1980) Simone de Beauvoir and Existentialism. *Feminist Studies* **6** (2): 277–89.

Lemaire, A. (1970) *Jacques Lacan*. Translated by David Macey. London: Routledge & Kegan Paul. 1977.

Lerner, L. (1983) *Women and Individuation*. New York: Human Sciences Press. (Special Issue of *The Psychoanalytic Review* 1982, **69** (1).)

Lewin, M. (1984) The Victorians, the Psychologists, and Psychic Birth Control. In M. Lewin (ed.) *In the Shadow of the Past: Psychology Portrays the Sexes*. New York: Columbia University Press.

Lewis, C. (1985) Men's Involvement in Fatherhood: Variation Across the Life

Span Suggests that Impressions of Historical Change are Over-Inflated. *Bulletin of the British Psychological Society* **38** (February): A21.

Lewis, J. (1985) The Debate on Sex and Class. *New Left Review* **149**: 108–20.

Lewis, M. (1981) Self-Knowledge: A Social Cognitive Perspective on Gender Identity and Sex-Role Development. In M.E. Lamb and L.R. Sherrod (eds) *Infant Social Cognition*. Hillsdale, NJ: Erlbaum.

Lloyd, G. (1984) *The Man of Reason: Male and Female in Western Philosophy*. London: Methuen.

London Women's Liberation Campaign for Legal and Financial Independence and Rights of Women (1979) Disaggregation Now! Another Battle for Women's Independence. *Feminist Review* **2**: 19–31.

Lorber, J., Coser, R.L., Rossi, A.S., and Chodorow, N. (1981) On *The Reproduction of Mothering*: A Methodological Debate. *Signs* **6** (3): 482–514.

Lowe, M. (1983) The Dialectic of Biology and Culture. In M. Lowe and R. Hubbard (eds) *Woman's Nature: Rationalizations of Inequality*. Oxford: Pergamon Press.

Maccoby, E.E. and Jacklin, C.N. (1975) *The Psychology of Sex Differences*. London: Oxford University Press.

Maccoby, E.E. and Jacklin, C.N. (1980) Sex Differences in Aggression: A Rejoinder and Reprise. *Child Development* **51**: 964–80.

McGhee, P.E. and Frueh, T. (1980) Television Viewing and the Learning of Sex-Role Stereotypes. *Sex Roles* **6** (2): 179–88.

McIntyre, A. (1972) Sex Differences in Children's Aggression. *Proceedings of the 80th Annual Convention, American Psychological Association* **7**: 93–4.

McKenna, J.J. (1983) Primate Aggression and Evolution: An Overview of Sociobiological and Anthropological Perspectives. *Bulletin of the American Academy of Psychiatry and the Law* **11** (2): 105–30.

Macpherson, C.B. (1962) *The Political Theory of Possessive Individualism: Hobbes to Locke*. Oxford: Oxford University Press.

Mahler, M. (1975) On the Current Status of the Infantile Neurosis. *Journal of the American Psychoanalytic Association* **23**: 327–33.

Maisner, P. and Pulling, J. (1985) *Feasting and Fasting*. London: Fontana.

Malcolm, J. (1982) *Psychoanalysis: The Impossible Profession*. London: Picador.

Malcolm, J. (1984) *In the Freud Archives*. London: Jonathan Cape.

Marcus, D. and Overton, W.F. (1978) The Development of Cognitive Gender Constancy and Sex Role Preferences. *Child Development* **49**: 434–44.

Marcus, S. (1976) Freud and Dora: Story, History, Case History. *Representations*. New York: Random House.

Marcuse, H. (1955) *Eros and Civilization*. New York: Vintage Books.

Martin, M.K. and Voorhies, B. (1975) *Female of the Species*. New York: Columbia University Press.

Martineau, H. (1877) *Harriet Martineau's Autobiography, Vol. 2*. London: Virago. 1983.

Marx, K. (1852) *The Eighteenth Brumaire of Louis Bonaparte*. In *Karl Marx and Frederick Engels. Selected Works*. London: Lawrence & Wishart. 1970.

Masson, J.M. (1985) *Complete Letters of Freud to Wilhelm Fliess 1887–1904*. Cambridge: Harvard University Press.

Meltzer, D. (1978) *The Kleinian Development. Part III: The Clinical Significance of Bion*. Perthshire: Cluny Press.

Menzies, I. (1975) Thoughts on the Maternal Role in Contemporary Society. *Journal of Child Psychotherapy* **4**: 5–14.

Merchant, C. (1980) *The Death of Nature: Women, Ecology and the Scientific Revolution*. San Francisco: Harper & Row.

Merk, M. (1985) Psychoanalysis and the 'Perverse': Theoretical and Historical Perspectives. London History Workshop seminars.

Michael, R.P. (1968) Gonadal Hormones and the Control of Primate Behavior. In R.P. Michael (ed.) *Endocrinology and Human Behaviour*. Oxford: Oxford University Press.

Michalowski, H. (1982) The Army Will Make a 'Man' Out of You. In P. McAllister (ed.) *Reweaving the Web of Life: Feminism and Nonviolence*. Philadelphia: New Society Publishers.

Milavsky, J.R., Kessler, R.C., Stipp, H.H., and Rubens, W.S. (1982) *Television and Aggression*. New York: Academic Press.

Mill, J.S. (1869)*The Subjection of Women*. Oxford: Oxford University Press. 1975.

Miller, J.B. (1976) *Toward a New Psychology of Women*. Harmondsworth: Penguin. 1978.

Millot, C. (1985) The Feminine Super-Ego. Together with Discussion by J. Mitchell, J. Rose, and Others. *m/f* **10**: 21–38.

Mischel, W. (1966) A Social-Learning View of Sex Differences in Behavior. In E.E. Maccoby (ed.) *The Development of Sex Differences*. Stanford: Stanford University Press.

Mitchell, J. (1974) *Psychoanalysis and Feminism*. London: Allen Lane.

Mitchell, J. (1976) Women and Equality. In A. Oakley and J. Mitchell (eds) *The Rights and Wrongs of Women*. Harmondsworth: Penguin.

Mitchell, J. (1980) On the Differences Between Men and Women. *New Society* **52** (917): 234–35.

Mitchell, J. (1983) Feminine Sexuality: Interview – 1982. *m/f* **8**: 3–16.

Mitchell, J. (1984) *Women: The Longest Revolution*. London: Virago.

Moi, T. (1981) Representation of Patriarchy: Sexuality and Epistemology in Freud's Dora. *Feminist Review* **9**: 60–74.

Moi, T. (1982) Jealousy and Sexual Difference. *Feminist Review* **11**: 53–68.

Morgan, K.P. and Ayim, M. (1984) Comment on Bem's 'Gender-Schema Theory and Its Implications for Child Development: Raising Gender-Aschematic Children in a Gender-Schematic Society'. *Signs* **10** (1): 188–96.

Morgan, M. (1975) *The Total Woman*. New York: Pocket Books.

Mulvey, L. (1975) Visual Pleasure and Narrative Cinema. *Screen* **16** (3): 6–18.

New, C. and David, M. (1985) *For the Children's Sake*. Harmondsworth: Penguin.

Newton, E. (1984) The Mythic Mannish Lesbian: Radclyffe Hall and the New Woman. *Signs* **9** (4): 557–75.

Nicholson, J. (1984) *Men and Women: How Different are They?* Oxford: Oxford University Press.

Nightingale, F. (1859) Cassandra. In Strachey, R. (1928) *The Cause*. London: Virago. 1979.

Oakley, A. (1976) Wisewoman and Medicine Man: Changes in the Management of Childbirth. In A. Oakley and J. Mitchell (eds) *The Rights and Wrongs of Women*. Harmondsworth: Penguin.

Oatley, K. (1984) Depression: Crisis without Alternatives. *New Scientist* **1413** (7 June): 29–31.

O'Connell, A.N. (1980) Karen Horney: Theorist in Psychoanalysis and Feminine Psychology. *Psychology of Women Quarterly* **5** (1): 81–93.

Omark, D.R., Omark, M., and Edelman, M. (1973) Dominance Hierarchies in Young Children. Paper presented at International Congress of Anthropological and Ethnological Sciences, Chicago.

Ophuijsen, J.H.W. van (1924) Contributions to the Masculinity Complex in Women. *International Journal of Psycho-Analysis* **5**: 39–49.

Pahl, J. (1985) *Private Violence and Public Policy*. London: Routledge & Kegan Paul.

Paludi, M.A. (1984) Psychometric Properties and Underlying Assumptions of Four Objective Measures of Fear of Success. *Sex Roles* **10** (9/10): 765–81.

Parker, R. (1984) *The Subversive Stitch*. London: The Women's Press.

Parker, R. (1985) Images of Men. In S. Kent and J. Morreau (eds) *Women's Images of Men*. London: Writers & Readers Publishing Cooperative.

Parsons, T. (1964) *Social Structure and Personality*. New York: Free Press.

Peck, E. and Senderowitz, J. (1974) *Pronatalism: The Myth of Mom and Apple Pie*. New York: Thomas Y. Crowell.

Pedersen, F.A. and Bell, R.Q. (1970) Sex Differences in Preschool Children Without Histories of Complications of Pregnancy and Delivery. *Developmental Psychology* **3**: 10–15.

Pedhazur, E.J. and Tetenbaum, T.J. (1979) Bem Sex Role Inventory: A Theoretical and Methodological Critique. *Journal of Personality and Social Psychology* **37** (6): 996–1016.

Perry, D.G. and Bussey, L. (1979) The Social Learning Theory of Sex Differences: Imitation is Alive and Well. *Journal of Personality and Social Psychology* **37**: 1699–712.

Peters, U.H. (1985) *Anna Freud: A Life Dedicated to Children*. London: Weidenfeld.

Philipson, I. (1982a) Narcissism and Mothering: The 1950s Reconsidered. *Women's Studies International Forum* **5** (1): 29–40.

Philipson, I. (1982b) Heterosexual Antagonisms in the Politics of Mothering. *Socialist Review* **12** (6): 55–77.

Piaget, J. (1932) *The Moral Judgement of the Child*. Translated by Marjorie Gabain. Harmondsworth: Penguin. 1977.

Pilbeam, D. (1973) An Idea We Could Live Without: The Naked Ape. In A. Montagu (ed.) *Man and Aggression*. New York: Oxford University Press.

Pingree, S. (1978) The Effects of Nonsexist Television Commercials and Perceptions of Reality on Children's Attitudes About Women. *Psychology of Women Quarterly* **2** (3): 262–77.

Powell, G.N. and Butterfield, D.A. (1984) If 'Good Managers' Are Masculine, What Are 'Bad Managers'? *Sex Roles* **10** (7/8): 477–84.

Prutzman, P. (1982) Assertiveness, Nonviolence and Feminism. In P. McAllister (ed.) *Reweaving the Web of Life: Feminism and Nonviolence*. New Society Publishers.

Rachman, S.J. and Wilson, G.T. (1980) *The Effects of Psychological Therapy*. Oxford: Pergamon.

Rada, R.T., Laws, D.R., and Kellner, R. (1976) Plasma Testosterone Levels in the Rapist. *Psychosomatic Medicine* **38**: 257–68.

Rada, R.T., Laws, D.R., Kellner, R., Stivastava, L., and Peake, G. (1983) Plasma Androgens in Violent and Nonviolent Sex Offenders. *Bulletin of the American Academy of Psychiatry and the Law* **11** (2): 149–58.

Ramas, M. (1980) Freud's Dora, Dora's Hysteria: The Negation of a Woman's Rebellion. *Feminist Studies* **6** (3): 472–510.

Raps, C.S., Peterson, C., Reinhard, K.E., Abramson, C.Y., and Seligman, M.E.P. (1982) Attributional Style Among Depressed Patients. *Journal of Abnormal Psychology* **91**: 102–08.

Rich, A. (1975) *Adrienne Rich's Poetry*. Selected and edited by B.C. Gelpi and A. Gelpi. New York: Norton.

Rich, A. (1976) *Of Woman Born: Motherhood as Experience and Institution*. New York: Bantam Books. 1977.

Rich, A. (1977) Mother Right. *The Dream of a Common Language: Poems 1974–1977*. New York: Norton. 1978.

Rich. A. (1980) Compulsory Heterosexuality and Lesbian Existence. *Signs* **5** (4): 631–60.

Richman, N. (1974) The Effects of Housing on Pre-School Children and Their Mothers. *Developmental Medicine and Child Neurology* **16**: 53–8.

Riley, D. (1983) *War in the Nursery*. London: Virago.

Robinson, S. (1984) The Art of the Possible. *Free Associations* (Pilot Issue): 122–48.

Rose, J. (1982) Introduction. In J. Mitchell and J. Rose (eds) *Feminine Sexuality*. London: Macmillan.

Rose, J. (1983) Feminine Sexuality: Interview – 1982. *m/f* **8**: 3–16.

Rose, R.M., Gordon, T.P., and Bernstein, I.S. (1972) Plasma Testosterone Levels in the Male Rhesus: Influences of Sexual and Social Stimuli. *Science* **178**: 643–45.

Rosenow, J. and O'Leary, M. (1975) Locus of Control. Research on Alcoholic Populations: A Review. *International Journal of Addictions* **13** (1): 551–78.

Rossi, A. (1973) *The Feminist Papers*. New York: Bantam.

Rotter, J.B. (1966) Generalized Expectancies for Internal Versus External Control of Reinforcement. *Psychological Monographs* **80** (609): Whole Number.

Rowbotham, S. (1972) *Women, Resistance and Revolution*. New York, Vintage Books.

Rowbotham, S. (1973a) *Hidden From History*. London: Pluto Press.

Rowbotham, S. (1973b) *Woman's Consciousness, Man's World*. Harmondsworth: Penguin.

Rowell, T.E. (1966) Forest Living Baboons in Uganda. *Journal of Zoology* **149**: 344–64.

Rowell, T.E. (1974) The Concept of Social Dominance. *Behavioural Biology* **11**: 131–54.

Rowland, R. (1984) *Women Who Do and Women Who Don't Join the Women's Movement*. London: Routledge & Kegan Paul.

Rubin, G. (1975) The Traffic in Women: Notes on the 'Political Economy' of Sex. In R. Reiter (ed.) *Toward an Anthropology of Women*. New York: Monthly Review Press.

Rubin, G. (1984) Thinking Sex: Notes for a Radical Theory of the Politics of Sexuality. In C.S. Vance (ed.) *Pleasure and Danger: Exploring Female Sexuality*. London: Routledge & Kegan Paul.

Rubin, L.B. (1983) *Intimate Strangers*. London: Fontana.

Ruddick, S. (1980) Maternal Thinking. *Feminist Studies* **6** (2): 342–67.

Ruehl, S. (1982) Inverts and Experts: Radclyffe Hall and the Lesbian Identity. In R. Brunt and C. Rowan (eds) *Feminism, Culture and Politics*. London: Lawrence & Wishart.

Russell, G. (1985) Narcissism and the Narcissistic Personality Disorder. A Comparison of the Theories of Kernberg and Kohut. *British Journal of Medical Psychology* **58** (2): 137–48.

Rustin, M. (1982) A Socialist Consideration of Kleinian Psychoanalysis. *New Left Review* **131**: 71–96.

Rustin, M. (1983) Kleinian Psychoanalysis and the Theory of Culture. In F. Barker, P. Hulme, M. Iversen, and D. Loxley (eds) *The Politics of Theory*. Colchester: University of Essex.

Ryan, J. (1983a) Psychoanalysis and Women Loving Women. In S. Cartledge and J. Ryan (eds) *Sex and Love*. London: The Women's Press.

Ryan, J. (1983b) Feminism and Therapy. The Pam Smith Memorial Lecture. London: Department of Applied Social Studies, The Polytechnic of North London.

Safouan, M. (1975) Feminine Sexuality in Psychoanalytic Doctrine. In J. Mitchell and J. Rose (eds) *Feminine Sexuality*. London: Macmillan. 1982.

Sartre, J.-P. (1944) *Being and Nothingness*. Translated by Hazel Barnes. New York: Washington Square Press.

Saunders, J.B. de C.M. and O'Malley, D. (1950) *The Illustrations From the Works* of Andreas Vesalius of Brussels. Cleveland and New York: World Publishing Company.

Saxton, M. (1981) Are Women More Moral than Men? An Interview with Psychologist Carol Gilligan. *Ms* (December): 63–6.

Sayers, J. (1982) *Biological Politics: Feminist and Anti-Feminist Perspectives.* London: Tavistock.

Sayers, J. (1983) Is the Personal Political? Psychoanalysis and Feminism Revisited. *International Journal of Women's Studies* 6 (1): 71–86.

Sayers, J. (1984a) Psychology and Gender Divisions. In S. Acker, J. Megarry, S. Nisbet, and E. Hoyle (eds) *World Yearbook of Education 1984: Women and Education.* London: Kogan Page.

Sayers, J. (1984b) Feminism and Mothering: A Kleinian Perspective. *Women's Studies International Forum* 7 (4): 237–41.

Sayers, J. (1985a) Sexual Contradictions: On Freud, Psychoanalysis and Feminism. *Free Associations* 1: 76–104.

Sayers, J. (1985b) For Engels: Psycho-Analytic Perspectives. Unpublished manuscript.

Sayers, J. (in press) Science, Sexual Difference, and Feminism. In B.B. Hess and M.M. Ferree (eds) *Women and Society: Social Science Perspectives.* Beverly Hills: Sage.

Sayers, S. (1973) Mental Illness as a Moral Concept. *Radical Philosophy* 5: 2–8.

Sayers, S. (1985) *Reality and Reason: Dialectic and the Theory of Knowledge.* Oxford: Blackwell.

Schneiderman, S. (1983) *Jacques Lacan: The Death of an Intellectual Hero.* Cambridge: Harvard University Press.

Schreiner, O. (1927) *From Man to Man.* New York: Harper & Row.

Scott, J. and Tilly, L. (1975) Women's Work and the Family in Nineteenth-Century Europe. In E. Whitelegg *et al.* (eds) *The Changing Experience of Women.* Oxford: Martin Robertson. 1982.

Segal, H. (1973) *Introduction to the Work of Melanie Klein.* London: Hogarth.

Seller, A. (1985) Greenham: A Concrete Reality. *Journal of Applied Philosophy* 2 (1): 133–41.

Sharpe, S. (1976) *'Just like a Girl': How Girls Learn to be Women.* Harmondsworth: Penguin.

Showalter, E. (1977) *A Literature of their Own: British Women Novelists from Brontë to Lessing.* Princeton: Princeton University Press.

Simmonds, P. (1985) A Kind of Liberation. *The Guardian* (6 May): 6.

Smetana, J.G. and Letourneau, K.J. (1984) Development of Gender Constancy and Children's Sex-Typed Free Play Behavior. *Developmental Psychology* 20 (4): 691–96.

Smith, C. and Lloyd, B. (1978) Maternal Behaviour and Perceived Sex of Infant: Revisited. *Child Development* 49: 1263–265.

Smith, P. (1974) Aggression in a Preschool Playgroup: Effects of Varying Physical Resources. In J. de Wit and W.W. Hartup (eds) *Determinants and*

Origins of Aggressive Behavior. The Hague: Mouton.

Smith, P.K. and Connolly, K. (1972) Patterns of Play and Social Interaction in Pre-School Children. In N. Blurton Jones (ed.) *Ethological Studies of Child Behaviour*. London: Cambridge University Press.

Smith, P.K. and Green, M. (1975) Aggressive Behavior in English Nurseries and Play Groups: Sex Differences and Response of Adults. *Child Development* **46**: 211–14.

Spence, J. (1984) Masculinity, Femininity, and Gender-Related Traits: A Conceptual Analysis and Critique of Current Research. In B.A. Maher and W.B. Maher (eds) *Progress in Experimental Personality Research* **13**: 1–97.

Spender, D. (1980) *Man Made Language*. London: Routledge & Kegan Paul.

Stayt, Y. (1984) Taking Sides. BBC Radio 4 broadcast (8 November).

Sternglanz, S.H. and Serbin, L.A. (1974) Sex Role Stereotyping in Children's Television Programs. *Developmental Psychology* **10** (5): 710–15.

Stone, L. (1979) *The Family, Sex and Marriage in England: 1500–1800*. Harmondsworth: Penguin.

Strachey, R. (1928) *The Cause*. London: Virago. 1979.

Strange, P. (1983) *It'll Make a Man of You: A Feminist View of the Arms Race*. Nottingham: Mushroom Books/Peace News.

Symonds, A. (1973) Phobias After Marriage: Women's Declaration of Dependence. In J.B. Miller (ed.) *Psychoanalysis and Women*. Harmondsworth: Penguin.

Taylor, B. (1983) *Eve and the New Jerusalem*. London: Virago.

Temperley, J. (1984) Our Own Worst Enemies: Unconscious Factors in Female Disadvantage. *Free Associations* (Pilot Issue): 2–28.

Thompson, S.K. (1975) Gender Labels and Early Sex Role Development. *Child Development* **46**: 339–47.

Thompson, S.K. and Bentler, P.M. (1973) A Developmental Study of Gender Constancy and Parent Preference. *Archives of Sexual Behavior* **2** (4): 379–85.

Tieger, T. (1980) On the Biological Basis of Sex Differences in Aggression. *Child Development* **51**: 943–63.

Timpanaro, S. (1974) *The Freudian Slip*. Translated by Kate Soper. London: New Left Books. 1976.

Tinsley, E.G., Sullivan-Guest, S., and McGuire, J.M. (1984) Feminine Sex Role and Depression in Middle-Aged Women. *Sex Roles* **11** (1/2): 25–32.

Turner, R.M., Giles, T.R., and Marafiote, R. (1983) Agoraphobics: A Test of the Repression Hypothesis. *British Journal of Clinical Psychology* **22**: 75–6.

Uglow, J. (1983) Out of the Sick Bed into the Swim of Things. *The Guardian* (25 March): 11.

Ullian, D.Z. (1984) 'Why Girls are Good': A Constructivist View. *Sex Roles* **11** (3/4): 241–56.

Ullian, D.Z. (1976) The Development of Conceptions of Masculinity and Femininity. In B.B. Lloyd and J. Archer (eds) *Exploring Sex Differences*. London: Academic Press.

Ullian, D.Z. (1977) The Development of Conceptions of Masculinity and Femininity. Unpublished Ph.D. thesis. Cambridge: Harvard University.

Urwin, C. (1984) Power Relations and the Emergence of Language. In J. Henriques, W. Hollway, C. Urwin, C. Venn, and V. Walkerdine *Changing the Subject: Psychology, Social Regulation and Subjectivity*. London: Methuen.

Vogel, L. (1983) *Marxism and the Oppression of Women*. London: Pluto Press.

Walker, L.J. (1984) Sex Differences in the Development of Moral Reasoning: A Critical Review. *Child Development* **55**: 677–91.

Walkerdine, V. (1985) Science and the Female Mind: The Burden of Proof. *Psych Critique* **1** (1): 1–20.

Walkerdine, V. (in press) *The Master of Reason*. London: Methuen.

Walkowitz, J. (1982) Male Vice and Feminist Virtue: Feminism and the Politics of Prostitution in Nineteenth-Century Britain. *History Workshop* **13**: 79–93.

Walters, M. (1976) The Rights and Wrongs of Women: Mary Wollstonecroft, Harriet Martineau, Simone de Beauvoir. In A. Oakley and J. Mitchell (eds) *The Rights and Wrongs of Women*. Harmondsworth: Penguin.

Webster, C. (1981) *Biology, Medicine and Society 1840–1940*. Cambridge: Cambridge University Press.

Weeks, J. (1981) *Sex, Politics and Society*. London: Longman.

Weeks, J. (1982) Foucault for Historians. *History Workshop* **14**: 106–19.

Weeks, J. (1985) Psychoanalysis and the 'Perverse': Theoretical and Historical Perspectives. London History Workshop seminars.

Weir, A. and Wilson, E. (1984) The British Women's Movement. *New Left Review* **148** (November–December): 74–103.

Weir, J. (1895) The Effect of Female Suffrage on Posterity. *American Naturalist* **29**: 815–25.

Weissman, M.M. and Klerman, G.L. (1981) Sex Differences and the Epidemiology of Depression. In E. Howell and M. Bayes (eds) *Women and Mental Health*. New York: Basic Books.

Weitzman, L.J., Eifler, D., Hokada, E., and Ross, C. (1976) Sex-Role Socialization in Picture Books for Preschool Children. In Children's Rights Workshop (eds) *Sexism in Children's Books; Facts, Figures and Guidelines*. London: Writers & Readers Publishing Cooperative.

Whiting, B. and Edwards, C.P. (1973) A Cross-Cultural Analysis of Sex Differences in the Behavior of Children Aged 3 Through 11. *Journal of Social Psychology* **91**: 171–88.

Wilby, P. (1985) Boys are Best. *The Sunday Times* (17 March): 37.

Wilden, A. (1972) *System and Structure: Essays in Communication and Exchange*. London: Tavistock.

Williamson, J. (1978) *Decoding Advertisements: Ideology and Meaning in Advertisements*. London: Marion Boyars.

Wilson, E. (1983) *What is to be Done About Violence Against Women?* Harmondsworth: Penguin.

Wilson, E. (1984) Forbidden Love. *Feminist Studies* **10** (2): 213–26.

Wilson, E.O. (1975) *Sociobiology: The New Synthesis*. Cambridge: Harvard University Press.

Winnicott, D.W. (1945) Primitive Emotional Development. *Collected Papers*. London: Tavistock. 1958.

Winnicott, D.W. (1956) Primary Maternal Preoccupation. *Collected Papers*. London: Tavistock. 1958.

Winnicott, D.W. (1960) Ego Distortion in Terms of True and False Self. *The Maturational Processes and the Facilitating Environment*. London: Hogarth. 1972.

Winnicott, D.W. (1965) *The Family and Individual Development*. London: Tavistock.

Winnicott, D.W. (1971) *Playing and Reality*. Harmondsworth: Penguin. 1974.

Wittig, A.F. (1984) Sport Competition Anxiety and Sex Role. *Sex Roles* **10** (5/6): 469–73.

Wollstonecraft, M. (1792) *A Vindication of the Rights of Woman*. Harmondsworth: Penguin. 1975.

Woolf, V. (1938) *Three Guineas*. London: Hogarth.

Young, W.C., Goy, R.W., and Phoenix, C.H. (1964) Hormones and Sexual Behavior. *Science* **143**: 212–18.

Name index

Abel, E. 84
Abraham, K. 143
Alexander, S. 91–2, 99, 111
Andreas-Salomé, L. 101
Andrews, J.G.W. 155
Angelou, M. 174
Anyon, J. 118, 178
Aquinas, T. 86
Archer, C.J. 26
Archer, J. 26, 100
Aristotle, 86
Astell, M. 3, 176
Austen, J. 170–71

Bandura, A. 24, 26
Barrett, M. 89, 94
Barrett Browning, E. 124
Bartlett, F.H. 125
Beck, A.T. 142
Beckwith, J. 18
Bell, R.Q. 6
Bem, S. 28–9, 93
Benjamin, J. 72–5
Bernays, M. 101
Bernheim, H. 122
Bernstein, I.S. 11
Betterton, R. 106
Bingham, S. 29, 171
Bion, W.R. 105, 160–61
Birch, H.G. 10
Birke, L. 11
Birnbaum, D.W. 25

Blackwell, E. 127
Blake, W. 49, 131, 154
Blakeman, J. 13
Blanchard, K.H. 29
Bleier, R. 10
Blurton Jones, N. 6
Bogdanovich, P. 152
Boswell, S.L. 18
Bott Spillius, E. 161
Bourne, G. 28
Brenner, J. 5
Breuer, J. 121–22
Bronte, C. 170, 176–77
Brook, E. 178
Broughton, J.M. 19, 70
Broverman, I.K. 118
Brown, G. 141
Brunswick, R.M. 85
Buck, C. 45–6
Buss, F.M. 177

Campbell, B. 5, 27, 64, 148, 150, 178
Cano, L. 28, 29
Caplan, C. 124, 173
Carlson, H.M. 29
Chasin, B. 10
Chasseguet-Smirgel, J. 37
Chesler, P. 138
Chodorow, N. 64, 67–77, 79–80
Chudleigh, M. 176
Cline, S. 44, 93

Cloward, R.A. 179
Cobb, N.J. 25
Cohn, N. 60
Coker, D.R. 14
Coleridge, S.T. 142
Collins, L.J. 25
Comfort, A. 129
Conran, S. 73
Coote, A. 27, 178
Cott, N. 43
Cotter, N. 168
Coward, R. 27, 85, 94
Crawfurd, H. 177

Damon, W. 27
Davidoff, L. 155
Davies, E. 20
Davies, H.A. 155
Davies, M. Llewellyn, 5, 148
Davis, A.J. 25
Deaux, K. 154
de Beauvoir, S. 23, 74, 92, 128,
    171–72
Delamont, S. 129
de Saussure, F. 79, 86
Descartes, R. 83
de Vore, I. 7
Dickson, A. 30
Dinnerstein, D. 49, 57–8, 60, 62–3,
    99
Dixon, B. 25
Dodge, K.A. 8
Doolittle, H. 45–6, 170
Doyal, L. 178
Drummond, M. 178
Durkin, J. 18
Durkin, K. 25, 28, 93
Dusek, V. 11
Dworkin, A. 150, 173

Eccles (Parsons), J. 18
Ehrenreich, B. 20, 168
Ehrensaft, D. 178
Ehrhardt, A.A. 9, 10

Eichenbaum, L. 144–45, 178
Eisenberg, N. 14
Eisenstein, Z. 93, 95
Eisenstock, B. 25
Eliot, G. 170
Ellis, S. 170
Elpern, S. 29
Engels, F. 5, 36, 134
Ernst, S. 178
Evans, M. 171
Evans, R.G. 29

Fagot, B.I. 27
Fairbairn, W.R.D. 64–6, 68
Fee, E. 178
Ferenczi, S. 123
Finch, J. 178
Fisher, M. 155
Flax, J. 73
Flerx, V.C. 26
Fliess, E. 125–26
Ford, I. 175
Foreit, K.G. 25
Foucault, M. 46, 105, 118
Franken, M.W. 26
Fraser, A. 170
Freud, A. 101
Freud, S. ix–x, 13, 22, 37–8, 40,
    45, 49–50, 65, 67, 76–82, 85–6,
    90, 94–5, 100–17, 119–37, 139–
    44, 151–56, 162, 173, 178–80
Frieze, I.H. 154
Fromm, E. 57

Gallop, J. 84
Garrett Anderson, E. 20, 174
Garrison, D. 40
Geis, F.L. 25
Gillick, V. 73
Gilligan, C. 18–20, 70, 72–3, 75
Gilman, C. Perkins 121
Glover, E. 80
Goldberg, S. 9
Goldman, E. 167

Goodstein, R.K. 154
Graydon, J. 21
Greenberg, J.R. 68
Griffin, S. 60
Grünbaum, A. 122
Guntrip, H. 139

Hafner, R.J. 154
Hall, C. 155, 170
Hall, Radclyffe M. 171
Harris, B.J. 43, 87, 176
Harris, O. 59
Hartsock, N. 72
Hedges, E.R. 121
Hegel, G.W.F. 74
Heiser, P. 29
Herik, J. van 88
Hinshelwood, R.D. 157
Hirshfeld, M.A. 141
Holland, S. 148
Hollis, P. 20, 170, 172, 175
Hollway, W. 151
Horner, M.S. 28
Horney, K. 36–42, 48, 62–3, 65, 79–80, 99
Housman, J. 72
Hudson, B. 118
Hutt, C. 4, 9
Hyde, J.S. 7, 13

Ingleby, D. 179
Irigaray, L. 42–9, 79
Isard, J. 154

Jaggar, A. 157
Johnson, L.B. 12
Johnson, S. 35
Johnston, J. 85
Jones, A.R. 172
Jones, E. 101, 124
Joseph, B. 162
Joslyn, W.D. 10
Jung, C.G. 95

Kagan, J. 15
Kalisch, P.A. 25
Kaplan, E.A. 106
Keane, M. 170
Keller, E.F. 18, 72–3, 75
Kernberg, O. 82
Kerr, M. 5
Klein, M. 49–63, 64–5, 67, 72, 79–80, 82, 105, 119, 136, 143–47, 156–62
Knight, J. 28
Koblinsky, S.A. 26
Kohlberg, L. 12–22, 37
Kohut, H. 41, 68, 82
Krafft-Ebbing, R. von 28, 124
Kreuz, L.E. 10
Kristeva, J. 92, 171
Kuhn, D. 13

Lacan, J. 43–7, 78–95, 99, 132
Laing, R.D. 67
Lampl de Groot, J. 108
Langlois, J.H. 27
Laplanche, J. 103
Lasch, C. 41
Lawrence, M. 127
le Doeuff, M. 74, 172
Lemaire, A. 88
Lenin, V.I. 30
Lermontov, M.Y. 139
Lerner, L. 71
Lévi-Strauss, C. 86, 90
Lewin, M. 135
Lewis, C. 71
Lewis, J. 5, 92
Lewis, M. 13
Linton, E. 20, 170
Lloyd, B. 7, 26
Lloyd, G. 72
Lorber, J. 71
Louden, A. 59
Lowe, M. 11

McClintock, B. 73

Maccoby, E.E. 3–11
McGhee, P.E. 25
McIntyre, A. 6
McKenna, J.J. 8
Macpherson, C.B. 83
Mahler, M. 68
Maisner, P. 127
Malcolm, J. 125, 131
Marcus, D. 14
Marcus, S. 131
Marcuse, H. 83
Martin, N.K. 8
Martineau, H. 171–72
Marx, K. 180
Masson, J.M. 125
Meltzer, D. 94, 161
Menzies, I. 60
Merchant, C. 59
Merk, M. 111, 132
Michael, R.P. 10
Michalowski, H. 12
Milavsky, J.R. 24
Mill, J.S. 101, 120, 174
Miller, J.B. 150
Millot, C. 134
Mischel, W. 23–4, 26
Mitchell, J. 38, 82, 86, 88–9, 91–2, 95, 176
Moi, T. 132, 152
More, H. 168
Morgan, K.P. 29
Morgan, M. 168
Mulvey, L. 106

New, C. 178
Newton, E. 128, 171
Nicholson, J. 11, 18
Nightingale, F. 129, 138–39, 142, 172

Oakley, A. 59
Oatley, K. 142
O'Connell, A.N. 41
Omark, D.R. 4

Ophuijsen, J.H.W. van 106

Pahl, J. 152, 178
Paludi, M.A. 28
Parker, R. 60, 170
Parsons, T. 70
Peck, E. 27
Pedersen, F.A. 6
Pedhazur, E.J. 28
Perry, D.G. 24
Peters, U.H. 101
Philipson, I. 71, 178
Piaget, J. 55
Pilbeam, D. 8
Pingree, S. 25
Pizzey, E. 73
Popp, A. 173
Prutzman, P. 30

Rachman, S.J. 179
Rada, R.T. 10–11
Ramas, M. 5, 132
Raps, C.S. 140
Rich, A. 35–6, 41–2, 44, 46–9, 63, 73
Richman, N. 141
Riley, D. 71–2
Rilke, R.M. 35
Robinson, S. 180
Rose, J. 92, 105
Rose, R.M. 10, 11
Rosenow, J. 154
Rossi, A. 124, 127
Rotter, J.B. 153
Rowbotham, S. 35, 38, 89, 170, 173, 175, 177
Rowell, T.E. 8
Rowland, R. 168
Rubin, G. 89–91, 157
Rubin, L.B. 71
Ruddick, S. 72
Ruehl, S. 47
Russell, G. 82
Rustin, M. 60, 161
Ryan, J. 72, 178

Safouan, M. 85
Sartre, J.-P. 85, 128
Saunders, J.B. de C.M. 87
Saxton, M. 19
Sayers, J. 3, 26, 46, 60, 72, 102–03,
    128, 139, 178
Sayers, S. 95, 125, 180
Schlafly, P. 168
Schneiderman, S. 83
Schreiner, O. 173–74
Scott, J. 83
Segal, H. 144–46, 159–60
Seller, A. 148
Shakespeare, W. 37
Sharpe, S. 25
Showalter, E. 176
Simmonds, P. 21
Smetana, J.G. 16
Smith, C. 7
Smith, P. 6–7
Spence, J. 29
Spender, D. 44
Stayt, Y. 3
Sternglanz, S.H. 25
Stone, Lawrence, 175–76
Stone, Lucy 124
Strachey, R. 20, 142, 170, 177
Strange, P. 12
Stratton, D.R. 152
Symonds, A. 154, 158

Taylor, B. 176
Temperley, J. 60, 157
Thompson, S.K. 13–14
Tieger, T. 4
Timpanaro, S. 123
Tinsley, E.G. 29

Tolstoy, L. 152
Trollope, A. 68
Turner, R.M. 155

Uglow, J. 129
Ullian, D. 15–17, 158
Urwin, C. 68, 75, 105

Vesalius, A. 87
Vogel, L. 30, 178

Walker, L.J. 19
Walkerdine, V. 72, 139
Walkowitz, J. 175
Walters, M. 172
Webb, B. 172
Webster, C. 129
Weeks, J. 47, 94, 118
Weir, A. 167
Weir, J. 20
Weir Mitchell, S. 121
Weissman, M.M. 142
Weitzman, L.J. 25
Whiting, B. 4
Wilby, P. 28
Wilden, A. 88
Williamson, J. 84
Wilson, E. 47, 128, 167, 178
Wilson, E.O. 7
Winnicott, D.W. 57–8, 66–71, 77,
    94, 118
Wittig, A.F. 29
Wollstonecraft, M. 176
Woolf, V. 176

Young, W.C. 9

Subject index

activity 20, 27, 40–2, 47–8, 75, 83–7, 90–3, 104–08, 111–12, 114, 118–19, 124, 134–36, 138–39, 142, 148, 155–56, 167–71

agency 75, 83–6, 92, 118, 155–56, 168; *see also* activity

aggression 3–4, 6–13, 16–17, 24–8, 50–7, 66, 113, 118, 142, 154, 157–60

agoraphobia 127, 150, 154–56, 158

ambivalence: *see* hate, love

anaclesis 104

anality 50–3, 81, 85, 103–06

androgyny 28–9, 90

anger 25, 140–44, 146–48, 154, 157–59

Anna O. 121

anorexia 127

anti-feminism 20, 59–60, 168

anxiety 15, 18, 20, 36–7, 39–40, 50–3, 56–7, 60, 82, 114–15, 127, 143–46, 154–60; night-time 52–3; persecutory 50–1, 57, 145, 159

assertiveness 3, 22, 28–30, 69, 75, 167, 170

attribution 150, 154

autism 68, 82

autoerotism (e.g. thumb-sucking) 42–3, 53, 86, 103–04, 125

autonomy 23, 68, 74–6, 154, 175; *see also* independence

battered women 5, 130, 152, 174, 177–78

bisexuality 40, 131–33, 136

breast 49–51, 62, 66, 80–1, 86, 103–04, 146

capitalism 30, 83–4, 89, 91, 95

caring 19–20, 47, 55, 58, 76–7, 106–07, 125–26, 129–30, 145, 167, 175

castration 85–8, 107–09, 113–14, 116, 119, 133–35

catharsis 120–21

cathexis 81, 109–10, 141, 143–44

childbearing 3, 5–6, 28, 35, 37, 42, 102, 124, 177

childcare 4–5, 37, 57–8, 62–3, 66, 70–5, 94, 102, 167, 177–78; *see also* caring

class 5, 89, 102, 121, 127, 129, 141, 155, 174–78

clitoris 156

collective action 42, 47, 92, 94, 118, 136, 147–48, 174–76, 181

condensation 86

consciousness x, 36, 39, 65, 67, 74, 77, 82, 93–4, 100, 102, 107, 109–10, 112, 114–19, 121–26, 130–31, 135–37, 144, 152, 155, 158, 162, 168, 179–81

contempt 56, 60

denigration 13–14, 37–8, 42, 51, 56, 58, 60

dependence 20, 41, 46, 56–7, 60, 68, 73–6, 93, 123, 144, 150–51, 154

depression 29, 50, 56–7, 60, 119, 136, 138–49, 150, 156, 158, 180

desire 39–40, 42–3, 53, 82, 85–7, 89–91, 108–17, 122–23, 125–35, 142, 151, 153, 155–56, 163, 168, 171, 173, 180; *see also* wish

disavowal 115

discrimination 38, 41, 94, 167–68, 172

displacement 86, 127, 153–55

dominance ix, 3–11, 15–17, 26, 30–1, 35–6, 38, 40, 49, 57–8, 62–3, 73, 89, 111, 118, 130

Dora 103, 115, 126–27, 130–32

dreams 43, 80, 90, 95, 101–03, 107–08, 110, 115–17, 121, 126, 130, 145, 155, 158–59, 173; nightmares 52, 180

dress 14–15, 21, 102, 104, 106, 170–71

eating 51–2, 54–5, 59–60, 104, 123, 127, 144

ego 13, 50, 64–8, 80–2, 104, 113, 119, 122, 124–25, 134–36, 143, 156, 158, 180; psychology 41, 68, 80, 82–3; splitting of 64–7, 82, 160

Elisabeth von R. 122–23

Emmy von N. 76–8

empathy 19, 40, 65, 73, 76–7

envy 35–41, 51, 53–8, 60, 62, 88, 160, 162, 173

essentialism 31, 41–8, 79

Eve 3, 18, 58, 65, 87, 178

exhibitionism 39, 81, 105

faeces 53, 81, 103

father 14–15, 39–40, 45, 53–5, 60–

2, 75, 85–8, 95, 105, 108–09, 113–15, 126–27, 131–32, 134–35, 139–40, 171

femininity 4, 7, 12–13, 20–3, 25, 27–9, 31, 38–41, 43–8, 59, 69, 70, 76–7, 88, 95, 101, 104, 106–08, 111–14, 119, 124, 139, 155, 161–62, 168, 170

fixation 134–35, 180

food 5, 8, 54–5, 59–60, 81, 102, 104

fort-da 105, 133

free association 116–17, 122, 124, 145, 179

frustration 12, 24, 48, 50–1, 65, 67, 133, 140–42, 144, 146–48, 154, 159, 162, 168

gender ix, 11, 13–18, 20–8, 30–1, 36, 70, 75, 79–80, 90, 113; constancy 14, 16, 21; identity 13, 69–70, 91; *see also* femininity, masculinity

genitals 29, 37–9, 42, 50–1, 81, 87, 106–07, 109–10, 114, 116–17, 173

gratification 39, 48, 50, 55, 65, 67, 80, 85, 104, 108–10, 112–14, 118–19, 128–31, 133–35, 153, 155–56, 168

guilt 29, 39, 109, 140, 145

hallucination 66, 80, 86, 110, 114–18, 127–28, 131, 133, 143, 180; *see also* primary process

hate 50, 56–7, 60–2, 65–7, 82, 110–11, 127, 141, 143, 147, 150

helplessness 123, 142, 154, 157

heterosexuality 39, 90–1, 102, 131–33

homosexuality 12, 28, 39, 90, 94, 131–33; *see also* lesbianism

hypnosis 121–22, 124, 136

hysteria 44, 46, 51, 76, 120–25, 127

id 82, 134
idealization 37, 42, 51, 53–4, 56,
    58–60, 62, 82
identification 47, 66, 69–72, 75,
    80–2, 84–8, 92–3, 108, 112, 116,
    130, 132, 134, 143, 158; projec-
    tive 160–62
ideology 36, 76, 83–4, 88–9, 92–3,
    95, 111, 155
illusion x, 46, 68, 82–4, 93, 113,
    129–30, 153, 157, 161, 180
imaginary 44, 46, 80–2, 87–8, 94
incest 40, 109, 114, 116, 118, 125–
    27, 134–35
independence 28, 56–8, 60, 68, 73–
    7, 95, 118, 151, 154, 171, 175
individualism 19, 48, 72, 76–7, 83–
    4, 88, 118–19, 136, 147, 172,
    174, 179–81
instincts 63, 65, 67; component 50,
    81, 143; Death 62, 133–34; ego
    104; Life 62, 133–34; sexual 50,
    81, 103–04
interpretation x, 61, 82, 135, 144–
    46, 152, 158–61, 179
introjection x, 50, 65, 82, 119, 136,
    138–41, 143–44, 146–47, 158,
    161

jealousy 110, 126, 151–53
jokes 21, 27, 30, 102, 139, 153

Katharina 124
kinship 83, 88–90

language 42–5, 47, 82–3, 86–8, 91–
    5, 105
lesbianism 47, 73, 85, 91, 93, 111,
    132, 171; *see also* homosexuality
liberation 20, 46, 94, 101, 167, 173,
    178, 180
libido 85, 95, 104, 133–35, 141
Little Hans 105–09
locus of control 153–54

loss 56, 140–46, 154, 158
love 50, 54, 56–7, 60, 62, 67, 73,
    82–3, 90, 93, 110–11, 126, 140–
    44, 147, 156

mania 56, 60
marriage 9, 28, 71, 85–6, 93, 101,
    107, 112, 123–24, 127–29, 148,
    154, 177
masculinity 12–13, 16, 20–1, 23–5,
    27–9, 31, 36, 38–41, 45, 47, 69, 72,
    88, 104, 106, 110–14, 117–19, 136,
    138–39, 168, 170–72
masochism 39, 41, 47, 91, 108–09,
    112–13
masturbation 39, 85, 107–09, 114
mergence 65–6, 69–72, 74–7, 82
mirror 43, 68, 82; stage 81–2,
    84–6; *see also* imaginary
morality 16–20, 29, 55, 72, 130,
    138, 168–69
mother 14–15, 26, 35–9, 41, 45–6,
    49–62, 65–75, 77, 80–1, 85–8,
    90, 93, 95, 104–09, 111, 114–17,
    126, 128, 141–42, 145, 161–62
mourning 138–40, 146–47
mythology 58, 60, 81, 95, 126

narcissism 39, 65, 68, 81–2, 85,
    109–10, 113, 118–19, 141–43, 173
negative therapeutic reaction 134
neurosis 29, 39–41, 55, 77, 102–03,
    114–17, 119–37, 138, 141, 143,
    179–80

objects 39, 80, 103–04, 114, 133,
    140, 143–44, 155, 157; bad 50–
    1, 64–5; good 50, 56, 64–5, 82,
    146–47; external 51, 141, 156;
    internal 51, 140, 146; part 50,
    56, 81; whole 50, 56, 81, 109
obsessions 52, 55, 103, 114, 116–
    17, 127, 152
Oedipus 39–40, 44–6, 79–80, 85,

87–90, 95, 101, 126, 134
omnipotence 56–7, 68
orality 44, 49–52, 80–1, 85, 104, 127, 131–32, 143

pain 41–2, 57, 60, 105, 108, 113, 123, 133, 136, 144, 150, 160
paranoia 50, 58, 119, 149–50, 156, 158, 180
parapraxes (e.g. slips of tongue) 102, 123
passivity 23, 39–43, 47, 75, 85, 90, 104–08, 111–14, 119, 134–36, 142, 168, 176
patriarchy 86–9, 91–2, 95; *see also* father
penis 37–9, 41, 45, 62, 81, 85, 90, 102, 106–09, 111, 114, 117, 135–36, 173
phallus 45, 81, 85–8, 90, 107, 109, 114, 116–19
phantasy 36–7, 39, 49–51, 53, 55, 57, 60–2, 92–3, 95, 108, 125–26, 131–33, 145, 147, 160, 179–80
phobias 52, 114, 154; *see also* agoraphobia
pleasure 41–4, 46, 56, 102–08, 112, 119, 133, 144; principle 133, 143, 180
pornography 60, 175
power 35, 41, 44, 58, 87, 138, 147–48, 151, 157, 180
pregnancy 53, 107, 112; *see also* childbearing
primal scene 111–12
primary: gain 129, 133, 155; narcissism 65; process 80, 86, 110, 115–16
projection x, 29, 50, 51, 54–5, 110, 119, 136, 143, 150–62
property 5, 15, 18, 35, 174
prostitution 93, 175
psychosis 110, 115
punishment ix, 6–7, 15, 27–8, 35,

52, 55, 108–09, 113, 134, 147, 154, 174

rape 10–11, 39, 60
Rat Man 103
rationalization 34
realism 56–8, 62, 110, 129
reality 56, 100, 113–14, 117, 126, 129, 150, 180; external 62, 65–9, 80, 143, 147, 151–52, 154–56; internal 62, 66–7, 143, 156; material 92, 95, 111, 125, 157, 179–80; principle 95, 143; psychical 95, 125, 157, 179–80; testing 57, 147, 154
regression 65
reinforcement (reward) ix, 6, 11, 22–3, 26–7, 30, 113, 155, 157–58
religion 38, 58, 60, 87, 91, 114
reparation 57, 146–47
repetition compulsion 134
repression x, 76–7, 80, 85–6, 88–9, 109–10, 113–14, 116, 118–24, 126–29, 134, 138, 143, 155, 172
resistance ix–x, 39–42, 63, 77, 85, 89, 91–3, 95, 99, 118, 122–24, 134–35, 176
retaliation 37, 51–3, 55, 61, 147
revenge 36, 52, 59, 130, 160
revolution 30, 36, 90, 141, 176
rights 18–20, 35, 48, 72, 90, 99, 121, 124, 153, 173, 175, 177–78

sadism 81, 91, 108–09, 112
schizoid states 50, 65, 68, 82
Schreber 110
science 18, 38–9, 66, 73, 88, 95, 100, 124–25, 139, 176, 178
secondary: gain 129, 133, 155; process 110; revision 100, 115–16
seduction 66, 103, 106–07, 124–26, 155
separation 56, 60, 65, 67–73, 75–6, 105, 130

sexual difference ix, 3–4, 6–7, 9, 11, 13, 17–18, 23, 25–6, 29, 37, 43–6, 47–9, 69, 72–4, 78–80, 85, 87–8, 91–2, 99–102, 107, 109, 111, 114–15, 119–20, 132–34, 136, 143, 168, 173, 178

sexual identity 12–14, 22, 88, 91; *see also* gender identity

sexual intercourse 36, 43, 53, 109–12, 114

sexuality: infantile 31, 36–7, 39, 85–6, 102–10, 125–28, 135

socialism 30, 36, 99, 173

splitting 50–1, 64–7, 102, 158–60

spoiling 51

stealing 18–19, 36, 53–4, 62

stereotypes 17–18, 20, 22, 23, 25, 48, 59, 151; *see also* femininity, masculinity

submissiveness 3, 8, 25, 38–9, 41, 135, 141, 167–68

subordination ix–x, 3, 5, 38, 40–2, 63, 74, 77, 88–90, 93, 99, 101, 111, 113, 123, 135–36, 145, 151–52, 155–57, 171, 176, 180

suffrage 35, 172, 174

suicide 139–40

super ego 134

symbolism viii, 45, 58–9, 86–8, 95, 105, 111, 116, 150, 158

therapeutic alliance 134, 143

therapy x, 55, 83, 101–02, 120–22, 130–37, 143–49, 156, 158–62, 167–68, 178–79

thinking 28, 41–2, 47–8, 72, 80, 86, 105, 110, 115–16, 122

toys (e.g. dolls) 9, 13–14, 24, 27, 52, 54, 55, 61, 104–05

tranference 131–32, 135–36, 144–46, 158–59, 179; counter- 132, 161

trauma 77

unconscious 31, 36–7, 47, 53, 58, 62, 80, 82, 86, 88–9, 92, 101–03, 110–11, 113–18, 126–27, 130–35, 139–41, 144, 151–52, 155, 158–60, 179–80

vagina 37, 39

violence 10–12, 43, 94, 112, 157

voyeurism 43, 105–06

wish 14, 19, 36, 58, 80, 85, 101–02, 107, 110, 114, 116, 135–36, 147, 153; *see also* desire

Wolf Man 107–08, 113–14, 139

work 5, 15–17, 26, 29, 42, 59–60, 64, 70–1, 83, 91, 93–4, 102, 111, 142, 157, 167, 171, 174–78

working through 144, 146